Thatcher

Nicholas Wapshott is Deputy Features Editor of *The Times* and author of a biography of Peter O'Toole to be published in August this year. Born and brought up in Gloucestershire, he graduated from York University and began his career in journalism in 1973 with *The Scotsman*. In 1976 he joined the staff of *The Times*, and he now specialises in British politics and the stage and cinema.

George Brock is Assistant Features Editor of *The Times*, where he divides his time between writing political features and being a commissioning editor for the opinion-editorial page. Born in Oxford, he graduated from the University there and began his career on an evening paper in Yorkshire in 1973, leaving there three years later to join *The Observer*, where he specialised in home affairs and Northern Ireland. He is co-author of SIEGE: SIX DAYS AT THE IRANIAN EMBASSY (1980).

Both authors are married and live in London.

Also by George Brock

SIEGE: SIX DAYS AT THE IRANIAN EMBASSY
(co-author)

Thatcher

NICHOLAS WAPSHOTT and GEORGE BROCK

Futura
Macdonald & Co
London & Sydney

A Futura Book

First published in Great Britain in 1983
by Macdonald & Co (Publishers) Ltd
London & Sydney

First Futura edition 1983

Copyright © Nicholas Wapshott and George Brock 1983

ISBN 0 7088 2433 1

Photoset in North Wales by
Derek Doyle & Associates, Mold, Clwyd
Printed in Great Britain by
Hazell, Watson & Viney Ltd, Aylesbury, Bucks.

Futura Publications
A Division of
Macdonald & Co (Publishers) Ltd
Maxwell House
74 Worship Street
London EC2A 2EN

Contents

TO KAY AND LOUISE

Acknowledgements

We would like to thank the participants in the events we describe for agreeing, as policemen have it, to help us with our inquiries. Most interviewees asked not to be identified and we record thanks to past and present Cabinet ministers, Downing Street staff, senior civil servants, MPs and personal friends of Mrs Thatcher in Grantham and elsewhere who have been generous with their time. We were lucky to enjoy the help of Noelle Judkins, Valerie Smith and Jean Moffat who typed the manuscript with skill and speed.

CHAPTER ONE

Life

She rarely sleeps more than five hours. As soon as she is awake, she turns on the radio, tuned in permanently to Radio 4. Denis sleeps in his own bedroom suite. She hears the network open with the six o'clock news. Then she makes a point of listening to Farming Today, which briefs farmers on stock and cereal prices, and will often remember a detail to mention to Peter Walker, the Agriculture Secretary. She likes nothing better than to keep her colleagues on their toes by dropping facts which she is not expected to know into general conversation, outflanking a minister on his own territory. She stays tuned for the Today programme, which she listens to in the bathroom and while having breakfast. The way it covers political topics often irritates her.

Margaret Thatcher lives above the shop, as her father did before her. There is a flat on the top floor of the pair of houses which make up 10 Downing Street, and it is at the disposal of the Prime Minister, although neither James Callaghan nor Sir Harold Wilson took up the option. The Thatchers live there with their son, Mark. Their daughter, Carol, continues to live at the family home in Flood Street, Chelsea. The bedroom, like the other rooms, is plain and slightly old-fashioned, with a bathroom en suite. There is nothing lavish about the design; it is more like a hotel room than a Prime Minister's bedroom, although she had it redecorated in her own choice of colour, old gold, and at her own expense. The rest of the flat is similarly comfortable, moderately well-appointed and quiet. But it is essentially a service flat and there is no question of luxury.

The radio is her only source of news in the early morning. She does not read newspapers, preferring her press secretary, Bernard Ingham, to make up a digest of press quotes for her. The radio allows her to do two things at once. That flexibility is important, because the early part of the morning is the only time she has for herself and her family. From eight o'clock until two the following morning, there is little private life. She herself eats little breakfast, often simply an apple, but Denis likes a cooked breakfast and he cannot cook. There is no domestic staff at No. 10, so the Prime Minister must cook her own husband's breakfast in the small kitchen in the flat — the only kitchen in the building. She considers it part of her duty, part of her routine, but she would prefer to be doing something else. She told an old friend, visiting No. 10 for the first time, 'Do you know that I do not have any domestic help here? If I have a second term, I will have to have some help.'

The early morning is also the time for personal matters, such as the dentist, the hairdresser, the dressmaker and clothes shops who will send a selection to suit her. During 1982 and 1983, Thatcher's teeth were growing troublesome and she made a succession of 8.15 appointments with the dentist. In 1982, she had a number of teeth capped, which slightly changed her enunciation and removed a distinctive gap between the teeth at the front of the right side of her mouth.

After her close friend, Airey Neave, was murdered, it was considered too dangerous for her to continue her usual routine of twice-weekly sessions with her hairdresser, John Howson, at his salon in Thurloe Place, Kensington. Since then, he has come to her at least twice a week at 8.30 in the morning.

She has fine hair which demands a lot of attention if it is to retain the impeccable shape that she prefers. She has long abandoned the extravagant sculptured hair-dos of the Opposition years in favour of a more manageable, more dignified, less severe style. Howson takes his assistants, Trudy Greaves, a shampooist, and Brian Carter, a hair tinter, up to the small bathroom in the flat where there is all the essential equipment: a hood hair-dryer, rollers, shampoo and conditioner. Thatcher dislikes blow drying. Her hair is so fine that it needs to be set in rollers after it has been permed to give it body. She also dyes her hair. She was originally fair, but by 1976 the hair was white. Now she is a brunette, thanks to Carter, who dyes the hair on a Sunday, when there is enough time for the elaborate process. Often she will begin her working day while waiting for her hair to dry under the hood.

She is helped in managing the personal side of her life by Caroline Stephens, who is married to her former political adviser, Richard Ryder. Stephens advises her on her dresses and her general appearance, continuing the job once performed by Lady Guinevere Tilney, and undertakes all the tasks of a personal assistant, from summoning speech writers to restocking the drinks cabinet. She knows Thatcher as few others do and is well-liked by all, mainly because she offers no direct political advice and is able to defuse a number of potentially awkward situations.

Shortly after 8.30, Thatcher will be given the first Prime Minister's brief of the day, a document marked 'Restricted', which opens with a diary of the day's principal events — everything from 'Mr Butcher addresses Greswold School PTA computer evening, Solihull', to '25th anniversary of CND launch' — and includes the press digest, a review of the morning newspapers, written by Ingham to include short, often amusing comments about the way various stories have been handled. He notes particularly how government business has been covered and assesses the success of 'helpful' letters and articles. It is written for her eyes only and contains lines like 'Gallup says your lead has dropped from 12.5%; but Marplan gives you lead of 21%', and 'You urge people to buy British food; *Express* leader sings praises', even '*Mail* highlights the fact that you don't travel by train; Gordon Bagier puts down question why? I say reason is security. But *Mail* thinks it's not the full story.' The digest runs to about six pages each day. The only paper she takes to supplement the digest is the *Financial Times*, although she will have seen the early edition of the *Daily Telegraph* the previous evening.

Every day is slightly different. There is a rolling programme which keeps pace with the changing arrangements of the day, the week and the month ahead. The main agents of the Prime Minister's day-to-day schedule are her principal aides: a team of private secretaries, each a career civil servant, who take responsibility for various areas of the PM's concern. Under her Principal Private Secretary, Robin Butler, are John Coles, who specialises in foreign affairs, Tim Flesher, home affairs, Michael Scholar, economics, and Willie Rickett, who looks after Parliamentary affairs and, in particular, the Tuesday and Thursday afternoon sessions in the Commons – Prime Minister's Question Time. These men make up the Prime Minister's Private Office, which is on the ground floor of No. 10. Butler and Coles share a room which is connected to a more crowded room containing Flesher, Scholar, Rickett, her diary secretary and a duty clerk, part of a 24-hour Prime Ministerial messenger service. Butler has not yet attained the level of influence of his predecessor, Clive Whitmore. Once, when Francis Pym, then Defence Secretary, said he had not yet made up his mind about the Sea Eagle missile, Thatcher is reported to have said, 'Then Clive and I will have to do it for you. We always do.'

The working day for most of the staff starts at 8 a.m. and everyone who works at No. 10 arrives by the front door, which has no knob. The policeman outside knocks for someone to admit entry. In all, about 100 people work at No. 10. The Private Office and the Press Office are joined by the Political Office, made up of Ian Gow, Thatcher's Parliamentary Private Secretary; her Political Secretary; the 'garden girls', the secretarial team who work on the ground floor at the back, overlooking No. 10's walled garden which backs onto Horseguards' Parade; and a number of key advisers, such as Ferdinand Mount, her chief policy adviser, Sir Anthony Parsons, her chief foreign policy adviser, Roger Jackling, defence adviser, and David Wolfson, her Chief of Staff. Then there are messengers, drivers, telephonists, cleaners, security guards and police. Security measures are tight: one aide of Mount's, Christopher Monckton, was forbidden to bring in a word processor, lest he use its memory to smuggle out the contents of files.

On Tuesdays and Thursdays, the days of PM's Question Time, Rickett has an 8.30 or 9 o'clock appointment with Thatcher for a preliminary discussion about what is likely to be raised. All queries will have been logged in the day's Commons order paper. Some will be specific; but the most difficult questions to prepare for are those which are vaguely worded or, the usual formula for a rogue question, ask when she will be visiting a particular constituency. The sting will be in the supplementary question, for which no notice is given. Thatcher and Rickett will survey the day's news for likely supplementaries and he will be despatched to research information so that the Prime Minister will not be caught by surprise. They will meet again later that morning for a full-scale preparation.

At 9.30 there is often a meeting of ministers, usually members of a specific Cabinet committee, a sub-group of the full Cabinet, whose members are chosen because of their knowledge of and sympathy towards the Prime Minister's point of view. The most important are the 'E' committee, the principal economic policy body, and the 'OD' committee, short for the Oversea and Defence committee. The existence of all Cabinet committees was kept secret by every PM until Thatcher announced in the Commons the existence of four of the more important ones, shortly after she became Prime Minister. However, the membership of each committee is a secret, and secrecy continues to extend to the existence of the vast majority of these Cabinet bodies. Thatcher has minimized the number of Cabinet committees. During her first four years, she established only 130, whereas James Callaghan created nearly two hundred committees in his brief time as Prime Minister.

Every Thursday there is a Cabinet meeting, usually either at 10.30 or 11. Very often, the previous Cabinet committee will still be meeting in the Cabinet room at the time the full Cabinet meeting is due to start. Most of the Cabinet will arrive shortly before the time appointed, by official car — Lord Hailsham sometimes cycles — except for Geoffrey Howe, the Chancellor, and Michael Jopling, the Chief Whip, who can use the connecting doors between Nos 11 and 12 Downing Street. Each Cabinet member has his appointed position at the table according to his importance in the pecking order. The table is boatshaped and Thatcher sits in the centre with her back to the fireplace, looking out

over the Horseguards'. In her first Cabinet, Whitelaw and
Soames sat at her left, and on her right was the Cabinet
Secretary, Sir John Hunt, then Gilmour, Walker and Jenkin.
Directly opposite her sat Lord Carrington, with Lord
Hailsham on his left, Geoffrey Howe, Pym and Prior on his
right. The proceedings of Cabinet meetings are meant to be
secret, but internal dissent was so substantial during the first
two years of her government that the twists and turns of
personality and argument inside the Cabinet room were
regularly reported in the press. Thatcher likes to conduct
Cabinet discussion at a brisk pace and hurries on debates,
cramming eight full items into the two hours. The meetings
rarely overrun, nor does she allow them to stray from the
agenda. Rather than remain an aloof chairman, as most
other Prime Ministers have, she has proved combative and
argumentative. Although not relegated to the role of rubber
stamp, the Cabinet is more a decision-endorsing than a
decision-making body under Thatcher. As one Cabinet
Minister put it, 'Her instinct is not to have a Cabinet.'

She keeps her ministers well up to the mark by herself
being well briefed on the issues. She does not like what she
calls 'unstructured conversation', the chummy man-to-man
chats which have historically lubricated the business of
most previous Prime Ministers. Her advisers will only see
her about twice a week, but will hand her a number of memos
and briefs. This causes some of them anguish, for they do
not wish to overload her with work, yet know that she will
read everything that is put before her.

It is her attention to detail which makes her preparations
for PM's questions so gruelling. She takes the two weekly
performances very seriously and devotes an enormous
amount of her time to them: far more than any other post-
war Prime Minister. She likes to anticipate every likely
angle of attack so as not to be taken by surprise, even
though many questions are friendly and are asked by MPs
on her own side by arrangement. On Tuesdays and
Thursdays, all staff are expected to work through
lunchtime, as Thatcher does herself. Although there are no
permanent catering arrangements, a woman comes in on
those days and makes food for everyone, what one staff

member called 'good nursery food'. Thatcher works
through lunch at her desk in her first floor study which
looks out towards St James's Park, scribbling notes over the
briefing notes. She will be further briefed by Ian Gow, her
Parliamentary Private Secretary, whose principal function it
is to keep her in touch with the feelings of her party in the
Commons.

Her treatment of Question Time is typical of her
approach to most government business. It has been said
that she has a 'searchlight mind', which can beam strongly
onto individual subjects and quickly become familiar with
and understand them. She lacks the broad-brush approach
or lofty perspective by which Harold Macmillan
instinctively determined where the Government or the
British should stand. She lacks the overriding vision of a
future Britain which Edward Heath held when championing
the European dimension. Some argue that her searchlight
concentration provides a perspective of its own, as the beam
swings from subject to subject. Others suggest that it offers
little of the imagination or inspiration necessary for political
leadership. One close aide, admiring her powers of
concentration, said, 'She would hate to hear it, but she
would have made a good administrative-grade civil servant.'
A senior Conservative was even less flattering: 'She is a jolly
good ADC, nothing more. Political leadership needs more
than the capacity to get things done.'

One of the main reasons for Edward Heath's defeat in the
1975 leadership election was that he had grown out of touch
with his constituents: the Tory MPs. Thatcher determined
early on that she would not allow the same mistake to be
repeated and found in Gow a loyal and obedient informant.
He works an immensely long day, starting at Downing
Street at 7.45 and seldom leaving the Commons bars until
the early hours.

On evenings when Thatcher has to be around the
Commons to vote, she will also be conspicuous around the
bars and dining rooms. Gow will precede her, encouraging
back-bench MPs to come and talk to her or to sit at her
table. She also chats to all and sundry when waiting in the
lobby during voting, unlike Heath who with his close aides

stayed away from the main body of backbenchers. Her forays into the tea room and the dining rooms at the Commons can be awkward occasions, as backbenchers waver between telling the PM what they think and repeating what she wants to hear. Often she will talk about the government, running it down, as if she had nothing to do with it. She is the only Prime Minister to have regularly used the cafeteria. Her favourite dish is buck rarebit: toasted cheese with an egg on the top.

It is Gow who passes out messages direct to MPs and also reports back to her on feelings and gossip around the House. He is nick-named 'Supergrass' and operates like a parallel whip, always to be seen in the Commons bars, gathering intelligence. He has been much criticised by the Conservative left for passing back to the PM more praise from right-wing MPs than criticism from the left. He has also been criticised for his continuing friendship with Enoch Powell. Thatcher gets good service from him and it has been suggested that the reason he has not been promoted to the Government as a minister is that he is too valuable – and too powerful – in his present job.

Between 2.30 and 3, Thatcher is taken by car from Downing Street to the Commons, stepping out of the front door into a deserted street, cordoned off by police since the IRA bombings in Hyde Park. The car in which she travels the short distance is fitted with bullet-proof glass and bodywork, which makes the doors heavy to open. Two other cars travel in the convoy, each filled with police. She will take with her at least a private secretary and will make straight for the Prime Minister's room directly behind the Speaker's chair as soon as she reaches the Palace of Westminster. After a last-minute conference with close aides, she will expect to sit down in her usual seat, directly in front of the mace on the government front bench, at 3. At 3.15 she will start answering the first of about fifteen questions from both sides of the House, very often punctuated by additional questions from senior members of the Opposition front bench. Her performance at Question Time, although not as skillful as those of either Harold Macmillan or Sir Harold Wilson, is robust and she considers the occasion a central part of her duties as Prime Minister, although the whole thing only takes fifteen minutes. When Sir Nigel Fisher attempted, through the Speaker, to have the questions made more specific, so that the answers could be more adequately prepared, it was made clear that Thatcher enjoyed the element of surprise in the ritual. One close colleague is reported to have said, 'She thinks that Questions are her hotline to the British people. She believes there is this terrible weight of bureaucracy and government on top of everyone, so she has to appeal over its head.' It also satisfies what many close to her recognise as the elements of an actress in her, the need consciously to perform in front of an audience.

What happens next depends upon Commons business. Even though she is Prime Minister, she is still an ordinary member of the Commons for voting purposes. She has a pair, arranged ad hoc by the whips, and will troop through the lobby like the rest. If there is to be a vote at 7 pm, it is likely that she will move her entire private office from Downing Street to the Commons for the rest of the afternoon. Otherwise, if a vote is not to be taken until 10 pm, she returns in the cars to Downing Street. The security arrangements are more elaborate for the return journey, as he car must drive the long way around Parliament Square. The first car, one of three Daimlers or a Rover 3500, leaves the Commons car park, past the policemen at the gate who have held up the traffic, and lingers on the inner edge of the square. Her own car then sweeps out and drives directly to No. 10, with the other following closely behind. Watching over Thatcher's security at all times, and usually physically very close to her, is Superintendent Gordon Cawthorne.

A return to No. 10 will probably mean another Cabinet committee meeting or a briefing session on an imminent event. A visit from a foreign prime minister will entail preparations for talks. Usually such a visit will be marked by a dinner at Downing Street in his honour. There will be a photocall with the visitor in the chequer-floored entrance hall of No. 10, and there will be small-talk while the photographers take pictures of Thatcher with her guest in front of the fireplace. There will then be about twenty minutes of confidential talks between the two leaders without officials present, before they make their way to a reception at 7.45 for dinner at 8. Such dinners take place in the State Dining Room on the first floor, and the meal, cooked by a team of outside caterers, will be eaten under the gaze of portraits of Nelson, Pitt, Wellington and Charles James Fox.

The decoration of No. 10 has changed very little since Thatcher became Prime Minister. She has changed the wallpaper in her study and altered some of the furniture, banishing French furniture in favour of more plain British pieces, borrowed from the Victoria and Albert Museum. She has also increased the number of portraits of famous Britons to hang on the walls, introducing Nelson and Wellington, and, as a scientist, a portrait of Priestley and busts of Farraday, Davy and Newton, a Grantham hero. The Tate Gallery lent her three Turners after she visited the British Embassy in Paris, which also has three. She has borrowed from her friend Lord Brownlow, of Belton House, near Grantham, both silver and a ceramic casket depicting Grantham scenes. She has been careful about the division between her public and private occupation of No. 10, not least in how the expenses are shared between them. In the beginning of her time there, she became involved in a row with the management of the government hospitality fund because not enough was being done to help her meet expenses. In the end, Lord Soames, as head of the Civil Service, had to step in and tell his civil servants to relax.

She does a lot of private entertaining at No. 10. Sometimes she opens it for fund-raising events and she and Denis greet all the guests as they make their way up the main staircase, which is decorated by black-and-white portraits of every Prime Minister, ending with a colour picture of Callaghan. Thatcher once remarked to a visitor, 'Doesn't it spoil the set?' There is no room for another portrait, her own, to which she has responded, 'Don't worry, I'll push all the others down.' She invariably kicks her shoes off at the end of a reception, stands up on a sofa and gives an impromptu speech about No. 10 being a tied cottage. She is an energetic hostess, introducing people to one another and working at making the party successful. She stays until very late, often between 11 and 11.30, waiting until the principal guests leave before going up to the flat and starting on her boxes, the red leather brief cases inscribed in gold with the words 'Prime Minister', which contain papers which she must have read by the morning. Ian Gow provides a black box of parliamentary matters. She will work well into the night, stopping usually at 2 am, but quite often going on until 3. She has been growing progressively more tired as the years of her premiership have gone on, but still usually outstays those about her.

Thatcher likes to write speeches late at night, an elaborate and time-wasting procedure which has shortened over the years as time has become more scarce. Only very important speeches are now written in this way. Caroline Stephens summons by telephone a number of speech writers who are currently in favour. Draft after draft is thrown away and it is rarely before the rejects reach double figures that Thatcher begins to get near what she is hoping to say. Discarded words can be smuggled back into the text. As one writer put it, 'You can recycle stuff from the waste-paper basket.' She is keen on homilies and will scrabble in her handbag to find a scrap of paper on which is written a phrase which she considers particularly pertinent. Her dictionaries of quotations are filled with her underlinings. Some of the phrases which she suggests sound banal to the writers, who giggle among themselves later. 'It was a bit of R.C. Sheriff's "Journey's End" mixed with cracker-barrel philosophy,' said one. 'You could make them up easily enough. I always imagined that the Thatcher Christmas crackers had quotes of this sort inside.' Since her election in 1979, Thatcher has been keen to avoid phrases which she considers would sound out of place in the mouth of a Prime Minister. She often misses jokes, so humorous lines are avoided in case they are misunderstood. She does allow, however, Alfred Sherman, the Director of Studies at the Centre for Policy Studies, to crack his own peculiar brand of joke and she indulges him rather like a licensed jester, often pretending to cuff him around the head. There is plenty of alcohol available, although she herself makes a whisky and soda last the night. But often there is a lack of food. She has taken to preparing and cooking baked potatoes for the team,

Late nights at Downing Street are also the times when she likes to have a good political philosophical argument. She prefers people who disagree with her, although she does not like to be contradicted or interrupted, and she likes to hear views or facts that she has never heard before. Unlike most other Prime Ministers, she actually enjoys hearing argument for its own sake. She was particularly impressed by Sir Anthony Parsons when he asked her, politely, to let him finish his point before she reacted to it. At other times she has been likened by one regular confidant to a two-way radio: she either talks at you or listens attentively; there is no dialogue. She also prefers to hear practical proposals instead of mere intellectual gymnastics. At one meeting of the Tory Philosophy Group, a regular forum for Tory thinkers across a wide range of views which meets at the home of Jonathan Aitken in Lord North Street, she scolded Enoch Powell: 'Be constructive, Enoch. Be constructive.' Denis usually makes his excuses and leaves such late-night discussions and has been known to fall asleep in front of the television in another room. If it grows very late and he is still awake, he comes in and breaks up the party, reminding them of work the next day.

Night time is also when Thatcher catches up with her correspondence. She is a compulsive bread-and-butter letter writer and cannot allow a type-written letter to pass her without adding a few words of her own in her own hand. It is a genuine impulse, prompted by a real concern for other people. She often irritates her aides by going out of her way to thank someone or make sure a kindness is paid to a friend. In Grantham in 1982, she was dining at the Angel Hotel when she discovered that the chef's wife had recently had a baby. She defied her staff and demanded that the chef come to her table so that she could congratulate him personally. She is also extraordinarily generous, both in her private possessions and in spirit. She has an easy knack of remembering not only everyone's name, but also the names of their wives and children, which comes from more than just an impulse towards good politics. She is particularly understanding about personal difficulties in her colleagues' private lives, especially those who have marriage problems, and always asks what is to happen to the children. She has been known to contact the chairman of a local constituency party of an MP involved in a personal scandal, advising that he should be allowed to solve his own problem without harassment. After her former PPS, Fergus Montgomery, was found guilty of shop-lifting, she deliberately walked arm-in-arm with him through the Central Lobby of the Houses of Parliament.

But, like most Prime Ministers before her, Thatcher has come to depend upon the country retreat of Chequers in Kent for her quiet and relaxation, and she misses her former weekend home at Scotney Castle. Even at Chequers she is not alone, and when the convoy sets off from Downing Street on a Friday evening, it contains a private secretary, two Special Branch men, a 'garden girl' and, if necessary, a press officer. Sometimes she invites visiting politicians or heads of state to spend the weekend with her and she has also invited the Cabinet en masse. The first time that the members of the Cabinet were invited to Chequers, one of the WRAF personnel waiting on table at dinner accidentally spilt a plate of beef down Geoffrey Howe's front. Thatcher leapt to her rescue, saying, 'Don't worry, dear. If the Chancellor of the Exchequer can't afford a new suit, you certainly can't.' But mostly she looks to Chequers for some peace and quiet. She particularly enjoys going to the small local church for the morning service on a Sunday. She is taken by car, but usually walks back. The less obtrusive security arrangements allow her a freedom and relief seldom found elsewhere. Every Prime Minister plants a tree at Chequers: she has chosen a copper beech tree given by a lawyer friend.

It is at Chequers that she tries to lead a normal family life. Mark and Carol have taken friends there for the weekend. Denis practices putting on the lawns, with a policeman acting as a caddy. And Christmas is celebrated at Chequers. Christmas Day itself is a quiet affair and she often returns to her boxes. When Christopher Patten wrote to complain about what he considered to be her demotion of the Conservative Research Department, she read the letter out to the family on Christmas Day. Private secretaries were surprised on Christmas Day 1982 when she telephoned them, wished them a happy Christmas, then continued with the conversation as if it were a normal working day. As there is little chance to watch television during the week, Thatcher orders up videotapes of her favourite programmes to watch over the holiday. The Christmas 1982 selection included episodes of Yes, Minister and Barchester Towers. Boxing Day is a more festive day and a number of family friends are invited. Denis's sister Joy is there, as is Ronald Millar, dramatist and speechwriter, who usually takes her a book as a present and sometimes plays the piano. Gordon Reece, her publicity adviser, is invited.

It is with Ronald Millar that she has gone to the theatre, en famille, once to The Two Ronnies, a television favourite of hers, which she found too rude for her taste; another time to 'Waters of the Moon', with Ingrid Bergman and Wendy Hiller, at the Haymarket, when, despite a heavy cold, she insisted on attending the backstage party. She also enjoys opera and always mugs up on the score beforehand.

Too much relaxation, however, does not suit her. She likes to go skiing, and while in Switzerland, will make a point of dropping in on some Swiss economists and bankers and on the British scientific research station there. Civil servants in the Department of Education still remember the shock of seeing their secretary of state arrive back a week early from a boating holiday in France. During the summer of 1979, she was persuaded by Lord Margadale to relax at his home on the island of Islay in Scotland, a country retreat often used by Tory leaders, who would enjoy the rough shooting during the day and the archaic playing of rowdy house-party games in the evening. The regime did not suit Thatcher, who announced after two nights that the entertainment was not to her liking and that she would therefore retire to work in her room which was, unhappily, directly over the noisy party. She thumped several times on the floor to no avail, then decided to put on her overcoat and escape the bonhommie by going for a brisk walk. A police dog promptly chased after her and brought her down in the heather, much to her embarrassment and that of the policemen who were meant to be protecting her.

There is also little time for reading, once all the red boxes have been finished. On a plane, Thatcher will take a spy thriller and John Le Carré is a favourite author. She once considered knighting him. But for content she prefers Kipling and has a large collection of his works at Flood Street, many of them bound in leather by herself. But being Prime Minister does not allow much time for poring over a good book and Kipling is consulted only rarely now, usually for checking a quote for a speech.

Many close colleagues, and at least two former Prime Ministers, question whether her work ought to take up so much of her time. Thatcher puts in more hours than any Prime Minister has since the war. Part of the industry is generated by her compulsion to be constantly busy. She seems more interested in politics as a means of occupying her energy than as a means of wielding power. If she lost an election, she would miss the work more than the power. As Carol told a neighbour, 'Goodness me! If Mum loses the election, what are we going to do with her?'

CHAPTER TWO

Grantham

Margaret Thatcher is fond of calling herself a 'conviction politician', by which she means that she depends for her inspiration upon a profound set of beliefs. She is guided by an inner mechanism which instinctively tells her whether she considers an action is right or wrong. She does not need to ask whether a new set of circumstances suits a particular body of doctrine. She is confident that the deep conviction which guides her will always keep her on the right track.

She acquired this deep-rooted conviction, by her own admission, during her childhood in Grantham, from her family, in particularly her father, Alfred Roberts, and from the Methodist Church. Added to these influences were the lessons learnt from living above her father's shop, where home and trade went hand in hand, and from the political life carried on in that shop by her father and his friends. Thatcher has taken her early life and used it as a touchstone to identify the old-fashioned values that she holds, admires and would like to restore to Britain. To explore the facts of her upbringing is to investigate the foundations of her philosophy. Under her premiership, Britain is being judged by, and in some respects led back to, the moral atmosphere and standards of the small business community in Grantham between the wars.

Grantham is today a market town much like it was before the Second World War. During the thirties the population was around 30,000. Much of its importance is as a focus for the farming community in the flat Lincolnshire countryside which surrounds it. The passing trade which came first with the stage coaches, then with the railways, then the motor traffic heading north and south on the Great North Road, the A1 from London to Edinburgh, has diminished. Yet, despite a modern by-pass, as much traffic

thunders today past the shop, now a restaurant, where
Alfred Roberts lived, as it did in the thirties. Then, situated
between the coal fields of Nottingham and the grandeur of
the Vale of Belvoir presided over by the Duke of Rutland,
Grantham was an average-sized town. It was big enough to
have the resources to support the communal services of
libraries, schools and parks; small enough to be dominated
by a tight group of men of moderate ability.

By the thirties, the town's traditional sources of wealth
had gone into sharp decline. The massive Victorian
expansion of railways and engine-building, which had vastly
increased both the population and the housing stock in the
nineteenth century, had slowed. The town's main employer,
Ruston and Hornby, which during the First World War had
converted its capacity for steam and diesel-engine
production into the manufacture of armaments, found the
slump in demand for both railways and arms too much to
bear. It went bankrupt, pushing thousands onto the dole.
Although the misery experienced was not as severe as that
in the steel works, shipbuilding plants and coal mines in the
North and in South Wales, Grantham was badly hit by the
Depression.

Alfred Roberts was not directly affected by the slump.
He was one of seven children from a family of rural
shoemakers from Ringstead in Northamptonshire. Bad
eyesight prevented him from following the close leather
work which his family had done for four generations.
Instead, he left school at twelve and made his way to
Grantham, where he was promised a job as an apprentice in
Clifford's, a grocer's shop in London Road, in the market
place. Although he had little formal schooling, a victim of
inadequate school provision, Alfred Roberts was highly
intelligent, and he held ambitions to become a teacher.
Without qualifications, however, such ambitions were idle
and he felt a lasting regret that his mind had not been
stretched by higher education. He made amends, as best he
could, by a strict regime of self-education through library
books, which he devoured at speed.

He was an ardent Methodist, worshipping twice each
Sunday at the Wesley's Chapel in the south of the town,

and he became active in the church, training to become a local preacher, the Methodist equivalent of a lay preacher. It was at the Wesley's Chapel that he met Beatrice Stephenson and her parents. Daniel Stephenson was a railway cloakroom attendant who also looked after the lost property office at the station, and his wife Phoebe, born Phoebe Crust, was a farmer's daughter trained as a factory machinist. They had been married in the village of Boston in Lincolnshire in 1876. The young Alfred Roberts was a strikingly handsome man, six feet three inches tall, with a shock of curly blond hair which had looked almost white since he was a boy. His brilliant blue eyes shone through the thick lenses of his glasses and he had fine facial features and a slender frame. The courtship between Alf Roberts and Beatrice Stephenson was long and formal and during their engagement they saved from his small wage in the shop, where he had at the age of twenty-one been promoted manager, and from her small income as a seamstress. Their plan was to buy a shop of their own, with enough living accommodation to bring up a small family.

Alfred Roberts had been manager at Clifford's for a year when the First World War broke out. He presented himself for military service, but was turned down because of his poor eyesight. By 1917 the couple had saved enough to get married at the Wesley's Chapel and to buy a business of their own, a small sub post-office and grocery store at No. 1 North Parade, hard by the busy Great North Road on the way north out of Grantham. Apart from the shop, there was a room directly behind it, and two floors above: enough room to live in and, eventually, to raise children. The couple took things cautiously. Alf Roberts had, in buying the shop, taken out a mortgage on the property and he was anxious about meeting the payments. There would be no extra money to start a family for some time and it was not until four years after the marriage that the first child was born and christened Muriel. The Roberts family had by this time, for convenience, transferred their allegiance to the Finkin Street Methodist Church, only about half a mile from the shop on North Parade.

Roberts and his wife were diligent workers and the shop

proved a success, known for its good service and friendly welcome. It became possible to expand the business to the two adjacent shops at 3 and 5 North Parade. The dividing walls between the three shops were taken down and one large shop was made, with the sub post-office at the end of a long L-shaped counter which ran the length of the back wall and turned to the section where the cooked meats were kept. The shop was kept well stocked, with as much as possible on display, stacked on the shelving which lined the walls.

The Roberts could feel proud of themselves. They had, together, moved into the bottom of the middle class – the first generation on either side of their families to have done so. With the help of the mortgage, they had joined the ranks of the self-employed, leaving the vagaries of an employer for the more manageable demands of their customers, each one of whom could claim to be their true employer. Saving ill health or accident, they were reasonably secure and could expect to earn a comfortable living. This is the family into which Margaret Hilda Roberts was born on 13 October, 1925, in a first-floor room above the shop.

As a home it was not lavish. There was no piped hot water and each bedroom held a washstand with jug and bowl. The lavatory was outside in the yard. There was no garden to play in. All of the furniture was second-hand, not only because it was cheaper but because Alf Roberts thought it better made than the modern. The shop and house were filled incessantly with the rumble of motor traffic from the busy road outside and they could also hear the hiss and squeals of the railway sidings not far away. By the standards of the 1980s, it seems a mean way to live, but before the war Alf Roberts would have been thought to be offering his family a secure, comfortable, privileged home compared to most of those about him. As long as his health held out, he was not likely to suffer unemployment. The shop made enough to allow Beatrice not to go out to work, but to help in the shop, run the house and bring up the children. They could afford to remain a close family and both parents could spend a great deal of time with the two girls.

Alf Roberts continued to make good progress. He opened

a second shop on the corner opposite the school which
Muriel attended, the Huntingtower Road Elementary
School. He had continued his church work, regularly
preaching in village churches, and had become closely
involved with the Grantham business community. He
allowed his name to be put forward as Grantham Chamber
of Trade candidate for the Borough Council. Although most
of his commercial colleagues were Conservative Party
members there was a tradition among them that party
politics should be kept out of local government. Most of
them, including Roberts, stood as Independent candidates.
It was as an Independent that he was elected. Although in
later life he was to identify more closely with his
Conservative colleagues on the council and would support
his daughter, Margaret, in her political ambitions, he never
became a member of the Conservative Party. He admired
the political ideals of the Liberal Party and, in particular,
the National Liberal wing which had joined Stanley
Baldwin's coalition, and it is the view of Tom Bourne, the
Conservative agent in Grantham for twenty-eight years
since the war, who knew Alfred Roberts well, that his
instincts were of a moderate Labour kind. He had been
prevented from adopting this as his true political colour
because of the strength of the local Co-operative
Movement, which was effectively the Labour Party in
Grantham. It was not only more left wing than Alf Roberts
would have wished, but was directly antagonistic, through
its cooperative retail shops, to anyone who owned a shop of
his own.

It was, then, as the daughter of a local councillor that
Margaret Roberts set off to school on 3 September, 1930.
Although there was a church school just behind the shop in
North Parade, Alfred Roberts preferred to send his
daughters to the local county school, about a mile away,
which was modern — built in 1914 — and had a good
academic reputation. It was built to a regular plan, common
after the First World War, with seven classrooms running
the length of one side of a central corridor and a school hall
on the other. It was a tidy school, presided over by a Miss
Winifred Wright and her deputy, Miss Doris Rollings. The

school inspector, HMI Mr J. MacInnes, described it in his report of 1935 as giving 'an all-round moral, social and physical training which endears it to the parents and pupils. The freedom and the happiness of the latter are apparent: the fruits of the physical education – which is fostered by the supply of milk to over 100 daily.' Margaret and Muriel Roberts both took their milk money to school each Monday. They walked the mile to school with other children from North Parade, cutting underneath the railway, and made the journey four times a day, returning home for lunch as there were no school meals provided.

Margaret was clearly a bright girl – much more so than her elder sister – and was allowed to start school when still not yet five years old, which put her in a class with children considerably older than herself. She was well able to hold her own. She is remembered by her classmates as a quiet, serious, neatly-dressed and groomed little girl who sat at the back of the class where well-behaved children were placed. She was a generous child and always shared the chocolate she was given by her parents after lunch. Her obvious intelligence and articulateness gave her a considerable degree of confidence, particularly with adults. At the age of nine, when her headmistress, in congratulating her on winning a poetry reading prize at a local drama festival, said, 'You were lucky, Margaret', she replied, tartly, 'I wasn't lucky. I deserved it.' She was intellectually precocious and when she was only nine-and-a-half she was moved into the scholarship class, at the very end of the corridor opposite the headmistress's study, to try for a place at the local girls' grammar school. On 13 July, 1936, the headmistress's daily log read, 'A scholarship has been granted to Margaret Roberts, as although she is very young (10yr 6m) her work was exceptionally good.'

For the first ten years of her life, Margaret was brought up in the company of her maternal grandmother, Phoebe Stephenson, a fiercely Victorian woman with strict morals and a habit of delivering homilies. Two of her favourite sayings, engraved in her grand-daughters' memories, were 'If a thing's worth doing, it's worth doing well', and 'Cleanliness is next to godliness.' Phoebe Stephenson's morality pervaded the house. Alfred and Beatrice Roberts were hardly liberal in their approach to home life and the up-bringing of children and their attitudes were hardened by the presence of Beatrice's mother, whom they did not wish to offend. Both families were strongly Methodist and both girls were brought up in an old-fashioned intimacy with the church. They were sent to Sunday school twice each Sunday, in the morning and the afternoon in the schoolroom at the back of Finkin Street Church, and were also expected to accompany their parents and grandmother to both morning and evening services. Alf Roberts had become a well-known and much sought-after local preacher and used to tour local villages, speaking from notes in a measured style, concentrating on the spiritual side of Christianity rather than its practical application. It was a skill which had stood him in good stead at the council meetings.

The church followed the family back into the home and involved them during the week. The whole family would take part in the regular Finkin Street musical occasions, presided over by the organist, Wilfred Allen, and they joined in the Biblical plays, in which Margaret once played an angel. Beatrice Roberts would go to the Wednesday sewing meetings, both girls would go to the Friday youth club and each Sunday evening the family would either invite a number of the congregation back to supper in North Parade or they would themselves be invited elsewhere, to continue discussing the issues raised by the sermon and become more acquainted with the visiting preacher. The Roberts family were completely teetotal and no alcoholic drinks were offered. Alfred Roberts was also a strict observer of the Sabbath. The girls were forbidden to play games on a Sunday, even snakes and ladders. No Sunday newspapers were allowed. Although Beatrice baked on a Sunday morning, the only work to be done was the shop book-keeping. Alf Roberts was also fiercely opposed to the opening of the four Grantham cinemas on Sundays and to the opening of the council swimming pool and tennis courts in the park. It was not until wartime, when troops and airmen from the local airbase were deprived of entertainment on their only free day, that he relented.

The Roberts girls were not spoilt. Pocket money was small and only rarely supplemented by a half crown or half sovereign, for a birthday or as a reward for a good school result, which the children were automatically expected to put into savings. The cinema was reserved for a special treat, and holidays, spent in a self-catering boarding house in Skegness, were for only a week and accompanied only by Mrs Roberts, while Alfred Roberts minded the shop. He would usually try to arrange that his week's holiday would coincide with Bowls Week, as he much enjoyed being a member of the Grange Bowling Club in Grantham.

From Beatrice, the girls learnt a great deal about practical skills and housekeeping. The Roberts divided their tasks in a conventional way for the time, with Alfred minding the business and all that it entailed and Beatrice helping in the shop where she could, but being principally responsible for cooking, cleaning, mending, dressmaking and other housewifely duties. Beatrice and Alfred Roberts were not intellectual equals, and where he would almost certainly have gone to university had he been born thirty years later, Beatrice would not. However, her dressmaking was first class and brought in a great deal of the savings which had allowed the couple to buy the North Parade shop. She continued making clothes for herself and her daughters, which they thought was a mixed blessing, until they left home, and she also taught them both needlework. She taught them how to bake and cook as well. Beatrice Roberts baked twice a week, on Thursdays and Sundays, with a full range of cakes, biscuits, bread and pies. And, having baked, she instructed her daughters in the direct-help approach to good works. She would always bake too much and would send one of the girls to take some of the freshly baked produce to those old people and families in the neighbourhood who were less fortunate than themselves. It was a country practice brought into the town. From Beatrice Roberts the girls learnt the disciplined routine of pre-war housework, with turns at doing the washing with a dolly and boiler. She also taught them how to paint and wallpaper a room.

The girls were expected to take their turns at odd jobs in the shop during the holidays and after school. They were given useful tasks, such as cutting and weighing the butter, which arrived in huge slabs, or weighing out the sugar or tea, which came in big chests. Their father encouraged the girls to become interested in the life he was leading outside the shop. His corner by the bacon slicer was an informal forum for all sorts of local businessmen, mainly colleagues from the council or the Chamber of Trade. They would chew over municipal matters and often national and international politics: the National Government under Stanley Baldwin; the prospect of rearmament; the rise of the dictators in Italy and Germany; the cause and effects of the Depression. Of the two girls, it was Margaret who took an interest in those conversations and was encouraged by her father to join in. The Roberts were a close-knit family and both parents attempted to be even-handed in their approach to their children, but Margaret and her father developed an especially close relationship because of their shared interests. Both were keen readers. From the age of ten, Margaret was allowed to go shopping for the family on a Saturday and was despatched en route to the public library next to the town hall to fetch books for both parents. Alfred wanted specific ones, usually a biography, a history or something on welfare. Beatrice was content with a novel. Alfred involved Margaret from an early age in his local government affairs. If an interesting speaker arrived in the town and he could not attend the meeting, Margaret was sent and expected to recount the main points of the argument.

He also involved her in the nuts and bolts of politics: the canvassing; the knocking up; the presenting of the candidate. She was enraptured by it from the start. Her first experience was in the 1935 General Election when the whole family worked to support Victor Warrender, the National Government candidate. Margaret was aged ten and she was given the task of running between the tellers outside the polling stations and the party committee rooms, taking the lists of those who had voted so that party workers could remind the faithful to turn out. She also took part in the election to return 'Plain Arthur' Eatch, a local builder and councillor who became Mayor of Grantham. And, of course, she worked hard in her father's elections, until he was elected alderman by his Conservative and Independent allies.

Alfred Roberts became an increasingly busy man in the local community and he explained his progress to Margaret as he went along. He was President of the Grantham Rotarians in 1936. He had been elected the youngest alderman in Grantham and proved a strong chairman of the borough finance committee. In 1937, he was on the celebration committee for the borough's coronation celebrations and is pictured in the souvenir guide as chairman of the finance sub-committee, in his gold-rimmed spectacles and round-edged detachable collar. He maintained his association with the Grantham Chamber of Trade and became a governor of both the major grammar schools in Grantham, including the one which had awarded the scholarship to Margaret, the Kesteven and Grantham Girls' School. When she was in the sixth form, he was appointed chairman of the school governors. He continued his busy round of local preaching and became a trustee to several village churches near Grantham. It was the example of Alfred Roberts which inspired his daughter Margaret towards a career in public life.

Margaret also possessed a similar nature to Alfred Roberts'. Both were incessant workers who found it difficult to relax. He was never still. The shop was open in the morning, to catch people on their way to work, and would stay open until six each night: except Thursday, which was early closing; Friday, when it shut at seven; and Saturday, when it remained open until eight o'clock at night. Alf Roberts would stay in the shop as long as it was open and only deserted his counter when other pressing engagements competed for his time. His work for the church was very time-consuming and he had, like his parents before him and his wife's family, integrated a great deal of his family's social life into the life of the church. It is important that it was the Methodist Church which was the fundamental influence on the early formation of Margaret's character.

Methodism is a down-to-earth interpretation of Christianity, which dismisses as ineffectual much of the intellectual approach to notions of good and evil. It is a deeply practical interpretation, so that when, early in 1970, Alfred Roberts died, the family gave to the Finkin Street Church, in a ceremony attended by Muriel and Margaret, a lectern with a brass plaque, rather than a merely decorative epitaph. The church in Finkin Street, like most other Methodist churches, is a clean, tidy, uncluttered amphitheatre. There is no stained glass, no altar. The centre of attention is the pulpit, the means whereby the congregation is led to God. It is the opposite of the disguised acceptance of social hierarchy to be found in Anglican churches and services. And the nature of the message is straightforward, too, giving direct advice about putting Christianity into practice.

The same could be said of growing up above a grocer's shop. Margaret Roberts was brought up in a household where work and home were compartments of the same building. The family used the shop as an extension of its sitting room and the room immediately behind the sub post-office was used simultaneously as an office, a room for entertaining salesmen and a sitting room, where either Alfred or Beatrice could retire and eat a meal. This confusion between private and public life was further enhanced by the council business which was conducted over the counter in the shop. The shop served as a privately-owned council committee room, where Peek Freans jostled for attention among the parks and recreations. Margaret Roberts did not suffer from the notion so commonly held by the British upper and middle classes that the market is somehow distasteful, because to her the market was home. Living above the shop, only an ungrateful daughter could deny that the market was ethical, honest and gave its just rewards to the hard working.

A similar logic inspired Alfred Roberts' experience of politics. Whatever his profound political beliefs, the reason that he was chosen to represent the interests of the Chamber of Trade was that he was a shopkeeper, one of the business community. He may always have resisted the final transfer of his Independent status to the full-blooded Conservative

label, when after the war the Labour Party dictated that
council elections be fought on party lines, but he had
practical reasons for backing the people he did. He and his
family were close friends of the other tradespeople in
Grantham and their families. They shared the same outlook,
understood the same problems, faced the same difficulties.
They became involved in local politics as a way of helping
themselves. They were not inspired by deep ideological
motives. They involved themselves in local politics because
it was a sensible thing to do. They were substantial
ratepayers and it was in their interests to minimize the
business contribution to the town's spending and ensure
that little was spent for the borough's benefit outside their
local community.

Tradespeople served on the council to protect their trade
from anyone with a bias against business, especially
Socialists. Alfred Roberts recognised this and he had his
reservations about some of their attitudes. All those who
remember him recall a man of more liberal social beliefs
than his fellow Independents, and particularly interested in
the foundation of the modern welfare state in wartime.

With such a father, there is no obvious explanation for
why Margaret should have plumped so firmly for the
Conservatives, rejecting the cavils which held her father
back from joining them in name. She first learnt the
business of politics among small-town businessmen whose
notions of self-determination were mixed with municipal
pride and a commitment to working for their ends in the
public domain – which is not necessarily the same as a
strong commitment to public service. From the time in 1935
when she first helped at a parliamentary election, she was
working for the Conservatives, and perhaps her father's
reservations were of small influence compared to the
encouragement she received from the others. But her
political allegiance was not obviously important because she
was not considering a political career. As she told Patricia
Murray about her work, aged ten, for Victor Warrender, 'It
never occurred to me that one day I would be in the same
position. But as far as actually going into politics was
concerned – no! There was absolutely no question of it

because I couldn't possibly have afforded it ... It was
beyond my vision because I always had to think in terms of
a career in which I could keep myself.'

The first step towards any career of substance was
winning the scholarship to the Kesteven and Grantham
Girls' School. It was a traditional grammar school which
began with a preparatory section, nicknamed 'The Kindo',
which fee-paying girls could join aged five. At the age of
eleven, when fee-paying girls had just left III Lower, a
number of scholarship girls arrived from state schools, as
did Margaret Roberts in 1936. There were two streams and
she was placed in IIIB, the slow stream, which had, as
might be expected, a dearth of scholarship girls, who had
mostly been placed in IIIA. Both forms were made up of
about thirty-two girls. The school consisted of five houses –
Brontë, Austen, Eliot, Rosetti and Browning – and at the
beginning of each new school year, the house captains
would pick names from a hat. Margaret Roberts found
herself in Brontë, a house which had a reputation for girls
who were good at games and gym. At the end of the year,
Margaret was top of her form, but was not moved into the
bright stream. In 1937, the year an old girl of the school
became the first female mayor of Grantham, she started in
IV Lower B and continued her excellent academic
performance, ending the year with an outstanding report
and, once again, coming top of her class. She was also made
a form monitoress. The headmistress, Miss Williams, who
had been with the school since its foundation in 1910,
decided then to move her up to the 'A' stream and she
continued there for the next three years. Her school report is
a remarkable document, still kept by the school. She held an
impeccable record, winning a D for distinction in each of
her years and coming top of her class each year except the
fifth, when she came second. Each year the headmistress's
report says much the same thing: 'Margaret is ambitious
and deserves to do well.' Her average marks never fell below
seventy per cent. The only subject which she found
impossible was art.

She was a studious girl, but enjoyed the dramatic society,
which made her at one time consider becoming an actress,

and also question and answer sessions at the end of visitors' lectures, as long as the subject was current affairs. She is well remembered by a girl in the year above her, Margaret Goodrich, for cross-questioning Bernard Newman, the expert on spying, with a confidence not normally expected from such a young girl. Another girl, Madeline Edwards, remembers that this forwardness irritated many of her classmates, who used to whisper to each other, 'She's at it again,' or 'Trust Margaret.'

Margaret seemed to be immune from the pack-mentality which infects schoolchildren and had taken to heart something which her father had told her. His advice to her was, 'You do not follow the crowd because you're afraid of being different — you decide what to do yourself and if necessary you lead the crowd, but you never just follow.' And there was more advice from him of a similar sort: 'You make up your own mind. You do not do something or want to do something because your friends are doing it. You never say, well, they're doing it, that's why I want to do it.' To an extent, Margaret Roberts was a girl apart. She came from a home which forbade many of the pursuits outside the school which her friends enjoyed. Instead, she and Muriel depended for most of their social life upon the Methodist Church. They were fully aware of what they were missing, but did not question their parents' influence. Margaret does not remember going to a dance until she arrived at Oxford University.

At the girls' school, Margaret Roberts had been surrounded for two years by girls of a very different social background. Their parents paid the school fees with comparative ease, whereas her father, even with the means-tested scholarship, found the fees a significant burden on the tightly-managed household budget.

When Margaret was thirteen, her sister Muriel left school, then home, to take a five-year course in physiotherapy in Birmingham. She qualified and returned to work in Grantham, first at the hospital, then visiting patients in their homes. The fact that Muriel was out in the world — and bringing home things like make-up and lipstick — gave a new twist to Margaret's ambitions. Having rejected acting, she decided to join the Indian Civil Service, partly under the influence of Kipling. But she came across the unromantic mind of Miss Dorothy Gillies, a Scot who had taken over as headmistress on the retirement of Miss Williams in 1939. Miss Gillies, in the first of several battles of will, pointed out that it was very difficult for women to succeed in the Indian Civil Service and that very few were even accepted. Margaret replied, 'That sounds a very good reason for trying to get into it.'

It was eventually decided that Margaret should at least attempt to go to university and that, as a preliminary, she would specialize in the sciences at Higher School Certificate level. As she explained, 'That was a period when we were dazzled by what it could achieve. We thought there were no problems that could not ultimately be answered by science.' Her ambition of a university place was encouraged by her father, who regretted his own lack of education and lived many of his ambitions through his daughter, who could benefit from the egalitarian advances established in the generation between them.

Grantham was close to many RAF aerodromes and wartime increased the business of the town. Once again, the town converted its productive capacity to munitions. The girls' school had to make many adjustments. There were sandbags, quick sales in aid of war weapons, warship weeks and Ministry of Information cinema shows. Most amusing, perhaps, was having to share the school buildings with the Camden High School for Girls, from London, which had been evacuated. The local girls studied in the mornings, from 8:30 to 12:30, and then were excused afternoon school while the Camden school took over. Other lessons were squeezed in at a big house called Stonebridge, near the Preparatory Department, and during half terms, when the Camden girls went home. This sharing system lasted until bombing in Grantham became so heavy that the Camden school was evacuated to Uppingham.

Alfred Roberts, too old for war service, became a great expert on the war, its causes and its military developments, and he would read each week up to three library books on the war alone. He read them so fast and so avidly that the

Grantham librarian, Mr Percy Willard, used to ask him questions to discover whether he really had read them. These stories relayed by her father, and the Churchill broadcasts, left Margaret with a strongly patriotic, dramatic and romantic view of those, like Airey Neave, who became wartime heroes.

Wartime also meant bombing. It was quite regular for the Roberts family to take refuge underneath the dining-room table on the ground floor — they had no cellar — and Margaret would take her homework with her. She had developed a tenacious concentration and once, during a School Certificate exam, she became so engrossed that, at the end, she was surprised to discover that there had been a noisy thunderstorm throughout.

It was forbidden for girls from her school even to walk home with boys from the King's School, the local boys' grammar school, and Margaret Roberts was not one to break rules. As Madeline Edwards recalls, 'I don't remember Margaret ever being interested in boys in that way. She was far too busy with her studies.'

Although Alfred Roberts worked for the war effort in all sorts of ways, adapting his council and church work to take in the new emergency, the Roberts family were not directly involved in the hostilities until one day they received a letter from the parents of an Austrian Jewish girl, Edith, asking them to help her escape from Vienna. Edith was Muriel's pen friend, acquired from a school project. Margaret had one, too, a French girl. Alf Roberts wrote back saying that he would be pleased to help in any way he could and that Edith was welcome to stay with them in Grantham. She arrived shortly afterwards and told the girls of life under Nazi occupation. As Margaret remembers, 'She would talk to us for hours about all the things that were happening, so we learned from her about the dreadful things that were going on there.'

Wartime also brought a coalition government and the return to power of many Labour figures. Alfred Roberts used to encourage Margaret to go to the town hall to hear visiting speakers, which, around this time, included Herbert Morrison, inspecting the local Air Raid Precautions service, and another socialist, A.V. Alexander, the First Lord of the Admiralty. In March 1942 there was a by-election in Grantham. There were two principal candidates: Sir Arthur Longmore, the Conservative; and William Kendall, a newly-rich arms manufacturer, running as an Independent. Kendall was well known to Alfred Roberts, who used to borrow books from him, but his flashy approach to his new wealth and his involvement in making profit from the instruments of war meant that Alfred — and Margaret — worked for the Conservative candidate. Instead of simply running between polling station and committee room, this time Margaret, aged sixteen, folded and posted leaflets. It did not help. Kendall was very popular locally. However temporary his boom in munitions was to be, it created a great deal of work locally and his image of a big-spending, high-living self-made local boy made good had obvious attractions over the staid, solid Sir Arthur. Kendall won by 367 votes. (In 1945 he pushed his majority, in a three-cornered fight, to 15,513.)

At school, Margaret was working towards the qualifications which would allow her to enter university. She had chosen chemistry and got on particularly well with her chemistry teacher, Miss M.P. Kay, whom the girls nicknamed Katie. Miss R.H. Dulton taught her biology and she also took mathematics as a third subject. The school leaving age at the time was fourteen and by the sixth form there were so few girls that both VI and Lower VI were taught together, alternate years providing half the syllabus.

It was in the sixth form that Margaret Roberts first met Margaret Goodrich, the daughter of Canon Harold Goodrich, vicar of Corby, a small village ten miles to the south of Grantham. They became close friends and have remained so. Their families and homes were rather different, the Goodrichs having reached a second generation of university entrance. Their home, an Elizabethan vicarage, was a civilized place, quite unlike the organised bustle of the flat in North Parade. Years later, when Margaret Roberts was newly engaged, she brought Denis to see the Goodrich family home and, in particular, a room laden with books. She revealed the awe in which she held such a monument to learning by saying, 'I so wanted to show Denis your library.' The Goodrich family had never thought of the room before as a library, merely a room with a lot of books.

Although Alfred Roberts would keep his daughter on the right lines and encourage her natural inquisitiveness, there were limits to his self-education. When it came to choosing a university and studying for the essential general paper, she depended upon Canon Goodrich for advice. She would arrive with a string bag full of rare and rationed items, such as butter, on her regular and rarely reciprocated visits to the Goodrich home in Corby.

The result of the conversations between the canon and the schoolgirl were that she should try at least for a university which would take her. She determined to approach Nottingham, and Bedford and Holloway Colleges at the University of London, but wondered whether she hadn't undervalued herself. Margaret Goodrich was planning to go to Somerville College, Oxford, and Margaret Roberts could see no reason why she should not try for the same place. Having decided, she approached Miss Gillies, who pointed out the many pitfalls that stood in her way. For instance, she would need to learn Latin, an essential prerequisite for Oxford, and there was no time. And, without saying so to her directly, Miss Gillies implied that, perhaps, she was having ideas above her station. She stormed away from the headmistress's study, grumbling, 'She's trying to thwart my ambition.' This apparent opposition from Miss Gillies made Margaret Roberts even more determined to proceed. As the girls' school did not teach Latin, she persuaded her father to employ Victor Waterhouse, the classics master at the King's School, to cram her in the subject. When Miss Gillies said that it was an impossible task and that she would not spend the school's money on entering her for an exam she was unlikely to pass, Margaret went to her father and returned to Miss Gillies' study with a cheque, saying, 'I have decided to go in for this exam, so will you please send off my forms?'

She was to exact her revenge on Miss Gillies many years later. In 1960 there was an Old Girls' dinner to celebrate the diamond jubilee of the school. She was the after-dinner speaker and was introduced by Miss Gillies, by this time retired, who used an incorrect Latin phrase. Margaret Thatcher, as she had become, seized her chance and corrected her old headmistress – a spiteful, unnecessary act which did not go down well with her assembled former school mates.

The quest for a place at Somerville continued. She had received warm and generous offers from Nottingham and Bedford College, London, but she continued with her preparations for the Oxford entrance examinations. Her crash course in Latin was successful and, in the late part of the autumn term of 1942, she went to Oxford for the first time, an overnight stay in Somerville, for the entrance exams. She took written papers in her science subjects, a general paper and an interview. She did well, but not well enough, as it turned out. She came equal first with another girl who was competing for the second – and last – time. The college awarded that girl the scholarship, but, as compensation, put Margaret Roberts on the waiting list for a place. It was a big disappointment.

Margaret was, in any case, wondering whether chemistry was the best subject for what she wanted to do. Although politics as a career was only a remote possibility for financial reasons, it was the thing which interested her the most. She had come to the conclusion that if she were finally to decide, after university, that politics was an option, she would be badly placed with a chemistry degree. She explained her doubts to Norman Winning, a Recorder friend of her father's who sat with him on the local magistrates' bench. She had taken a great interest in the court and thought that perhaps the law would have suited her and fitted her better for politics, were she to make that choice. Norman Winning told her not to worry, that he had a physics degree himself and that, if she were truly interested in the law when she had graduated in chemistry, she would be well placed to take a second degree and qualify for, say, the patents bar, where her scientific degree would put her at an advantage.

And so, in the autumn term of 1943, Margaret Roberts

returned to Kesteven and Grantham Girls' School for a third year in the sixth form. She was now at the top of the school. She had risen to become House Captain of Brontë, and was part of a highly successful first hockey XI. She had become Deputy Head Girl and, at the beginning of that term, she was summoned to Miss Gillies' study with Madeline Edwards to be told of their Higher results. Madeline Edwards' diary for that day reads, 'M.R. has passed.' The following day, both were summoned again to Miss Gillies' room and were appointed joint Head Girls, the first time the school had done such a thing. The term had begun three weeks earlier than usual, because there was a wartime scheme to spend three weeks of October on local farms, potato picking. Three weeks into the term, when, in normal times, the autumn term would just have started, Somerville sent a letter to Margaret Roberts inviting her to take up a place which had become unexpectedly available. She left school at once. The school, to its credit, gave her full honours and, for her three weeks in the post of Head Girl, marked her name on the roll of honour.

CHAPTER THREE

Oxford

In February 1983, the Prime Minister, Margaret Thatcher made a private visit to Oxford to unveil a bust of herself which now stands in the college buildings to which she had come as Margaret Roberts as an undergraduate in October 1943. In her brief speech, she paid compliment to Oxford as the place which was the break, where she had become herself and where the world had opened up. (She left the college that day to the sound of a small, but angry demonstration mounted by the undergraduates of 1983 against her economic policies.)

She arrived at Oxford an unsophisticated, lower-middle class Lincolnshire girl. By the time she left, four years later, she had acquired firm ambition, friends higher up the social scale and the qualification which had eluded her father. 'When I got there, I think the first thing I learnt was that for the first time in my life, you are totally divorced from your background,' she said later. She must also have realised that, to pursue a career either at the bar or in politics, she would need money – and more than she was likely to earn from being a chemist.

Somerville College, a modest network of red-brick and stone buildings at the southern end of the Woodstock Road, had girded itself with stiff academic disapproval against the inconveniences of war, but had been unable to keep them out entirely. One building had been surrendered to the Radcliffe Hospital as accommodation for male medical students, and was known to the college as the 'Isle of Man.' Two loggias looking onto the college lawns had had ponds sunk into them to supply water pumps in case of fire. The college had organised a 'trailer pump team' and there was a large Air Raid Precautions noticeboard carrying details of stirrup pumps, hoses, hydrants and fire escapes. In the academic year that Margaret Roberts arrived, members of the college acted as guinea pigs for some local research into malaria, designed to help the war effort in the South Pacific; 'they became markedly yellow,' the Junior Common Room archives record, 'but suffered little other inconvenience.'

Margaret was homesick. In her own words, 'When you've been at home, you have never known what it's like to be lonely. It's quite an experience the first time you come across it and it takes a while to make new friends.' Margaret Goodrich, who had arrived at Oxford two years ahead of her school friend, remembered seeing her often, once visiting her with her father and finding her disconsolately toasting crumpets in her room.

To be a woman and a scientist was to be twice removed from the main stream of undergraduate life. Incoming students were treated to a talk by the dean, the college fellow designated to supervise social and disciplinary matters – a more time-consuming duty then than now. Vera Farnell, the college's French tutor and dean, left notes on the conduct of the office dated October 1943 (the year that Margaret Roberts arrived) which gave a flavour of the time and include a 'script' for the talk to 'freshers'. It began with some guidance on the university's formal black and white dress: 'If you aim at looking appropriate and "right" and would avoid the risk of looking common and vulgar, or unfortunately dressed, avoid associating academic dress with any but the very discreetest of make-up. As smoking in academic dress is a university offence, so are brightly coloured lips and fingernails an offence against good taste.'

Male visitors were allowed in rooms only between 2 and 7 pm, and the same, no doubt frequently breached, limits applied to Somervillians visiting men's colleges. The dean was recommended to tell her new charges to 'guard the reputation of women in the university and in your own college ... women still have enemies within Oxford as well as outside.' The dean was supposed to 'make occasional perambulations in different buildings after 11.15 p.m.'

Social life was restricted by blackouts, and shortages of food, drink and men who were neither too old nor too young, those of the right age being mostly in the army. The war had lowered the age of the youngest undergraduates; Balliol, whose choir used occasionally to join up with a Somerville choir which included Margaret Roberts, had posted a notice which took note of an important wrinkle in the rationing rules. It read, 'Gentlemen under 18 may collect their bananas from the porters' lodge.'

Margaret joined the Bach Choir, the Scientific Society and a student Methodist group. Most important of all, she joined the Oxford University Conservative Association; it was the route out of the 'impersonal' world of the laboratory — the word she used to describe it afterwards — out of the dowdiness of Somerville, which was non-denominational and had always been considered middle-class by comparison with Lady Margaret Hall, which was Anglican and classy, and a route to a club of her own kind in an undergraduate world dominated by Liberals and Socialists and witty people reading arts subjects, interested in arts or sports. A world in which it might have been fashionable to be a woman, but it was not fashionable to be a scientist or a Conservative.

She has since denied an early vaulting ambition to be an MP or political meteor; even if the thought had occurred to her, the next few years suggest that she knew it was to be a long march. 'I worked all day,' she later said, ' ... a lot of laboratory work in the daytime and lectures in the early evening. I spent a lot of my time talking and discussing political matters, as I had done at home. But I knew I had to get my qualifications, then a job, and that political activity would have to come second to that. So I saw politics in terms of voluntary part-time activity, on a local level. Looking at it from a strictly financial point of view, at the time we are speaking of, MPs were paid £9 a week. I couldn't have done a proper job as an MP on £9 a week, to cover secretarial help and living in London as well as a constituency. I had no private income or trade union to back me. I just didn't think of being a Member of Parliament.' Attlee's unexpected election victory in 1945 was to change that: MPs were subsequently paid £1000 a year, making those impossible things more of a possibility. But Margaret's political ambitions had been clear to her friends at school, let alone at Oxford. Now they were explicit. She explained to Margaret Goodrich that she thought she had made a mistake in reading chemistry. 'I know I ought really to have read another subject for politics; I shall have to go and read law,' her friend remembers her saying in the summer of 1947 as she completed her degree.

She was profoundly affected by the war, perhaps more so than many of her contemporaries. Like most, she did spells of fire-watching and served at a forces' canteen. She felt the war as a moral issue, more than a political or military one. One of her favourite books, 'The Last Enemy' by Richard Hillary, was published in 1943 and she read it soon afterwards, often quoting the message of the last chapter. Hillary, a well-educated young airman recovering from injuries, witnesses the death of a woman after a bomb destroys her house:

'Her death was unjust, a crime, an outrage, a sin against mankind — weak inadequate words which even as they passed through my mind mocked me with their futility.

'That that woman should so die was an enormity so great that it was terrifying in its implications, in its lifting of the veil on the possibilities of thought so far beyond the grasp of the human mind. It was not just the German bombs, or the German Air Force, or even the German mentality, but a feeling of the very essence of anti-life that no words could convey. This was what I had been cursing — in part, for I had recognised in that moment what it was that Peter and the others had instantly recognised as evil and to be destroyed utterly. I saw now that it was not a crime; it was Evil itself — something of which until then I had not even sensed the existence. And it was in the end, at bottom, myself against which I had raged, myself I had cursed. With awful clarity I saw myself suddenly as I was. Great God, that I could have been so arrogant!'

Margaret canvassed for the Conservatives in the 1945 election campaign and at the end of that summer term she did the same in the villages surrounding Grantham in support of the local Conservatives. She warmed up audiences before the candidate arrived or spoke. She later recalled meeting an acquaintance and commenting on the result, 'Isn't the news dreadful?' 'Oh I don't know,' he said. 'I'm really rather pleased about it.' She and Muriel had been back to Grantham frequently that year: it was the year that Alderman Roberts spent as mayor. The previous summer vacation, Margaret had spent teaching science at Grantham's Central School for Boys. During the war, the school arranged a six-week August term, so that the pupils could be released later in the year to pick rose hips. She recalled, 'I used to go on until I knew they'd got it, and I wasn't prepared to let them go on until they'd got it. And you might have to come at it several different ways, particularly in mathematics.'

The end of the war brought an influx of officers and men to Oxford, and with them a breath of fresh air and experience. The Somerville which had been run by Miss Helen Darbyshire since 1931 was taken over by Dr Janet Vaughan, the first head of any Oxford college to be a scientist. Miss Darbyshire had exhorted her students to study in a disinterested way, for love of the subject and not for its use. She was fond of telling the story of an exceedingly able young mathematician who had successfully played the Stock Exchange to keep his mother and sister, but, she pointed out firmly, he had *not* studied mathematics to do that, but for the sake of the subject itself. Dr Janet Vaughan was of a somewhat different mould; she was already known in the world of medical science for her work on radiology and blood, and had spent the war putting her skills to very practical use – she had been a member of the first medical team into Belsen after its liberation.

She very quickly noticed Miss Roberts. 'She fascinated me. I used to talk to her a great deal; she was an oddity. Why? She was a Conservative – she stood out. Somerville had always been a radical establishment and there weren't many Conservatives about then. We used to argue about politics; she was so set in steel as a Conservative. She just had this one line ... We used to entertain a good deal at weekends, but she didn't get invited. She had nothing to contribute, you see.' Years after their Oxford careers, Margaret told Edward Boyle that her anger during Dame Janet's intermittent attempts at political re-education had helped develop her own political position.

But she was invited out on the Conservative circuits; as a political allegiance it may not have been fashionable, but this obscured its actual popularity. By 1946, it was the second largest society in the university after the Union. Editorials in the Association's *News Digest* would begin with sentences like, 'Mr Shinwell is at it again.' 'She has been painted as something of a blue-stocking,' said Maurice Chandler, who was OUCA's secretary when Margaret Roberts was president in the summer of 1946. 'I don't think her contemporaries would have said that.'

She gave, Chandler recalled, excellent parties: the food and drink did not run out and you could guarantee that you would meet someone you had not met before. An anonymous social columnist of the *News Digest* attended the Association garden party in the summer of 1947, Margaret Roberts' final term, preserving a snapshot of some intriguing faces. 'Mr Robert Runcie,' the column breathlessly recorded, 'was everywhere.' The Honourable Anthony Wedgwood Benn, then president of the Union and pressing for the admission of women who were at the time barred from membership, attended, wearing a red tie. 'Mr Peter Kirk told us of his nephew and Miss Roberts told us it was positively her last OUCA function.'

It was an important liberation. 'On Saturday nights, some girls at my school would go to dances or parties. It sounded very nice. I would like to have gone. But my sister and I didn't go dancing.' Oxford had changed that. 'As I got older, I was able to do things I hadn't been able to do earlier on. I went out to parties much more and came to love ballroom dancing.' Miss Roberts, as president of the sister association in the other place, attended the Cambridge University Conservative Association ball in the autumn of 1946. Edward Boyle, in those days something of a star at the Union, came to Maurice Chandler's room one day shortly before his sister was due to have her coming-out

dance at the Savoy. 'My mother's been working things out,'
he explained. 'Can you take Margaret?' Thus were social
arrangements made in those days. They were the days when
bright young undergraduates enjoyed repartee of this ilk:
'His dancing's irresistible.' 'Yes, *so* like a bulldozer.'
Margaret is remembered searching for the right chemical
formula for preserving as long as possible a carnation given
to her one evening by an admirer; she eventually settled for
the tried and tested method of dissolving an aspirin in water
and putting it in that.

With a Labour government leading post-war thinking
and reconstruction, political debate started on left-of-centre
ground: the topics of the time were profit-sharing plans and
discussions of 'co-partnership' with the unions. 'It seems to
be generally agreed,' said a *News Digest* leader of 1947,
'that the future organisation of industry will be divided
between public and private enterprise.' Anthony Crosland
was president of the Union in 1946; ex-POW
undergraduates included ex-Lance Corporal Fred Mulley.

In 1945, the Union – whose debates Mrs Thatcher later
dismissed as 'rather frothy' – narrowly rejected the motion
that the house would welcome a Conservative government.
But a year later, OUCA's president and her treasurer,
Edward Boyle, welcomed Sir Anthony Eden to Oxford with
a sherry party, just as the Association's membership went
over a thousand. Eden went on to a debate in the Union
where a motion saying that the Conservatives had no
constructive alternative to socialism was heavily defeated.
Speakers who came to the Association during Miss Roberts'
presidency included Captain Peter Thorneycroft, MP, who
subsequently kept in touch. Representing OUCA, its
president attended her first party conference in October
1946.

What kind of Conservative was she? Nobody would have
thought of her as out of the mainstream, said one of her
OUCA contemporaries, echoing several similar
descriptions. The undergraduate Conservatives were fond of
writing policy prescriptions for their party. Margaret
Roberts was a co-author of papers suggesting that the
decolonisation of Africa should leave national boundaries

as far as possible the same as tribal territories (an idea
which would still have a sympathetic hearing today) and
one on Conservative philosophy which inveighed against
over-reliance on reason and logic in the making of party
doctrine. 'There was no sign then of the things which mark
her out now,' said one of her colleagues. 'We were all
thoroughly middle-of-the-road, liberal kinds of
Conservatives. That was the style of those days. Sometimes
I really wonder how far the girl that we knew ... I just
wonder whether she is really all that far to the right.' There
was a right wing to student Conservative politics:
agressively social, fond of point-to-points, drunken male
dinners and unlikely to be sympathetic to ambitious young
ladies from Grantham. Nobody remembers Margaret
having any sympathy for them. 'One doesn't associate her
with ideas,' said another contemporary. 'The image of a
great woman of ideas and convictions is pretty good
rubbish. She was very nice but an absolutely hard-boiled
Conservative Association officer with no particular spark of
independent thought. She took Conservatism as it was
handed out. She was very determined to make a political
career for herself.'

In common with many chemistry students, Margaret
Roberts chose to take a fourth year of her course,
concentrating her work in X-ray crystallography. Most of
those who taught her or monitored her academic progress
saw a determined and thorough student, but not a brilliant
one. 'She was a good beta,' Dame Janet Vaughan
remembered, 'hardworking, competent. None of us ever
thought she would go very far. She was not the sort of
person to whom you say at the beginning of their last year:
now are you going to give up whatever it is and concentrate
on work, because if you do then you may get a first.'
Dorothy Hodgkin, the college's chemistry tutor and later
Nobel Prize winner, received clear, solid work from her
pupil and had the impression that she enjoyed her subject,
but also 'that she wasn't absolutely devoted to it'. Her tutors
were aware of her other interests. Professor Sir Harold
Thompson, who lectured to her twice a week for several
terms and supervised laboratory experiments, thought that

she looked intelligent and determined and remembers one of his colleagues saying, 'Well, I don't know where the hell that girl's going to, but she's going somewhere.' She left with a respectable second class degree.

The idea of becoming an MP must have seemed more real and possible with the contacts and experience of student politics. Her own description of the idea occurring to her places it at a party given one vacation in Corby, near Grantham, by Margaret Goodrich.

'I think it was a 21st birthday party to which I was invited. And it was quite a way away, so we stayed the night. And the great thing about parties isn't the party — it's really congregating afterwards in the kitchen (being a vicarage, it had quite a big kitchen), and you just sit down and you talk and you get whatever there is to eat — cup of tea, sandwiches — and you just sit down and talk. And of course, I was talking about politics. I so often was. And one person there just suddenly said, "Well, then, you'd really like to become a MP?" And it kind of crystallised everything which I wished to do. I said, "Yes, I would like to." '

However, it was hardly to be left to chance. She needed a job to support herself, but the next few years make it clear that she can never have seriously intended to be a research chemist. One of the recruiters touring the major universities in 1947 on what would nowadays be known as the 'milk round' was the head of research and development at one of the country's oldest plastics firms, British Xylonite. Stanley Booth usually recruited between eight and ten graduates each year to join seventy or so other graduates who mostly worked in his department. Theoretical research had produced several new plastics which were just being converted to commercial uses. At a plant employing just under three thousand people on the north bank of the River Stour opposite Manningtree, Essex, BX produced the raw materials which were elsewhere made into spectacle frames, baby pants, electrical insulation and plastic raincoats.

Margaret started work at a salary of £350 a year. Women recruits began at £50 a year less than male graduates, although Mr Booth remembers that all three

women he hired that year turned out to be better than their
male counterparts and their salaries were quickly brought
into line. She worked between the main factory and a
research station about two miles away; after a general
introduction to the work of the firm, she worked on
whatever practical problem had been put in front of the
department. She spent some time studying surface tensions
and working on the development of an adhesive for sticking
the newly-produced polyvinyl-chloride to wood or metal.
She was, said Mr Booth, 'very conscientious, very thorough,
hard-working. Not a lot of imagination, though. But that's
not a good quality in a politician — she would doubt herself
if she had too much imagination.'

She took digs ten miles away in Colchester in the large
house of a recently widowed mother of two, Mrs Enid
McAuley, and joined the local Conservative association.
She impressed her landlady as busy and obviously
determined to become a politician; she rapidly made herself
useful to the local party in the variety of ways in which any
local branch is grateful for voluntary energy: canvassing —
she is remembered as being proud of having canvassed for
Quintin Hogg in Oxford in 1945 — and running stalls at
fetes. One of her fellow members described her 'just a very
good sort'. Mrs McAuley recalls a well-turned out young
lady; 'nice suits, nice blouses, nice gloves.' The local party
had formed a 39/45 group for ex-servicemen which used to
meet in a Colchester pub and she was a regular attender at
the discussions. Iain Macleod and Enoch Powell spoke at
the fortnightly meetings during her time there.

Dressed in her Burberry coat, she would take the works
bus to the factory every morning. She recruited several of
her colleagues to the Young Conservatives and debated
across the canteen table. Stanley Booth recalls having
plenty of political arguments with his new chemist. 'Most of
us tended to be if anything on the left side in those days. I
was a bit older and I had seen the thirties at close quarters
and seen the need for a safety net. At the time her views
seemed rather simplistic. She'd come up not the hard way,
but the medium-hard way, and hadn't seen the thirties. She
believed then, as she believes now, that people should stand

on their own two feet. I'd come up the hard way and didn't quite see things like that. Now, of course, she's quite right: the safety net's grown too big and she's trying to cut it down.'

Mr Booth, reading and watching today's Prime Minister, says that her style has changed little. Her views, however, appear to have been conventional for the party of the time: she came to Colchester in the year of R.A. Butler's Industrial Charter. The Charter, which was to be discussed throughout the party to encourage what Butler called the 'two-way movement of ideas', represented a merger of pre-war economic Conservatism (cuts in public expenditure to finance tax cuts, some privatisation of nationalised industries, abolition of the closed shop) with concessions to the contemporary climate which favoured central planning and intervention (it accepted the need to aim for full employment, deficit budgeting, some nationalisation and regular cooperation between industry and the state). Her colleages do not recall their busy young graduate in connection with any particular position in party debate; one member described the 39/45 group as composed of people who had 'rapidly become disillusioned with the Socialist Utopia to which they had returned.'

In 1948 she went to the party conference at Llandudno, representing Oxford graduates. She was sitting during one session with a friend from undergraduate days, John Grant, a director of the bookshop Blackwell's, and on her other side sat John Miller, chairman of the Dartford Conservative Association. As she tells it, 'We all three walked out in the lunch-break down the Llandudno pier and my Oxford friend said to the chairman of Dartford, "I hear you're trying to find a candidate to fight the next election." "Oh yes," said John Miller, my chairman. "We shall need a very able young man. It's a very tough industrial area." "Oh," said my Oxford friend, "would you not consider an able young woman?" "Oh no, it's not that sort of area at all." "Well, would you just consider her?" "She can apply." And then he said that it was me. You see, I had not thought of applying at all. And then they brought along the women's chairman and she looked at me and then said: "Well, just apply." And that was how really I came to apply.'

She applied and went for interview in early 1949; with a Labour majority of almost 20,000 it could be no more than a training ground. But training grounds within easy reach of London are prized; she was one of 24 candidates who were whittled down to a short list of three. The entrants included two men who were beaten by their future leader but who later won Parliamentary seats: Trevor Skeet and Cranley Onslow. Several members of the selection committee argued hard against selecting a woman but they were a minority. The constituency had been unable to tempt the men they thought would do best. John Miller admitted at Margaret Thatcher's adoption meeting that the association had approached unsuccessfully four local businessmen to see if they would be prepared to stand.

It was an unusual selection in any terms, but particularly in a constituency of that kind: she was 23 when selected and the youngest woman candidate in the country. The local Young Conservatives, said their chairman Miss Mary Hamilton, were 'terribly bucked' that a young person had been chosen.

Dartford no longer exists as a Parliamentary division but was then a thin strip of the North Kent coast divided between light industry, working-class housing and commuter dormitories. There were three focal towns: Crayford, Erith and Dartford. The issues a candidate would be expected to address ranged from the local question of whether there should be double-decker trains on the North Kent railway lines to the wisdom or otherwise of the bulk buying of raw material by government for industry. The sitting member was a well-liked Labour veteran with a well-developed skill for publicity stunts, Norman Dodds.

Margaret's father came down to speak at her adoption meeting on 28 February 1949, telling the audience that the Conservative party now stood for the principles which the Liberals had defended when he was young. No member of the audience appears to have been awkward enough to raise the question of the gap between the two parties on trade with the empire; Alderman Roberts' daughter was campaigning vigorously in support of the Conservative 'imperial preference' policy at the time, which the Liberals were committed against. Only one vote was raised against the motion that she should be adopted as candidate and a collection was taken towards election expenses, for the general election could not be far away: £37-13s, which was then doubled by an anonymous supporter.

Her first move was away from the job at British Xylonite: she took a job in the research department of J. Lyons & Co. at Cadby Hall in Hammersmith and arranged to lodge in Dartford. The marking of time had stopped and the political career was about to begin; however hopeless the seat, it was a foot on the ladder and her youth and proximity to London guaranteed good publicity.

The other crucial change happened almost simultaneously. She had to return to Colchester for work the morning after her adoption meeting and was offered a lift by a constituency activist who had been at the meeting, a tall bespectacled extrovert called Denis Thatcher. He was a director of a family paint and chemicals firm in Erith and had once, unsuccessfully, fought a seat on Kent County Council as a ratepayer candidate. The relationship did not develop immediately. Mrs Thatcher was once asked by an interviewer whether it had been love at first sight. 'Certainly not,' she replied.

She commuted to London each day, catching the 7.10 train to Charing Cross and the 6.08 back again at night to be in time for meetings and canvassing. She had no car and so local party members used to take turns to chauffeur her about. Her work at J. Lyons & Co. involved the testing of processes and products. She worked on new fillings for Swiss rolls, investigated ways of preserving the foamy quality of ice cream and tested machinery to see that it was uncontaminated. She was discovering techniques of organisation which kept this activity in order. 'The great secret of life,' she said later, 'is turning 90% of it into habit. In that way you can keep it turning over – after all, you don't think about cleaning your teeth, it's a habit.'

She was rescued from cheerless digs by one of her chauffeurs, chairman of a constituency ward, Ray Woolcott. The Woolcotts had no children of their own and

Margaret paid no rent for her own room. She wrote constituency letters in front of the fire and frequently ironed her favourite black velvet dress. She was often taken out — one admirer used to send orchids. Occasionally, but not often, Denis Thatcher would arrive to pick her up, driving a large Jaguar and hooting outside. She was also being wooed by a Scottish farmer she had met at a dance in Colchester, Willie Cullen. He proposed and was turned down. Not long afterwards, he proposed to Muriel Roberts, whom he had met through Margaret, and was accepted.

The campaign of 1950, fought in atrocious January weather, nevertheless included a full round of open-air meetings, often one at lunchtime and a couple at night. Old-fashioned heckling was common and she impressed the newspaper reporters who visited the constituency in search of some light novelty with her combative approach. Norman Dodds adopted a style of avuncular affability towards his challenger and promised to take her to lunch at Westminster when the campaign was over. She addressed one meeting on the eve of poll to which the police had been called when fighting had broken out during a warm-up speech by a speaker deputed to keep the crowd interested until she arrived from a meeting at the other end of the constituency. The journalist and playwright Robert Muller was at the time London correspondent of the German-language magazine of the American military government in Germany. Asked by superiors to illustrate British democracy at work, he visited the battle in Dartford.

'I must say I thought that she was incredibly plucky in that safe Labour seat, not to say off her rocker. She seemed absolutely convinced that she was going to get it this time, that people would come round to her way of thinking. We took a picture of her with test tubes, I remember — she was quite aware of publicity and its value — and I think that Conservative Central Office were quite glad of her, she was a young starlet. I thought that it was a freakish thing to do; she was clearly never going to get into the House. She was fearless at meetings and pleasant but cool to meet; blinkered, determined, ambitious.' Muller's article recorded her promising that a Conservative government would end unemployment.

She did not understate her case. The election was a battle between two ways of life, 'one which led inevitably to slavery and the other to freedom.' Conservatism was not, she told one audience, for the privileged few, underlining the point with phrases which would raise an ironic smile today: 'What is the first tenet of Conservatism? It is that of national unity. We say one nation, not one class against each other. You cannot build a great nation or a brotherhood of man by spreading envy or hatred.' She was ambitious and well-behaved, but some touches of the later Thatcher showed through. The Labour Party, she told another audience, had proposals which 'looked so reasonable on the surface, but underneath were most pernicious and nibbled into our national life and character far further than one would be aware at first glance.' She recalled a metaphor of her father's about a caged bird: 'It has social security. It has food and it has warmth, and so on. But what is the good of all that if it has not the freedom to fly out and live its own life?'

It was the election which asked, 'Whose finger on the trigger?' and the *Daily Mirror* front page asking the question (about Churchill and his attitude to the cold war) appeared in many windows. Miss Roberts spoke in a few neighbouring constituencies, including to a ladies' luncheon club in Bexleyheath, where the candidate was Edward Heath. Amid a huge swing to the Conservatives, she reduced Dodds' majority to 13,000 but Attlee's government just survived. Whatever the actual result in the constituency, she was well launched; that summer she proposed the vote of thanks to Winston Churchill at a mass Conservative women's rally at the Albert Hall. Later that year, at a meeting of Conservative candidates, she met for the first time the escape hero of Colditz, Airey Neave.

Some time between the election of February 1950 and September 1951, she left the Dartford lodgings and moved into her own flat in St George's Square Mews, Pimlico. She was still going out with Denis Thatcher. 'We dined out from time to time,' she said, 'and went to the occasional cinema or theatre. But they were still rather dark days in 1949 and

1950; there wasn't a lot of gay life about.' He took her to his trade association's annual dance, and failed to impress her with the speed of his two cars. 'We had the same common interests,' she said on another occasion. 'He didn't half ask me some tough economic questions.'

Denis Thatcher was the grandson of an enterprising Kent farmer who early in this century found out that sodium arsenite made a good sheep dip and a better weed killer. The fruits of the successful exploitation of this discovery were passed on to Denis by his father in the shape of the Atlas Preservatives Company of which Denis was managing director and where he had worked since 1934. He was 36 when he met Margaret Roberts and had been married once before to Margaret Kempson (now Lady Hickman) during the war, in which he served with the Royal Artillery in Italy and France, winning a mention in despatches. The marriage had, in his own words, 'never got off the ground.' Because they had met and married in wartime they were 'never able to live together because I was in the army ... When I came back from the war, my wife and I were strangers.' They were divorced in 1946.

Carol and Mark were grown up before they learnt that their mother was their father's second wife. As the private life of the Thatchers was investigated in the wake of her victory over Ted Heath in 1975, Mrs Thatcher was asked why she had kept Denis's first wife a secret. She delivered a reproach worthy of Queen Victoria: 'One didn't keep it a secret he'd been married before. One wasn't asked. One just didn't talk about a thing like that.' One clearly didn't talk about it at home either.

Denis was a keen golfer and a rugby referee, on the committee of the local ratepayers' association, head of a reasonably prosperous family firm and owned a comfortable flat in Swan Court, off Chelsea's Flood Street. By the time he met his second wife, his tastes and habits were firmly fixed and marriage did not greatly change his style of life. He was not obliged then, as he is now, to play a part in her political life if he did not want to. His own working life took him out of the country from time to time. In September 1951, he came back from a holiday in France

and Spain and proposed to Margaret Roberts. She said yes.
The election of October 1951 had just been announced and
the couple consulted John Miller on whether they should
announce the engagement, or try to keep it a secret. Miller
advised delaying the announcement.

Both the candidate and the voters entered that election
with less enthusiasm than before; the meetings were
noticeably less well-attended. Less than three weeks before
the poll, Margaret was telling a reporter from the *Evening
Standard* that she had 'no time to spare for marriage'.
Speculation about the engagement emerged in the few days
before polling. She had celebrated her 26th birthday a few
days before. As the results produced a national
Conservative majority of seventeen, she reduced Dodds'
majority by another thousand – a modest and not
spectacular result.

The Thatchers were not married in Grantham: the
ceremony took place on a bitterly cold December day at the
Wesleyan Chapel in City Road, East London. It was a
Methodist service but by Alderman Roberts' standards
must have verged on the Anglican. The music was Handel's
Water Music, Bach's 'Jesu, Joy of Man's Desiring', and
Clarke's 'Trumpet Voluntary'; the hymns included
'Immortal, Invisible, God only wise' and 'Lead us, Heavenly
Father, lead us.' Prevented from wearing white by her
husband's previous marriage, the new Mrs Thatcher wore a
flamboyant dark blue velvet dress – a favourite colour and
material since childhood – with a Gainsborough-style hat
and ostrich feathers. It was the wedding of a minor
celebrity, with small pictures and paragraphs appearing in
the next day's papers. Around 50 guests went on to a
reception at the home of the chairman of Kent
Conservatives, Mr Alfred Bossom, in Carlton Gardens, just
behind Pall Mall. Food and drink was served by footmen in
breeches and short jackets. The honeymoon, the first
journey abroad of her life, combined Denis's business with
pleasure: they stopped in Portugal and Paris for business
and relaxed in Madeira. She returned home a Chelsea
housewife.

CHAPTER FOUR

The Bar

Margaret had married into the middle class and a new set of possibilities. Denis's income was an essential prerequisite for her political aspirations. She told Margaret Goodrich, when she took her around Parliament for the first time, 'I am very lucky because I have my own secretary. You know I could only do it on Denis's money.' Denis described his salary at the time as 'reasonable but not fantastic'. It was, however, large enough to allow his wife to stop work and start studying for the Bar.

Denis drove to work every day and his new wife studied law, aiming at the intermediate exams. The coronation of Queen Elizabeth began a spate of public speculation about the likely and desirable characteristics of the dawning 'Elizabethan Age'. Two months after she was married, the erstwhile candidate for Dartford addressed the issue in the *Sunday Graphic* in a rare piece of signed journalism headlined 'Wake Up Women!' The *Sunday Graphic* reminded its readers that the author's qualifications to write on the subject included the fact that she was only a few months older than the queen. 'Women can – AND MUST – play a leading part in the creation of a glorious Elizabethan era,' she said, deploring women who abandoned their careers for the sake of bringing up a family. The two could be combined: 'the idea that the family suffers is, I believe, quite mistaken.' She cited several examples of women who were then prominent in their professional fields, including Janet Vaughan, who combined marriage, children and work. 'Should a woman arise equal to the task, I say let her have an equal chance with the men for the leading Cabinet posts. Why not a woman Chancellor – or Foreign Secretary?'

'I should like to see married women carrying on with

their jobs, if so inclined, after their children are born,' she was quoted as saying. But, as she was ready to admit later, this was easier if you could afford the help. The Thatchers employed a live-in nurse immediately after the birth of their twins, and nannies thereafter. She was pregnant at the end of 1942 and accelerated her work towards the intermediate bar exam which she passed in the following May. The twins, weighing only four pounds each, were seven weeks premature, arriving in August instead of October. (Denis was out celebrating an English Test match victory when labour started and missed the drama.)

They were born, by Caesarian section, in the Princess Beatrice Hospital, Old Brompton Road; it was not an easy labour. Mrs Thatcher recalled later, 'I remember lying in the hospital ... And I remember thinking, if I don't, now I'm in hospital, actually fill in the entrance form for the final of the law, I may never go back to it. But if I fill in the entrance form now, pride will not let me fail. And so I did.' She took that final exam four months after the birth and was called to the bar early in 1954. The bar offered the prospect of good preparation for a return to politics without being too time-consuming or irregular in its hours. 'And they were small,' she said recently of the twins, '... they were going to need a lot of looking after. And of course they do become the centre of your life and you live for them as you've never lived for anyone else ... and yet, I knew that I had something else to give.'

There was no doubt that the something else Margaret Thatcher felt she had to give was to be given to politics, but there was a tenancy in a barrister's chambers to be secured first. She had met a senior barrister, Sir John Senter, QC, at a dinner at the House of Commons and Senter had taken a liking to her and offered to map out her path to a tenancy in his own chambers at 6 King's Bench Walk. He suggested two pupillages as preparation for specialisation in tax, which had replaced Thatcher's previous target, the patent bar. He proposed that she do six-month pupillages in Chancery chambers and common law chambers, and then come to pupil master in his set. She completed the first two, becoming briefly a colleague of Airey Neave's. At King's

Bench Walk she was under the supervision of a tax specialist, Peter Rowland. Tax work involves little or no court work, a good deal of 'devilling' in past precedents (often a job for the pupil), many conferences with clients, and requires a reasonable head for numbers. Thatcher started with the advantage that she was married to an accountant and used occasionally to take work home in order to ask Denis about it. She and Rowland would work on releases and indemnities, tax reconstruction schemes and liabilities for profits tax. They drafted a deed for a bishop in favour of his children. They worked on a case involving the Trinidad and Tobago ordinances; Rowland remembers sending his pupil to look them up.

At the end of the pupillage, in the early months of 1955, she was told that the chambers was contracting and there would not be room for her. It was an arbitrary decision taken by the head of chambers. Patrick Jenkin, also a pupil in the chambers, missed his own chance of a tenancy because of the shrinkage. Rowland said that it is possible that his pupil was the victim of a feeling that tax clients would not take a female barrister sufficiently seriously. She was apparently bitterly disappointed by this rejection. But she quickly found a tenancy at 5 New Square, where the clerk confined himself to saying before her arrival that he wished that she was a 'Miss' instead of a 'Mrs'.

She was a full-time tax barrister for five years and only began practising in her own right shortly before she was selected for Finchley. It left its mark on her style of operation. A civil servant who worked with her years later described her as essentially a critical mind and not a creative one, but with a remarkable facility for taking a brief and with the minimum of changes, making it her own. Her skill with a brief became one of her principal strengths as she rose at Westminster.

A colleague in New Square, Pamela Thomas, served with her on the Society of Conservative Lawyers; Thatcher was the first woman on the executive and Miss Thomas replaced her. The two women used to discuss politics at coffee each morning, and candidacies in particular. Thomas pointed out that applications were open for Hemel Hempstead, according to the *Daily Telegraph*. Her friend entered but did not make it. Miss Thomas recalls her politics of the time as to the right of the party, firmly critical of public ownership and the lack of action on trade union immunities, and firmly supporting Quintin Hogg over Suez.

In 1957, the rent for the flat in Swan Court was to be raised and a decision had to be taken about whether it was best to stay in the centre of London or buy a house in the country, which would be a more healthy place for the children to be brought up in. The Thatchers were house-hunting and found what they had in mind, a half-timbered, five-bedroomed mansion, The Dormers, in Locks Bottom, Farnborough, in the constituency of Orpington. In 1955 Thatcher had tried, and just failed, to become the prospective Conservative candidate there. It was closer for Denis to get to work at Erith, but it would mean that Margaret had to take the train in to London each day. The twins were, as yet, too young for school. They were cared for by a nanny each day. A cleaner was also employed. The house had a large garden which was considerably overgrown and a gardener was found, although, at the weekends, both Thatchers liked to garden. The children had recognisably different characters from the very beginning: Mark was active and tended to be irresponsible; Carol was more retiring, more gentle. Thatcher continued working full-time at the Bar, while looking after the twins as much as she could. She cooked them and Denis a breakfast each morning and, when they reached school age, drove them to school before taking the train. She would then try to be home by late afternoon. Often her work would keep her later. She worked to maintain the family closeness which she had enjoyed so much as a child. When the children were grown up, she admitted feeling guilty about the amount of time she had spent away from them. Once, when she and Denis went on holiday for a fortnight, she left the children in the care of her mother. She was surprised that it took a full day to get them used to her again. Before the twins were school age, they were taken on holiday to Westgate and Bognor Regis; then, as soon as they were five, the family holidays settled down into a routine visit to Seaview on the

Isle of Wight, first staying at a hotel, then hiring a house which became a favourite.

They had the normal range of childhood illnesses, including mumps, which she had not contracted as a child, and so she, too, fell ill with the disease. She did not subject her children to the severe regime of her own childhood, consciously allowing them to be indulged in a way that her parents' inadequate living could not provide. After having the children, she became a very light sleeper. The family went to the local village church each Sunday, but as soon as the children went away to school — Denis had insisted that Mark start at a boarding school at the age of nine — she no longer insisted that they go to church during the holidays. At about this time, the mid-fifties, she turned against the memory of Grantham and her modest beginnings. She once asked a schoolfriend, whom she had kept up with, whether she didn't envy those who had been to Cheltenham Ladies' College instead of Kesteven and Grantham Girls' School. Her mother and father now lived in a house called Allerton, across the road from the shop on North Parade. Visiting her parents in Grantham had become a bore. The innocent girl who had shown Denis with pride around her home in Grantham had grown away from her roots.

She was further distanced from Grantham when her mother died and her father remarried, a widow, Cissie Hubbard. Her husband, George, a farmer in the village of Eaton, near Grantham, had died when a car had driven into them as they were both crossing a road. Alf had met her when preaching locally. She had two sons and three daughters from her first marriage, all of whom had grown up by the time she married Alf Roberts. When her father remarried, Margaret confided to a friend, 'My father has married again. I suppose that's a good thing. She's a nice, homely little woman.' When her father died in 1970, the family gathered at the Methodist Church in Finkin Street to dedicate a lectern to his memory as has been mentioned before. Since then, most links with Grantham have lapsed, although she makes a point of paying a duty visit to her step-mother, who still lives in the house in North Parade.

Thatcher's political ambitions remained strong all

through the fifties and from very soon after the time the twins were born, she was looking for a seat. In 1955, she had not found one to suit her and had been preoccupied with the children. But in 1957, when she moved to Kent, she was looking round again.

Margaret had hoped to find a constituency close to home, for the children's sake. She had kept in close contact with the Conservative Central Office and spoke for them when asked. She took part, also, in the Conservative Candidates' Association meetings. She had spoken every day throughout the 1955 election campaign in marginal constituencies or where she knew the candidate. But although her loyalty was not in doubt, the fact that she was a young mother counted against her. She tried for the nearby constituency of Beckenham at the time of the 1957 by-election, and the selection committee flattered her on her abilities by putting her on the short list. She was turned down, however, because they felt that she should stay at home and look after her young children.

In the mid-fifties, a young middle-class mother was meant to be a housewife. This archaic approach did not please Margaret Thatcher, who promptly applied to become the candidate for Maidstone, also in Kent. Again she was on the short list and again she was turned down, for the same reasons, although this time she was runner-up. When she heard that the Conservatives were looking for a candidate at Oxford, she promptly applied, and found herself running against C.M. Woodhouse, at that time Director-General of the Royal Institute of International Affairs at Chatham House. Simultaneously, she applied for the safe Tory seat of Finchley, which was being vacated at the next general election by Sir John Crowder, an old-fashioned Conservative of the Old Etonian, county council – in his case Hampshire – school, who had represented Finchley since 1935. It was a plum seat. About two hundred hopefuls applied to be chosen as candidate, attracted by the size of the majority there: 12,000 over Labour. Finchley was further away than she wished, but she was in no position to be choosey. Her disabilities – as a career woman with young twins – meant that she must find a seat where she could. Finchley was at least within striking distance of both Kent and Westminster. It would be possible to take the seat without spending nights away from the children.

The seat of Finchley was a prime Tory outer suburban seat. There was little industry and, even in 1958, little council housing in proportion to the numbers of home owners. It was commuter territory, containing five Underground stations. The Conservative Party there was old-fashioned, like its member, rather staid and stuffy. They whittled down the large number of entrants, first to twenty-two, then, finally, to four, by asking each applicant the same questions, then marking their answers. One lost along the way was C.M. Woodhouse, who withdrew from Finchley in return for Thatcher withdrawing from Oxford. The Finchley short list contained three men, each of whom had similar backgrounds: Major Ian Fraser, MC, from Chipstead in Surrey, was 42 years old, retired from the Army, and had been educated at Shrewsbury; Major Thomas Langton, MC, from Binfield in Berkshire, was one year younger and had graduated from Jesus College, Oxford; Mr Francis Richardson, of Radclive Mill, Buckinghamshire, was 44 years old and educated at Balliol. By contrast, the fourth on the list, the blond, blue-eyed attractive Mrs Denis Thatcher, from The Dormers, Holwood Park Avenue, Farnborough, aged only thirty-three, was an exciting option. The climax to the selection procedure was a meeting of the constituency divisional council, to which each candidate would be asked to speak, after which voting would take place. If there was no clear majority, the fourth candidate would withdraw and there would be a second ballot, until a clear winner was elected. In the first round, Mrs Thatcher came second, with thirty-three votes, beaten by Major Fraser, who received forty-six. She had done unexpectedly well, particularly because she made the other candidates look too established, too traditionally Conservative for many of the young Conservatives and their leader, Frank Gibson.

At the second ballot, after an appeal by Gibson to reject the safe option, she was a clear winner. Denis was absent from the meeting, away on a business trip in Africa, and found out about his wife's success by chance, two days later, when he found a London *Evening Standard* on a plane from Johannesburg to Lagos. Although she had written to him, the letter had not arrived.

As soon as the voting was over, Thatcher was approached by Frank and Betty Gibson, who offered to mark her card, pointing out who was who in the small, close-knit world of the Finchley Tories. In a series of cocktail and tea parties, they introduced her and Denis to the leading lights of the Conservatives, the Chambers of Commerce, the Rotary Club and the other local dignatories. They were impressed by Thatcher's easy charm, and her ability to speak spontaneously, lucidly, without notes. Sir John Crowder had been remembered as a man who shuffled with a stack of prompt-cards on the lectern.

The constituency suited her personality well. In the late fifties, there was a significant difference between the character of Tory constituencies: in the countryside, they provided the old, patrician sort of Conservative member and in the suburbs, members who were meritocrats. Within London itself, there was a significant difference. In principle those seats in the south-west, which drifted into Surrey and Sussex, provided an old-style member; those in the self-made north-west, such as Finchley, were tending to replace the older Tories with people more like themselves. Like many seats in the north-west of London, Finchley had a large number of Jews living in the area, a significant section of the community likely to vote Conservative, but which would willingly change allegiance if their interests seemed to be served elsewhere. In 1957 the Finchley Golf Club, dominated by leading members of the Finchley Conservative Party, had turned down for membership a number of local Jews, who alleged that they were being excluded on grounds of race. In the row which developed, the Conservative Party became identified in Finchley with middle class anti-semitism. The Liberals in Finchley took advantage of this scandal and convinced a large number of Finchley Jews that their natural allegiance was with them. By 1964, the Liberal pitch for the Jewish community had been so effective that six of the nineteen Liberals on the Finchley council were Jewish. At the very least, the presence of a large number of Jews in Thatcher's home constituency has meant that she has always been well briefed on matters concerning Israel and the Middle East.

Finchley was and remains typical Thatcher territory, with a large home-owning population with mortgages. Finchley people are mostly upwardly mobile, living in fresh-painted houses in wide suburban roads. There is little inherited wealth and a large number of self-employed businessmen, many self-made. In 1957, when Thatcher was adopted for the seat, there were few immigrants. The working-class areas of the constituency were small and noticeably separate.

Thatcher approached the constituency and got to know it with a thoroughness the Conservatives had not seen before in Finchley. Local party organisation was poor and this accounted in part for the beginnings of a Liberal revival by the time of the 1959 general election. Still, as expected, Thatcher easily won her seat. Of the 69,123 electors who turned out to vote, which represented a massive 80.8 per cent of the constituency, over half voted for her. The result was.

M.H. Thatcher	29,697	(53.2%)
E.P. Deakins (Labour	13,437	(24.1%)
H.I. Spencer (Liberal)	12,701	(22.7%)

She arrived in the Commons with a majority of 16,260, amounting to 29.1 per cent.

The next election was not to be quite as straightforward. The Liberals were encouraged by the success of a strong parliamentary candidate, Manuella Sykes, in 1955 and of the Liberal candidates in Finchley council elections, who had won every seat available for two years in a row. A flush of rather unrealistic optimism among the Liberals ignored the size of the majority and started billing Finchley as a second Orpington. (Orpington, with a Conservative majority of 14,760 had fallen to the Liberal candidate, Eric Lubbock, at a spectacular by-election in March 1962). Finchley was to be the second front in a hoped-for Liberal assault on London.

The Liberals had backed their judgment by assigning to

the constituency one of their bright young hopes, a thirty year-old Cambridge graduate, John Pardoe, later Liberal member for North Cornwall, as the candidate. The Conservatives took fright and, in 1962, appointed to the constituency a competent full-time agent, who had proved successful when snatching the inner-London constituency of Baron's Court from Labour in 1959. At the selection meeting in 1957, Thatcher had been asked specifically what she would do to counter a Liberal revival and she had simply said that she would work harder to put across the Conservative message. And that is what she did. By 1964, she was fighting as a junior minister in Sir Alec Douglas Home's Government and was still the youngest woman in the House. She had been a great local success and had appeared on a Conservative television broadcast. She was attractive and conspicuous. Before the campaign started, a survey revealed that almost half her constituents were able to name Thatcher as their Conservative candidate – a remarkable achievement. In 1962, the Liberals won all the council seats up for election in Finchley and three out of five wards in Friern Barnet. The following years they again took all the seats available in Finchley, reducing the Conservatives to five out of twenty-four seats on the council, and taking over control. It looked like a close-run thing. But Thatcher was organised and worked hard, walking briskly into Tory committee rooms, throwing her coat back to Denis, who followed behind. She addressed ten full-scale meetings, pulling a total of about thirteen hundred people. And, although Pardoe was an easy target – a brash former socialist, who brandished a slide-rule whenever confronted with a voter who said a Liberal vote would be wasted and whom the *Jewish Chronicle* had mistakenly called a Jew – she stuck to national issues.

Ironically, the person writing a chapter on the 1959 Finchley campaign for the definitive series of general election studies by Nuffield College, edited that year by David Butler and Richard Rose, was Bernard Donoughue, later to become Harold Wilson's chief policy adviser. He got on very well with Thatcher and was generous in his description of her: 'For the Conservatives, Mrs Margaret

Thatcher, an attractive mother of twins, trained first as a chemist and then as a barrister, and now serving as a junior minister in the Government, was a formidable sitting member. She maintained a good personal relationship with the various groups in the Finchley community, including the trade unions. On the public platform she answered a wide variety of questions with a barrage of official statistics. Her political opponents clearly had a high respect for her.' And he cites her ability to master questions from the floor: 'Almost the only light relief came at a large Tory gathering where the first question was from a lady who wanted to know "why had the Conservative Government done nothing about the lavatories which won't flush ... it is not a laughing matter, it is happening all over the country." Thatcher negotiated this one with great skill and turned eagerly to the next hand raised, only to be asked "What is the purpose of life?" She later remarked, "You must not get the wrong impression of us; after all, this is Hampstead Garden Suburb." '

She won the seat, but with a substantially reduced majority. The result was:

M.H. Thatcher	24,591	(46.6%)
J.W. Pardoe (Liberal)	15,789	(29.9%)
A.E. Tomlinson (Labour)	12,408	(23.5%)

The majority was cut to 8,802, which represented a reduction of nearly a half of the 1959 figure, at 16.7 per cent. Still, it was a safe seat for a general election which had caused a change of government to Labour. The social make-up of Finchley helped her maintain her majority. More than a third of the electorate in 1964 were of the professional middle class, termed AB. Twice as many of them were educated beyond the age of fifteen as in the country as a whole. Over half were owner-occupiers and nearly sixty per cent were women. The Jewish section of the electorate – representing up to a fifth of voters – could find something to admire in her conspicuous devotion to hard work and her family.

Since then, the seat of Finchley, which, at the February 1974 general election became Barnet, Finchley, has been secure for her. She has twice, in 1970 and 1979, attracted an absolute majority of votes cast and her majority has never slipped below ten per cent. The fact that it is so close to the centre of London has meant that, even since she became Leader and Prime Minister, she has been able to continue regular visits to the constituency. She used it for keynote speeches during the leadership campaign and at the start of the 1979 general election campaign.

By the time she was an MP, the Thatchers had moved closer to her work at the House, to 19 Flood Street, close to where they used to have a flat. It is a modest town house, in a small, narrow street in a row of houses hard onto the road with a small amount of garden at the front. Some houses protrude; their's stands back.

The fact that both Margaret and Denis have worked has taken its toll on family life. The children were squeezed between their parents' respective careers. Margaret would still get up and cook breakfast for the family and would look unharassed by the time that she set off for the House, when she would either take a cab or drive in her battered, second-hand Vauxhall. Denis drove a company car with the number plate DT1. The garages were at the back of the houses, where children played, and the cars would usually toot as they went in and out. Margaret would always make a point of talking to the children and would remember each of their names, much to the irritation of one trio of brothers in the street, who used to remark to each other how unnatural such a faultless memory seemed. It was as if she was mocking them by remembering. As an MP, she was a celebrity in the street, much to her annoyance. She continued to be an early-morning housewife, rushing out each morning to do her shopping in the small, local shops of the King's Road and a more modest set of corner shops in a local parade. Later, when a ministerial car arrived each morning, she would often keep it waiting as she finished the daily shopping. She always appeared to be in a rush. Even when the children were home from school, it was unusual for the whole family to eat together. Margaret would prepare food which would be eaten when needed. There were few formal dinners, nor was there lavish entertaining.

It was most unusual for there ever to be politicians in the house and, most certainly, her home was not the centre of an elaborate political salon. She used to run the house in between everything else, depending only upon a regular cleaner to help out.

Clothes were always an expensive item in the household budget. Like most women in public life, her clothes were and are an essential part of the public image and it was important to her that there should be a regular change of outfit. She was lucky in as much as she is a petite woman who finds it easy to look neat and tidy. She is also lucky in that she can dress herself from off the peg. She used to eke out her budget by shopping at Marks & Spencer or buying out of season. Her blue velvet wedding dress did service for many years as an evening gown. She was also capable of making her own dresses and made her children's clothes very often, sometimes to their annoyance. She turned an old pair of curtains into duffle coats for the twins. There was no lavish living and much of the family budget was spent on supporting her political needs.

They used to economise in other ways: she and Denis did much of the home decorating. The children were not given a great deal of pocket money and Carol used to supplement that, when she became old enough, by baby-sitting for neighbours in Flood Street. Margaret's car was an old, unfashionable model and she would express surprise at anyone who could afford to buy a new one from private means.

The children were brought up very conscientiously, neither spoilt nor deprived of what other children had. They were taken to the theatre and the opera and the whole family would go around the corner to the cinema in the King's Road. The children were introduced to the delights of London, then left to enjoy them as little or as often as they wished. They were given things which their parents had not been allowed in their childhoods. Margaret was anxious that they should be brought up with a warm family life and regretted the fact that there were no close adult relations as there had been in Grantham. Still, she did duplicate the closeness of neighbourliness which she had enjoyed in her childhood by doing as her mother had done, taking a close but not over-intrusive interest in people around her whom she had befriended when they were in trouble. There are numerous examples of her giving a hand to friends in distress, in particular rescuing children from the discomforts of broken marriages. She kept in her drawing room a special drawer for children outside the family, with sweets and games inside.

Mark and Carol were very different children. Mark was a cross between both parents; Carol was like neither of them. He was sent to Harrow and rather enjoyed his mother's notoriety. In later life, he has taken advantage of her fame and has a tendency to name-drop. Carol is more independent and more anxious to divorce her life from her mother. When she was training to be a solicitor, she forbade her mother to pull strings on her behalf. She dislikes the limelight and she considers her mother's career to be inhibiting to her ability to lead her own life.

Her mother's career and her private life inevitably overlapped during her long love affair with the young, rich Conservative MP, Jonathan Aitken. He was handsome and had a reputation as a womaniser — a reputation which mother tried to stress to daughter when Carol appeared more serious about the relationship than Aitken. The romance continued while Carol travelled and worked in Australia. There was talk of marriage but the affair was ended by Aitken who soon after announced his engagement to Lolicia Azucki. The end of the friendship brought mother and daughter closer than before. Carol has few close friends and depended on her mother for solace. While working as a journalist, she continues to live in Flood Street, which was put up for sale in early 1983.

Mark, however, now lives in Downing Street and, unlike his sister, is normally accompanied by detectives. He is free-spending and has assembled a career and income on the strength of being Mrs Thatcher's son. He has advertised Japanese airlines, Marlboro cigarettes, Playboy Toiletries for men, Cutty Sark whisky and Japanese synthetic suede. He enjoys jet-set life, appears regularly in night clubs and gossip columns. The only occasion his mother has been seen in tears in public occurred while he went missing during a car rally across the Sahara in 1982. Those close to Mrs Thatcher say that they have never known her to be so worried. The reports of what had happened were, like the rally arrangements, confused. Before he was finally found by the Algerian air force, stranded with his co-driver by their car, reports reaching Downing Street first said that he was dead and then that he was safe. Two friends of the family put private planes at their disposal and Denis flew to the desert in a jet owned by Sir Hector Laing of United Biscuits. Mark reappeared looking surprised by the fuss and the relationship between father and son did not seem to be close or warm.

CHAPTER FIVE

The Commons

Thatcher's early parliamentary career was an impressive one. It began with good luck, winning a ballot which allowed her to introduce her own legislation. And she built upon that good fortune, impressing those members of the government with whom she worked over her Private Member's Bill, then building up a solid reputation for hard work and effective speaking in the Chamber. Her political apprenticeship was one of steady progress and she consciously worked towards a position in the Cabinet. Her ultimate goal — the highest she expected any woman to reach in her political lifetime — was that of Chancellor of the Exchequer. Her progress was not lubricated by any particular friendships among the leadership. (Until leader herself, she was never intimate with the ruling elite in the Party.) But she had established a close relationship with Keith and Helen Joseph. While remaining a dutiful member of the Conservative shadow team, she had begun compiling a set of beliefs of her own.

The new member for Finchley made a bold start to her parliamentary career. On her first day, she had herself photographed with a portly policeman on the door and was shown the ropes by her friends from the Kent constituencies around Dartford and from the Inns of Court Conservative Association. She also found swift success by coming runner-up to a new Labour MP, Richard Marsh, in the ballot for Private Members' Bills arranged in November 1959 by the Speaker. Second in the ballot meant a good chance of instigating successful legislation, if the measure chosen was not too contentious and if it met government approval and thereby was granted parliamentary time. She went into discussions with the Government Chief Whip, Martin Redmayne. Her immediate choice was to fill a gap in the law of contempt of court revealed during the recent case of Gunther Podola, who had murdered a policeman. It was, however, the opinion of the Attorney-General, Sir Reginald Manningham-Buller, whom the matter directly concerned, that, although Mrs Thatcher was a barrister, the proposed legislation was much too complicated to be handled by a new MP in a Private Member's motion. Instead, he was planning a government-inspired measure. She was not best pleased and made her feelings plain to the Chief Whip – not the person to cross so early in a career. The sort of measure which the Government would prefer to be handled as a Private Member's Bill was a piece of legislation which it would like placed on the statute book, but one which had contentious aspects which it did not wish to rebound on itself. Such a project was the reform of the law concerning the admission of the press to council meetings. The legislation governing such matters was embedded in the Local Government Act of 1933, which allowed councils to create whatever committees they choose – including resolving themselves into committee as a whole – thus undermining the Act of 1908 which only allowed councils to exclude the public – and thereby the press – from certain committee meetings.

The issue had come to the fore during a press printing strike, when some Labour councils had shown solidarity with the strikers by excluding from their meetings reporters who were working for newspapers produced by strike-breaking labour. The Watch Committee of Nottingham Council had excluded the press from the meetings which decided to suspend the city's chief constable for failing to inform them that some council members were being investigated by Scotland Yard. The Government was eager to change the law, but anxious not to upset the sensibilities of council members, particularly as many Tory councils also found exclusion of the press to be a useful manoeuvre from time to time. Although there was a commitment in the 1959 Conservative Manifesto to do something about it, a Private Member's Bill which proposed that the press and public should be admitted at all times, except when

confidential personal matters or contract information were
being discussed, was a politically appropriate solution
for the Government. The project was suggested to
Thatcher, who agreed to use her position as the runner-up
to the ballot to introduce the measure. The process of
drafting legislation was considered far too arduous for a
new member and so she was given the assistance of Sir
Lionel Heald, a former Attorney-General. She also required
the active help of Henry Brooke, the Minister for Housing
and Local Government. Brooke's instinct was to avoid
legislation and, instead, by threatening it, to introduce a
voluntary code of conduct which councils should follow.
The Association of Municipal Corporations made it clear
that they were opposed to a legal remedy, whereas the
newspaper publishers and the journalists who worked for
them were almost unanimously in favour. The Conservative
group on Thatcher's own council in Finchley were opposed
to resorting to law, preferring to use the discretion which a
voluntary code would allow. On 5 February 1960, a Friday,
Thatcher stood up in the Commons and made her maiden
speech, which, unusually, was the Second Reading of her
own Private Member's Bill. She said, 'I know that the
constituency of Finchley which I have the honour to
represent would not wish me to do other than come straight
to the point and address myself to the matter before the
House.' Then followed an extraordinary maiden speech,
lasting twenty-seven minutes, spoken without referring to
the notes in her hand, in which she lucidly explained her
Public Bodies (Admission of the Press to Meetings) Bill. The
chamber, usually empty on a Friday, as members leave for
their constituencies, had a rare crowd of about 100. (Denis
Thatcher was not present; he was on a business trip to the
Middle East.) Her performance was nearly faultless and
there was no apparent nervousness in her voice or manner.
Her case was well rehearsed and her argument loaded with
facts and figures. Of the £1400 million a year spent by local
authorities in England and Wales and the £200 million
spent in Scotland, she explained, 'less than half is raised by
ratepayers' money and the rest by taxpayers' money, and
the first purpose in admitting the press is that we may know

how those moneys are being spent.' Her bill would allow the press to be admitted as a right to full council meetings and those meetings which effectively discharged the functions of the council. Also, the press should be provided with the essential background information necessary to do their job of public scrutiny. She concluded, 'I hope that MPs will consider that a paramount function of this House is to safeguard civil liberties, rather than to think that administrative convenience should take first place in law.'

Praise came from all sides. Henry Brooke spoke of 'a fluency which most of us would envy' and predicted that her reputation would soon be extended. William Deedes, the driving force of the Peterborough column on the *Daily Telegraph*, was present, and the following day the column read, 'As a thirty-minute exposition, without a note, of a controversial and complex Bill, it was of Front Bench quality.' He went on to praise her for 'an uncanny instinct for the mood of the House which some members take years to acquire – and many never acquire at all.' Barbara Castle and Joyce Butler, both Labour members, praised the Bill. The three women in the Government were present for most of the speech and both Sir Lionel Heald and Henry Brooke spoke in support. But there was Labour opposition, particularly as the Bill was seen by many as a retaliation against those councils who had backed the printing strikers. And, unwisely for a measure which must progress without the protection of a government whip, Thatcher had chosen as her ten sponsors members who were all Conservatives. There was some Tory opposition, but the most substantial opposition came from Michael Stewart, who spotted its vulnerable point, criticising it as not a bill for the protection of the public, but a bill to promote an extension of the privileges of the press. None the less, the bill passed its Second Reading by 152 votes to 39.

Stewart's objection to the bill made the committee stage even more tortuous than usual. The Government conceded that he had a point and wished to overcome his objections, which might otherwise have caused the bill to fail. The solution was found by Henry Brooke's junior minister, Keith Joseph, who advised Brooke to put a motion before the Commons in government time, changing the title to the Public Bodies (Admission to Meetings) Bill, which would meet the Labour objections. Joseph was the Government representative on the committee stages of the bill and he and Thatcher became close political friends. Other changes were made in committee: councils were to be forbidden from forming themselves as a whole into a committee either before or during a full council meeting; and, to meet the opposition to the bill's narrowness, a public right of access to council meetings was established. Despite these hiccups, it was a considerable achievement for a new member not only to use a Private Member's motion for publicising a particular issue, but to succeed in steering legislation through the Commons. Thatcher's competence and determination were impressive to those who witnessed her in action and, during the unopposed Third Reading of the bill, on 14 May 1960, Keith Joseph paid tribute to her 'most cogent, charming, lucid and competent manner' which had contributed to the success of 'a delicate and contentious measure, perhaps not ideally suited for a first venture into legislation'. She had established for herself a good reputation among the class of '59 and drawn herself to the attention of the Chief Whip who was the controller of all Government patronage.

The success of the bill also widened her reputation, though some mileage was made by her opponents out of the fact that the Conservative group on the Finchley council not only refused to propose a motion congratulating their MP on her success, but determined never to allow the press into their general purposes committee. In May she was addressing the Junior Fashion Fair, asking for less ugly school clothing. In October she was addressing 550 women at a lunch at the Savoy to celebrate her being chosen as one of the six women of the year chosen by the Greater London Fund for the Blind, and let it be known that the person in history she would most like to have been was Anna Leonowens, whose autobiography 'Anna and the King of Siam' she had just read, because of her 'sense of purpose and the perseverance to carry out this purpose'. She was developing the necessary mental and physical stamina for a successful political career.

In November she fainted in the House and had to go home to rest – a rare lapse. There was an extraordinary published interview conducted by Godfrey Winn, who found in her the same regal qualities, 'the same flawless complexion', as the queen. She had been recruited by Reginald Maudling, President of the Board of Trade, to make a tour of the country pushing a government-sponsored export drive. And, because of her bill, she was chosen to appear and explain it in a party television broadcast at the time of the local government elections. In it she asked the viewer, in a single, long take to camera, whether he knew what his local council was doing. The public relations team at Conservative Central Office were keen to use her. Although they did not consider her to be a natural performer and her voice was very high, she was suitably attractive for television work. For many years, Thatcher was to be used as a token woman. In 1960, the only other Conservative woman to be used regularly for party promotion purposes was Pat Hornsby-Smith.

A member of the Cabinet at the time remembered her being singled out as an MP likely to do well, but this did not prevent her from occasionally opposing government policy. In March 1961, commenting at the annual meeting of her local party on the decision by South Africa to leave the Commonwealth, she suggested that in order to preserve the British system of democracy in newly-independent nations, a bill of rights should be included in their new constitutions. But she had a more important worry. She said, 'Having been a member of Parliament for eighteen months now, the thing which still troubles me most of all – and something which is fundamental to everything – is control of government expenditure. It is, in fact, very much more difficult than I ever thought it would be in theory.' And she continued, 'We are chasing after the hundreds and the thousands, but tending to let the millions go by. Sometime we must alter the system of public accountability and the nation must present its accounts to Parliament as a company does to its shareholders ... Until then, it will be extremely difficult to bring down and control government expenditure and, therefore, the level of taxation is not going to be considerably reduced.'

She was certain that taxpayers' money was being wasted. She had decided to make Treasury affairs her speciality, and accordingly took part in the debate following Selwyn Lloyd's first Budget. She showed a noticeable bias against the City in favour of business interests — a not unusual rhetorical stance among many leading Conservatives of the time. 'It is the speculator in shares that we want to get at — the person who is making a business of buying and selling shares, not to hold them for their income-producing properties, but to live on the profit which he makes from the transactions.' She went on to condemn the increase in tax on companies as inflationary.

In the same month, April 1961, she also made clear her opinions on home affairs and took part in a substantial back-bench rebellion. It was to do with an amendment to the Criminal Justice Bill. Sir Thomas More had, the previous February, introduced an amendment proposing that courts should have the power to inflict the cane for offenders up to seventeen years of age, and the birch for those between seventeen and twenty-one. Thatcher had supported the amendment. 'In our desire for humanitarian reform of offenders, we have lost sight of the purpose of the criminal courts and the aims of punishment,' she said. 'I do not accept that all offenders guilty of the most violent crimes are necessarily mental cases.' And she made clear that detention centres for the young were not providing the 'short, sharp shock' which they were meant to. When it came to the vote at the end of the debate in April, Mrs Thatcher had led the 67 rebels through the lobby, voting against the Government. Her act of disloyalty and her enthusiasm for corporal punishment did not, however, count against her later in the year.

On Monday 9 October, Margaret and her sister Muriel were meant to be meeting for lunch. A message came from Downing Street, asking her to be at Admiralty House after lunch for an appointment with the Prime Minister, Harold Macmillan. Although there were two posts vacant in the Government and Macmillan was expected to announce a reshuffle, she did not entertain any expectations. She thought that she might be summoned to be asked to propose or second the Loyal Address in reply to the Queen's Speech at the opening of the parliamentary session. She returned to tell Muriel that Macmillan had appointed her as Joint Parliamentary Secretary to the Ministry of Pensions and National Insurance, under John Boyd-Carpenter, in succession to Pat Hornsby-Smith. Although she had hoped for government office, she confided to Muriel that she would have preferred to wait until the children were a little older — they were eight. However, judging that in politics, as she told Muriel, 'when you're offered a job you either accept it or you are out', she accepted. Denis also missed this excitement, as he was in Japan on a business trip. She wrote him an air-mail letter, but he heard the news on the radio before it arrived.

She then began three years in the department, answering questions on pensions on behalf of the government for the first time on November 6. Her job was shared with Richard Sharples. She looked after enquiries, complaints and correspondence concerning national insurance and supplementary benefits; he with war pensions and industrial injuries. Although, when Boyd-Carpenter had been asked by Macmillan whether he was happy to have Thatcher on his team, he had sent a telegram back from Canada, which he was visiting, saying simply, 'Delighted,' the view was not shared by Sir Eric Bowyer, the permanent secretary at the department, or the other senior civil servants. Sir Eric thought that a young woman with two young children and a husband who travelled a great deal would not be able to work hard enough. Her style also rankled. 'She would turn up looking as if she had spent the whole morning with the coiffeur and the whole afternoon with the couturier,' he remembered. 'But we got at least as much work from her as from anyone else and probably a bit more.' Despite her habit of redrafting letters, the civil servants came to like her. She was quick to grasp a brief and proved competent in the House, both at answering questions and guiding legislation.

Her debut in the House as a ministerial speaker came on 14 March 1962, when, in answer to a Labour censure motion, she delivered a barrage of statistics and arguments which lasted for three-quarters of an hour. She was challenged to justify the Government's decision not to raise pensions and her justification covered every possible comparison and analysis of the pensioners' relative wealth, quoting figures for 1946, 1951, 1959 and 1962 and comparing pensioners in Britain with those in Sweden, Denmark and West Germany. The House of Commons was momentarily stunned by the avalanche.

As time went on, she became a more relaxed and more effective speaker, popular among back-bench MPs for her relish in assaulting the Opposition speakers. Richard Crossman described one performance as 'a good, professional, tough speech'. (The Chief Whip, Martin Redmayne, on the other hand, would have preferred more progress and less politics at the Despatch Box.) At the department she proved capable of application and concentration, sorting through the hundreds of queries raised by MPs about particular constituents' pension and social security matters. As the department was not in the forefront of political action, there was also time — rare for young government members — to consider future policy. She served under three ministers: Boyd-Carpenter, until his promotion to Chief Secretary of the Treasury in July 1962; Neil MacPherson; and Richard Wood. And she learnt about how the civil service responds to a change in its leadership, coming to the conclusion that civil servants tend not to put up advice which they think the minister will reject, restricting too narrowly the range of ideas and policy options available to a minister. She discussed her experience with other parliamentary secretaries, who used to have meetings to discuss general policies, sometimes attended by Macmillan himself.

The Liberal victory at the Orpington by-election began a long and uncomfortable period for the Macmillan government, then dogged by a succession of scandals, sackings and resignations, brought to an end by Macmillan's ill-timed retirement. A constitutional row ensued about whom the queen should send for to form an administration. In the confused leadership battle which developed, Thatcher was an admirer of R.A. Butler. She considered it too risky for Lord Home to go through the dangerous hoop of a by-election. However, when Sir Alec, as he became, eventually took up his seat in the Commons, she was 'perfectly happy' and continued in his Government. By the time of the October 1964 general election, Thatcher had been a loyal member of the government under two prime ministers, dutifully supporting the government's overtures towards membership of the European Economic Community, and remaining quiet upon the sacking of Selwyn Lloyd, who had been reluctant to increase government borrowing.

The Tory defeat of 1964 brought calls for a change of leadership. Against the brash, sharp Harold Wilson, Sir Alec Douglas Home looked stuffy and out of touch. Wilson was defending a bare overall majority of five and another election was expected to follow quite soon. New rules were formulated for the election of a Conservative leader – a new departure, following the fuss surrounding Home's 'magic circle' selection – and no sooner were they extant than there was pressure to use them. Like a cricketer walking from the crease, Sir Alec stood down without prompting. The two main contestants for the leadership, Edward Heath and Reginald Maudling, were from the same generation and position in the party. Thatcher thought that Home's departure was unnecessary, but on his resignation, had at first favoured Maudling. She knew him quite well and had admired his performance as Chancellor of the Exchequer. But before long she had changed her mind and decided to vote for Heath, who was generally considered to be likely to prove more robust opposition to the wily Wilson.

Until Heath's election, Thatcher had continued as Opposition spokesman on pensions. One of the disappointments of the October defeat for her had been the abandonment of a Pensions Bill. Heath left her as a general watchdog on the pensions issue, but also appointed her to become a shadow spokesman on housing and land. She criticised the Wilson Government in December 1965 for cutting the pensions of the 3,500 Britons living in Rhodesia after Ian Smith had declared unilateral independence the previous month. And she worked closely with — and impressed by her competence — Airey Neave on a policy for allowing state pensions for those aged over eighty, who had been too old to benefit from the existing scheme. Their collaboration consolidated a significant friendship.

Edward Heath, who had arrived as leader of the modern Conservative Party on his personal merit, used Thatcher's talents to the full, encouraging her to work across a range of subjects. She stood out as the only woman on the Opposition team, but had qualified as a sound performer at the Despatch Box. Heath genuinely admired her capacity for work. He encouraged her to become involved in policy-making and at the October 1965 party conference she delivered a key-note speech on the reform of the rating system, dismissing the notion of a local income tax as a wasteful duplication. She and Boyd-Carpenter went onto the attack over Labour's policy over a Land Commission, a state institution which would buy land for building development; its changes in the law over leaseholds. There was embarrassment, however, about criticising Labour's plan for an 'option mortgage' scheme, which would reduce the interest rates available for mortgages to those whose income levels prevented them from receiving the full benefits of mortgage tax relief, as the Conservatives were themselves considering a similar scheme.

After the March 1966 election defeat, Thatcher was switched to the shadow Treasury team, headed by Iain Macleod. Her determination not to be restricted, as a woman, to social issues had paid off. Her experience as a tax lawyer meant that she was well equipped to counter the proposals for a Selective Employment Tax (SET) invented by the Labour Chancellor, James Callaghan. During the Budget debate on 5 May, she went on the offensive in the House, boasting, amid giggles and gasps from both sides, that before the debate she had read every Budget speech and Finance Bill since 1946. On SET, she jeered, 'Oh, that Gilbert and Sullivan should be living at this hour. This is sheer cockeyed lunacy. The Chancellor needs a woman at the Treasury.' She accused the Government of discriminating against working mothers, who, as employers of child minders in the non-productive sector that SET was discouraging, were being severely taxed.

Iain Macleod was impressed by her performance. He told Nigel Fisher, MP, 'This one is a bit different. Quite exceptionally able. A first class brain', and he tipped her for Cabinet rank.

When on 20 July Wilson announced a freeze on prices and incomes and a Prices and Incomes Bill which would back it with the force of law, Thatcher joined Macleod in the Tory attack. Although they had, in the previous administration, instigated a voluntary prices and incomes policy, they argued that a statutory policy would prove too rigid and would entail cumbersome detailed controls. Although opposition to the measures stressed their inefficiency, Mrs Thatcher was personally convinced that statutory solutions to inflation were in themselves wrong. She became involved in the Conservatives' major review of taxation which would lead to formulating tax reform policies to be presented at the next general election. Again, her experience as a tax lawyer was recruited. After working for Macleod for only twenty months, she was promoted, on the recommendation of Peter Walker, into the Shadow Cabinet, as shadow spokesman on fuel and power.

Her first debate, on 26 October 1967, concerned the tragedy at Aberfan, where a Coal Board tip had buried a primary school and its children. Power brought Thatcher face to face with the nationalized industries and their problems. Her opposite number, Richard Marsh, was pushing Britain through steel nationalisation; there was a switch going on, weaning Britain away from nationalized coal towards nationalized electricity and gas, including new reserves found under the North Sea. The prospect of North Sea oil was also looming. But no sooner had Thatcher come to terms with the new brief than, a bare year later, she was switched again, to Transport, once again opposite Marsh. She had just missed shadowing Barbara Castle, who had moved to Employment. The legislative action had moved with her, leaving Thatcher to watch over the completed Transport Act. Again, no sooner had she taken in the complications of the transport debates and the powerful transport lobbies than she was once more moved, in October 1969, to Education.

Her Commons voting record on matters which the whips have deemed a free vote has been orthodox Conservative and reactionary. As well as advocating the return of corporal punishment within the first year of entering Parliament, she voted for the reintroduction of the death penalty in 1964, 1966 and 1969, although she voted against it in 1975, when there was a proposal to reintroduce hanging for terrorists. She voted against divorce law reform, abstained on homosexuality legalisation and voted in favour of the Termination of Pregnancy Bill, which she was later to criticise for being interpreted too liberally. She did not contribute to the Commons debates on any of these measures. She has always voted for British entry to the EEC.

On 10 October 1968, Thatcher delivered the Conservative Political Centre's party conference lecture at Blackpool. She followed the precedent of the occasion by describing the fundamentals of her belief and the direction that Conservatism ought to follow. It was her first systematic statement of philosophy and intent and therefore has special value, for although no one in the audience could know, this would be the philosophy of the Party's leader from February 1975 onwards. The speech (reproduced in its entirety in Appendix, p. 270) was reprinted as a blue-covered pamphlet, published by the Conservative Political Centre. It is significant that in 1968 when it was published, it did not create a stir, nor objections from the left of the Party. The arguments that it contains are not to a traditional right-wing formula, although most right-wing Conservatives would agree with everything that was written. It follows no specific antecedent of thought in the Conservative tradition, nor logical exposition of a deliberate argument. More, it is the articulation of a set of instincts and impulses reacting to events since the Second World War and, with hindsight, can be seen as the first presentation of the set of general beliefs and prejudices which make up Thatcherism.

What is particularly striking is that 15 years later Thatcher would agree with almost every word of it – indeed it might have been written as her first period of government came to an end. The principle themes of Thatcherism are exposed: the condemnation of an over-reliance on government and the way that government intervention in people's lives leads to the debilitation of the individual; the natural justice of the market and the folly of those who try to tamper with it or change its purpose; the total equation between individual freedom and economic freedom, between free choice and market choice, between political pluralism and economic competition; the dislike of large social or political units and bureaucracy as enemies of individuality and individual freedom; the declaration that the welfare state should be trimmed back, taking care of only those things which the citizen can't readily handle himself; the dismissal of materialism as nothing more than the means whereby individuals may enjoy their spending decision; the enthusiasm for tight monetary control; the promotion of family responsibilities; the contempt shown for the post-war political consensus.

But, to a great extent, the CPC speech is exceptional only in hindsight. At the time it went largely unnoticed. It was certainly not considered to be a major contribution to Conservative ideology. It did not confront the principle aims of the Conservative Party in opposition.

At the same conference, the chairman of the Party, Anthony Barber, described the four principles which would guide the next Tory government as: a belief in the importance of the individual and his right to choose; a recognition that prosperity and personal satisfaction would be more likely to come from private enterprise than state control; that those individuals who can shoulder greater responsibility should do so, leaving the state to help those who really need it; and to work in the interest of the whole nation, not one class. Iain Macleod, the shadow Chancellor, added that the priorities of Conservative economic policy were to reduce personal taxation, encourage savings, keep 'an iron hand' on public spending, review trade union legislation, return choice to the people, and 'get the government off the people's backs'. All these things could be found in the Thatcher lecture, but she went further. She questioned 'the extensive and all-pervading development of the welfare state' and 'the rapid spread of higher education' and the practicality of international idealism as a means for solving international problems. She went further than Macleod and criticised the dependence of successive chancellors, including Conservative ones, upon the notion of growth as a prerequisite for political solutions and, in a hostage to fortune, dismissed a statutory prices and incomes policy as a 'totally unacceptable notion'.

Even more remarkable, in hindsight, is the precocity of her words on economics. In 1968 she was declaring, 'We now put so much emphasis on the control of incomes that we have too little regard for the essential role of government which is the control of money supply and management of demand. Greater attention to this role and less to the outward detailed control would have achieved more for the economy. It would mean, of course, that the government had to exercise itself some of the disciplines on expenditure it is so anxious to impose on others. It would mean that expenditure in the vast public sector would have not to be greater than the amount which could be financed out of taxation plus genuine saving. For a number of years some expenditure has been financed by what amounts to printing the money.' Few Conservative Treasury spokesmen would have diagnosed the problems of the management of the economy in that way in 1968. Monetarism was by no means fashionable. Milton Friedman only rose to prominence in Britain during the early seventies. The Barber Chancellorship of 1970-74 most certainly did not live by Thatcher's dictum.

So, where did such a clear description of the fundamentals of monetarism appear from in 1968? Certainly it is unlikely that she wrote the whole of the speech herself and it seems possible that the section on the importance of restricting monetary growth was a piece of undigested wisdom from another source. But whom? The only person who was regularly preaching monetary continence was Enoch Powell — in 1968 recently sacked from the Shadow Cabinet and raising issues in public which split the Tory ranks on everything from Europe to immigration. In her CPC lecture, Thatcher said, 'The great mistake of the last few years has been for the government to provide or to legislate for almost everything. Part of this policy had its roots in the plans for reconstruction in the postwar period when governments assumed all kinds of new obligations. The policies may have been warranted at the time but they have gone further than was intended or is advisable.' This statement, taken with the plea for the money supply to be taken seriously, lest it would lead to the printing of money, is similar to Powell's views, neatly combined in a speech delivered as long before as 1957. But his sentiments remained the same – and still do. The 1957 Powell speech, delivered at Halifax, said: 'The Western nations, and our own among them, emerged from the war not only with a leeway of destruction and deprivation to make up, but with limitless, if laudable, appetites and ambitions for expansion and development of every kind, for the provision of facilities, services, security, for the expansion of the sphere of community action, for the economic enrichment and improvement of the life of the individual. How tempting to satisfy these ambitions at a greater rate than the nation was willing to make possible out of its production by taxation and savings! How simple and delightful to meet them by increasing the supply of money! The power was there; the temptation was there; and the sight of means to do ill deeds made ill deeds done – the ill deeds of debasing the currency and defrauding those who relied upon its value.' By 1968, then, Thatcher was at least preaching a Powellite economic interpretation of the post-war years, although there is nothing to suggest that he was involved in the writing of her CPC lecture. She was at least echoing his sentiments, although it seems that, by her subsequent silence, she was not fully able to apply that wisdom to the politics she was engaged in. However, her instinct towards 'sound money' – money which did not lose value through inflation – was identified at this time and nowhere were her feelings better expressed than by Enoch Powell. The 1957 Halifax speech continued, 'I do say that at the very heart of those measures is the Government's determination, at all costs, to equate the total of the

demands upon it with the total of the resources which can
be provided without inflation. Those resources in reality are
only two: taxation and borrowing from the public. But
taxation we want to see reduced further, while the readiness
of the public to save and to lend to the Government cannot
be conjured up with a magic wand. It depends in turn upon
the prospects for a stable value of savings and a sound
financial future.'

In its efforts to offer a more attractive alternative to the
state collectivist government of Harold Wilson, the Tories
were working across a broad front to return to a private
enterprise approach which would appear relevant and
dynamic. This revision of their aims, coupled with a
disengagement from the traditional patrician motives of the
generation before Heath, culminated in a much-celebrated
conference of the Shadow Cabinet held at the Selsdon Park
Hotel in January 1970. It gave birth to Wilson's crack
about Selsdon Man, a figure from prehistory which would
soon find itself extinct. Thatcher was absent from the first
day's meetings, but arrived at the Croydon hotel on the
second day, a Saturday, for discussions on the draft of a
Conservative election manifesto. The conference emerged
with a five-point legislative plan which she happily
endorsed. The Selsdon scheme, which was considered to be
noticeably more right-wing in tone than any previous
Conservative programme, consisted of: reducing the burden
of taxation and switching from direct to indirect means;
introducing legislation into trade union affairs, particularly
the settling of disputes; the provision of pensions for the
over-80s (which Thatcher had pushed for at the behest of
Airey Neave); and plans to reduce immigration. Thatcher
was pleased with the package and was later to say, in 1974,
'There is a lot of talk about Selsdon Man. Well, I was
Selsdon Woman.' At the end of the conference, she and
Denis drove quickly back from Croydon to a meeting in
Finchley, so that she would be there to hear the end of a
speech delivered by Powell. And she was the only member
of the Shadow Cabinet to wish him success in the 1970
general election.

CHAPTER SIX

Education

Thatcher's only senior ministerial experience before she became Prime Minister was three and half years at the Department of Education. It marked her permanently, although the effects were not immediately obvious at the time. She experienced the traditionally painful ministerial lessons of finding herself in charge of a policy – the conversion of schools to the comprehensive system – which suited neither her instincts nor those of many Conservatives. It was a policy which she was powerless to change, let alone reverse. And it became evidence for her later judgement that Conservatives were rarely able – and rarely seemed to want – to do anything but dilute reforms begun by the Labour Party.

But the most important impact of her job during the Heath government had little do do with education. She encountered for the first time the full complexity of the relationship between political will and its administrative application. It contributed to her subsequent distrust of the civil service as a whole. Her relations with civil servants at Education were good humoured enough, but since then she has sounded bitter about the quality and attitudes of the civil servants with whom she worked. She seems to regret the extent to which she accepted the prevailing notions of the time and of the department which she ran. Something similar was happening in her attitude to the whole range of the Heath government's policies, in particular the economic strategy of Anthony Barber. No sooner had the government fallen in the 'miners' election' of February 1974 than she was busy denouncing it in private.

Education, like 'law and order', has always been a subject to arouse strong feeling among the faithful who set the noise level at party conferences. Sir Edward Boyle, her old

Oxford friend, had been provoking murmurs of complaint by an insufficiently vigorous counter-campaign on the comprehensive school reform begun by Anthony Crosland and subsequently pursued by his successor, Edward Short. Boyle was badly received by the 1969 conference; disenchanted with political life, he decided to accept the offer of the vice-chancellorship of Leeds University and left the Shadow Cabinet. He had already been Secretary of State for Education once before and it seems unlikely that he would have been ready to do it again if he had still been in the Shadow Cabinet at an election. Thatcher, identified in the minds of some Conservative backbenchers with a tougher stand, was moved from shadow spokesman on Transport to Education. 'She is rather a pal of mine, I got on very well with her when she was at Pensions,' Richard Crossman wrote in his diary at the end of that week, 'and she is one of the few Tories I greet in the lobby. She is tough, able and competent, and, unlike Boyle, she will be a kind of professional Opposition Spokesman.'

The widespread view of her as likely to be less sympathetic to comprehensives than Boyle was drawn more from her general political antecedents than from any past interest in the subject outside her own family. The twins were now sixteen; Mark was at Harrow and Carol at St Paul's. In her early briefings with party officials, she asserted that she wanted to crusade as hard as possible against comprehensives, but was rapidly confronted by the limits to the extent to which she was likely to be able to commit the party. The conference simply promised to 'maintain the existing rights of local education authorities to decide what is best for their area' and said that Labour's attempt to force comprehensive schemes through was 'contrary to local democracy and contrary to the best interests of the children.'

The change from Boyle to Thatcher was more one of style than of substance. Boyle had not been, despite the allegations from grassroots party members and backbenchers, inclined to make Labour's comprehensive plans bipartisan, but had taken the view that a sudden change would be impossible and that the policy had to be steered gradually. He based his view on two facts with which any education minister had to contend. The Department of Education and Science has influence, but that is not the same as direct power and control; the department's sway over much of what happens in many schools is at best indirect. Second, the move to comprehensive schemes which were aimed at eliminating the selection and separation of school children of differing abilities at too early an age, had begun in the late 1950s and was liable to be almost as popular with education authorities controlled by Conservatives as with Labour councils. Crosland had attempted to speed up the pace of change by issuing the circular 10/65 which requested authorities to submit plans for comprehensive schemes; he had followed it with circular 10/66 which threatened to withhold building grants from authorities which did not obey. By the end of 1969, the majority of authorities were submitting schemes. Edwart Short went further and introduced a bill which would make submission of plans compulsory; it was introduced three months after Mrs Thatcher came into the education job and her Parliamentary task during that government's last few months was opposing it in committee and in the chamber.

In common with many Conservatives who read the opinion polls, she was not expecting to win the snap election called by Harold Wilson that summer; 'I'm not a natural optimist politically,' she once recalled. Her appointment attracted extensive publicity: although not the first woman education minister, she was the only woman member of the Cabinet and education was a subject more in the news in the early 1970s than is the case a decade later. Her relations with the education correspondents were already bad. She had spoken soon after her shadow appointment at a lunch of the education correspondents group and it had developed into a rancorous slanging match which left mutual suspicions that were to persist for years. Media visitors who were not education specialists were struck by her defensiveness and sense of injury over the coverage she had received. 'They were all snobs,' she said shortly after becoming the minister. 'No, I mean inverted snobs.'

The job was to be her first experience of the stresses and strains of a minister's job when dealing with a subject on which almost every adult member of the population has strong views. Her evangelistic style of promoting policy, although it disguised her caution and containment within the Cabinet line, gave her the appearance of being more ideological than was in fact the case.

On the vexed comprehensive issue, she was essentially against compulsion of local authorities rather than against comprehensive schools as such. She had very little choice: the move against selection by the eleven-plus was too far advanced to reverse, and even educationalists who were unenthusiastic about comprehensive schooling were equally unwilling to return to the eleven-plus, which had been widely discredited as a reliable method of selection. There was no alternative policy to turn to.

With circular 10/70, she very quickly rescinded the requirement for plans to be put forward, but found herself passing the large majority of schemes that came before her. In February 1973, she revealed during the course of a Commons debate that since taking office she had approved 2,650 proposals to change secondary schools and rejected only 115, or around 4% of the total. Speaking of her preparations in opposition one colleague said, 'She made quite a lot of it at the time, but she soon learnt. She thought that she could do something more radical than she could.' In fact, her line on secondary schools seems to have been a mixture of resignation in the face of the facts of life and of recognition of the absence of an alternative. She explained, 'People think that a minister has a great deal of power. They would be surprised if they knew how little one actually has.' She spoke admiringly in public of the grammar schools but never showed signs of wanting to develop a counter-policy which would halt the widespread move towards merging them with secondary modern schools.

Her relations with her private office and the department's senior civil servants were good. They recognised quickly that her intelligence and energies would not be a disadvantage to the department's reputation, that she was a considerable improvement on Short, who had been unpopular with his officials. 'She at least read what you wrote and had something worthwhile to say about it, which was more than you could say for him,' said one. They noted that she did not arrive with any manifesto commitments or crusading zeal which would make life difficult.

Her officials were agreed that she was generally courteous to those she dealt with. Her style with paperwork was brisk. She was careful not to push staff too hard, paid for the contents of the drinks cabinet in her office and was attentive to managerial courtesies such as attending the annual production of the staff amateur dramatic society. 'She's an actress,' said one mandarin. 'She has an image which she wants to project, something of queenliness. She is very conscious of the impression she is making.'

'She can give people the impression of being a bully,' a senior official recalled. 'You have got to have equally strong convictions to stand up to her and she will argue against you with tact and grace. If you don't, she walks right over you. When she first came, at the start of a meeting, she would tell you the answer to the question which you had gathered to consider. She was terribly quick on the draw and would interrupt before you had finished speaking. I think we did a lot to housetrain her.' After the election of February 1974, a hundred of the most senior civil servants paid their departing minister the rare compliment of asking her back for a farewell party.

She was fond of saying that she made up her mind about people very fast and was not often wrong. A long list of names to head an intensive one-year inquiry into teacher training produced no ministerial approval until the officials suggested Eric James, the vice-chancellor of the University of York. James was invited to Flood Street for a lunch cooked by Mrs Thatcher. She astonished the small group present by meeting James at the front door and announcing immediately after introductions were complete that she had invited him to lunch to see what he was like. He passed the test.

These relations between minister and officials would not be worthy of much note except for Thatcher's side of the story as it has emerged since those years. This is a description from one family friend: 'The lowest point in the water I ever remember Margaret getting was when she was at Education, when she realised what she wanted to do there was not going to come about. It was an impasse. If the minister arrived and wanted little change, it accepted that. Otherwise it was one extra (despatch) box of papers a night, just to keep you occupied. She looked more fagged out and was nearer to physical deterioration than I have ever seen her and it takes a long time to get to that stage; it really was an extraordinary thing. Denis was fussed about her health. I think she would say that it was the most strenuous time of her life and left her with the most satisfaction. And she didn't get what she wanted.' And this was her summary in 1983: 'There was a great battle on. It was part of this equalisation rage at the time, that you mustn't select by ability. After all, I had come up by selection by ability. I had to fight it. I had a terrible time.'

This frustration did not communicate itself to the officials she dealt with. 'If she says now that she had a terrible time at Education, that was not the minister I knew,' said one. Some of the strain on her was due to the bitter public rows which began erupting very soon after she arrived. Treasury-inspired rumour held that the first package of public expenditure cuts, announced four months after the Conservatives came to office, would be of the order of £300 million, of which a third was to be from education. She fought an effective defence of the departmental budget in the bilateral negotiations with Maurice Macmillan, Chief Secretary at the Treasury, and emerged with the worst cuts deferred or abandoned. It was in that round of cuts that her department agreed to the end of free school milk for seven to eleven year-olds at a saving of £8 million a year.

The ensuing furore made for poor relations between the minister and her senior officials – and with the Permanent Secretary, Sir William Pile, in particular – for several months. Thatcher accused them of failing to warn her of the strength of likely reaction from teachers and local authorities. They were adamant that they had not underplayed the risks.

Hindsight makes it look a peculiar row. Labour had

recently ended free milk for secondary schoolchildren: there was no row when, on receipt of an alibi in the form of a report finding no medical ill-effects, the next Labour government failed to restore it. It triggered protests, abuse and the first crop of nicknames: Milk Snatcher, Ice Maiden, Cave Woman, Open Refrigerator, Salome, and so on. It enhanced a reputation she had acquired for coldness. 'Something happens to her eyes,' one journalist had written in 1969, 'like a cold wind passing over a Norfolk beach.' She defended the decision doggedly but without flair. One woman who came to offer sympathy and a small piece of ammunition was Janet Young, then chairman of the education committee on Oxford City Council. The two women had first met as undergraduates at Oxford; Mrs Young had asked her education officials whether there was any truth in the allegation that there were medical risks in not giving children milk and they had said that there was none. Manchester Council for a time added a dash of cocoa to the milk and called it drinking chocolate, and gave it away, and one or two councils continued to simply give milk away until legislation brought them into line. Denis was sufficiently worried about the effect that the pressure of events was having on her that he suggested she should resign and give up politics.

She was the target of a concerted press campaign. 'At a time when Mr Heath's government is desperately seeking an image of compassion and concern,' wrote the *Sun*, 'Mrs Thatcher is fast emerging as a liability,' headlining the piece 'The Most Unpopular Woman in Britain.' 'Now Tell Us What You Think,' said the *Sun* and one Conservative agent in the North of England was caught inspiring his activists to write in her support. She was not the most popular person with her Cabinet colleagues or their wives. At a formal lunch at No. 10, at which she was present, an eminent guest was heard during a gap in the conversation asking if there was any truth in the rumour that she was a woman.

She was not a member of the Heath inner circle: as Education Minister, she sat in one of the seats furthest from the Prime Minister at the centre of the table and used to persuade her more senior neighbour, Joseph Godber, to ask

questions on non-education subjects so that she would have
a chance to ask supplementaries. Reginald Maudling was
sometimes heard complaining about 'that bloody woman
rabbiting on' as he emerged from Downing Street. Heath
had a limited respect for her and she did not feel close to
him. But he stubbornly resisted any suggestion that he
should move her in order to make life easier for the
Cabinet's education policies. The only time she came close
to being moved was for other reasons; when Peter Walker
was moved in November 1972 from Environment to Trade
and Industry, Heath offered him a choice of Thatcher or
Howe as junior minister for Trade and Consumer Affairs.
Walker chose Howe. In the end, Thatcher served an
unusually long stretch of three and a half years.

The image of the budget-cutter conjured by the 'milk-
snatcher' episode has masked that fact that the thrust of her
policies was strongly — and to a large extent successfully —
expansionist. For an ambitious departmental minister, an
expanding budget was not a disadvantage. She won an early
battle in Cabinet for an increase in funds for the rebuilding
of Victorian primary schools. She tenaciously pursued the
commitment to raise the school leaving age — which had
been delayed by the Labour government on grounds of cost
— and finally saw it through in January 1972 against some
light party opposition. She fended off proposals to abolish
the Open University. During her time, education spending
as a proportion of gross national product reached $6\frac{1}{2}\%$, for
the first time ever higher than spending on defence.

Expansion was indeed on the cover and at the heart of
the most important document which the DES produced in
her years. 'Framework for Expansion', a White Paper
outlining the strategy for education resources for the
coming decade, appeared in December 1972 to a good
reception from most of the lobbies whose interests were at
stake. It represented another successful negotiation with the
Treasury and No. 10, who required convincing that there
was a case for planning a major increase in public
expenditure. In her own words to the Schools Council in the
following March, 'When the Education White Paper talked
about expansion it meant expansion and not contraction ...

Taking altogether the policies outlined in the White Paper, covering threequarters of the service, annual expenditure could rise by nearly half – £960 million – over the decade.'

It was principally a civil service initiative, an attempt to produce an overall solution to several interconnected problems. During its preparation over the previous eighteen months, Thatcher occasionally sounded slightly suspicious of the fact that she had little idea of what was going on inside the various reviews which were to converge in the White Paper. The document planned expenditure for the coming decade: it had to be drafted to last through at least two governments without offending the minister in power at the time it was to be published. The mixture turned out to be right: Thatcher approved it with few amendments. There was an important omission on which she had insisted: no prescription was laid down for the development of education policy for the 16-19 age group, where ideas evolving in the educational establishment threatened the grammar schools, which Thatcher did not want to see undermined. Covering around three-quarters of total public spending on education, the White Paper set levels for the expansion of nursery education, the school rebuilding programme, the number of teachers, and suggested what kind of teacher training there should be and how resources should be allocated in higher education. 'I think that it was a historical accident that she happened to be at education when a number of major problems reached the point where they could be resolved in a related way,' said one man closely involved in the exercise, 'but she did have the kind of mind that was quite capable of thinking in those terms. Historically, she did more and got more for education than any other minister I served.' The fruits of this work did not last long: within a year, the money agreed by the Treasury had been withdrawn under the impact of the OPEC oil price rise.

The document continued to lay the stress on nursery education which had been a theme of Thatcher's public statements since the first debates over the location and scale of expenditure cuts. 'I sent my two children to a nursery school, just a couple of hours each morning,' she said, 'and

this is something that should be available to all who want it
... But nursery schools were especially needed in the
deprived areas. You found that, by the time children came
to school at the age of five, a lot of them were already
behind because they came from homes where no interest
was taken in the children, where the parents didn't talk to
them ... Of course the State can never take the place of
good parents ... But it can help redress the balance for
those born unlucky.' There was a very strong hint of Keith
Joseph's current ideas in that explanation; Joseph, along
with Thatcher the most successful member of the Cabinet at
expanding the size and spending of his Department of
Health and Social Security, was engaged in setting up an
inquiry into the 'cycle of deprivation'. The inquiry did not
report until the Conservatives were back in power again: it
failed to sustain his hypothesis that intervention to assist
children in the very early years of their lives was the best
way of redressing inequalities of opportunity. 'A lot of these
buildings,' Thatcher said after she had left Education, 'were
in areas where the children tended to have a poor home
background. Then you often found that these bad school
buildings also had bad equipment, and that it was very
difficult to get teachers to go there. So these children
suffered a triple deprivation, lacking a decent home, proper
school buildings and enough good teachers.'

Thatcher's reputation since her time at Education has
obscured the common denominator of her actual policies:
she had the forensic and intellectual skills to push through
schemes which were within the broad framework of
government policy, but she did not have the political weight
to step outside that framework. She may have supported the
idea (which has resurfaced during her own government) of
student loans, but she did not push it, knowing that Heath
was opposed because of his own experience as the
beneficiary of a student loan. She failed to persuade the
cabinet to support a move back to the eleven-plus. What she
has said since suggests that she would have liked to, but
these later statements may be coloured by the pattern of her
rhetoric in the eighties. The chairman of the backbench
education committee in the early 1970s was Angus Maude

and they appear to have cooperated well in exchanging intelligence on currents of opinion in the House and in the Department. She was occasionally frustrated by the education unions and lobbies: in trying to put through a change of policy over teachers' pensions, she was out-lobbied by Terry Casey, leader of the schoolmasters union, and the prospect of a backbenchers' mutiny forced her to pull back. One of her officials remembers her on the verge of tears.

The policies which brought such bad publicity for the first two years of her time were three: school milk, comprehensives and student unions. She published a consultative document in November 1971 suggesting that university and polytechnic authorities should take responsibility for the financing of student unions and outlining some regulations aimed at preventing union subsidies being spent on exotic political causes often far distant from the unions or the students themselves. Student marches streamed through the streets of university towns; she was mobbed at the Queen Elizabeth Hall, where most of the students due to receive awards refused to come forward to accept them. Within a few months the proposal was withdrawn in the face of opposition from not only students but university vice-chancellors and local authorities. It was nominally withdrawn for a year only but never reappeared.

A substantial proportion of her ministerial time was pre-empted by the steady stream of decisions to be made on comprehensive schemes. The 'Section 13' procedure requires the Secretary of State to assess the plans of a local authority in the light of representations from any interested party. The plans presented by Birmingham for the reorganisation of its 90 schools generated a petition against the proposal allegedly containing 1.3 million signatures, and a petition in favour with 24,000. Her decision was to exempt 18 schools from the scheme.

A more common difficulty was sometimes caused by the clash between the manifesto commitment, the autonomy of the local authority decisions, and parents' pressure. Depending on the argument, friends or critics have pointed to the fact that Thatcher passed more comprehensive schemes than any other minister before or since. It is an artificial measure of her attitude to comprehensives, since her period in charge of the decisions coincided with the peak of the change. No other minister would have had the opportunity to make so many decisions and it would have been literally impossible to refuse every local authority, particularly after it had been made clear that it was no longer compulsory for them to change.

This pragmatism was not sufficiently appreciated to prevent a small groundswell of complaint in the party; Thatcher survived conferences well — an earlier one had seen the appearance of her most spectacular hat, wide and decorated with a bold swirling pattern, which was a gift to cartoonists for several years afterwards — until 1973. There, one speaker from the floor lamented that 'we have policies certainly, but not a philosophy', and that parents 'have witnessed the wanton destruction of good schools in the cause of comprehensive education, on occasion helped by members of my own party.' Throughout her time as minister Thatcher resisted pressure to allow expansion of the number of direct grant schools and she spoke at that same conference against the idea — then being preached by Dr Rhodes Boyson — that there should be a voucher system in education.

'She was,' recalled one civil servant, 'what we think of as a good minister: she took what we gave her and fought for it. She did cross-examine and hector, but she was open to persuasion.' Attending international conferences for the first time, she started taking French lessons twice a week and taking cassettes back to Flood Street for extra study. At least one official who disagreed with her policies was struck by her unusual personality and approach to the job. He recalled one of his colleagues telling the minister that he did not think a particular policy would be popular. I'm not asking you whether it's popular, said Mrs Thatcher, is it the right thing to do? 'It may sound corny, but ministers who say and mean that kind of thing are unusual. I was very strongly impressed by her conviction of an objective outside herself; she did then and does now a great many things which other politicians would advise her not to do.'

She was not a member of the inner group of ministers which advised Heath on economic policy. Heath did not encourage members of the Cabinet outside that group to debate economic strategy. During and after the leadership election Mrs Thatcher's supporters hinted that along with Keith Joseph, she had objected to the U-turn away from austerity measures and had argued against it in Cabinet, but had finally not taken the step of resigning on the issue. She herself appears to have suggested this to several people afterwards.

There is very little evidence to sustain this idea. She was closer to Joseph than to most of her colleagues and he certainly did harbour doubts about Heath's change of heart which he was ready to voice in private. Several ministers who served in Heath's Cabinet are unable to recall her taking a strong individual line against the post-1972 policy, let alone any hint of resignation. She did drop a small word of encouragement to Jock Bruce-Gardyne, a member of a group of Conservative hard-liners opposing the Industry Bill and its subsidies for failing enterprises, suggesting that there were one or two people in the Cabinet who supported him. If she did ever consider resignation, it would have been a harsh choice; she knew she was not highly respected by Heath and he was unsympathetic to resignations. Her chances of returning to the front bench while he was still party leader would have been slim.

There was certainly little debate in that Cabinet between those supporting the change of tack and ministers who have subsequently become 'monetarist'. Thatcher was prone to say, in the arguments which followed Heath's defeat, that nobody in the early 1970s understood the full significance of the money supply. Cabinet ministers were not even given money supply figures until just before the February 1974 election. In private afterwards, Thatcher was not as critical of Anthony Barber's chancellorship as her developing public position on economic policy might have suggested: she told people that much of the timing of economic policy in that government had been wrong but much had also been misunderstood: the longer-term effects of the previous Chancellor's measures; the impact of the rise in commodity prices in late 1973; and the incomes policy, a mistake of presentation (it could not work without a consensus behind it) and not of doctrine. In general the fate of that government had been a lesson.

She had begun attending the monthly Hobart lunches at the British home of political market economists, the Institute of Economic Affairs, where she met, among others, Alan Walters. The contradictions of her policies cannot have been lost on her at the time – they were cetainly not lost on some of her critics from within her own party. She stressed repeatedly her belief in the importance of preserving and protecting parental choice: she had not done much to alter the range of choice either way.

In retrospect she gives the impression of someone learning about public relations the hard way. It was her first experience of the difficulties of defending policies against determined lobbies and since then she has never been as passive in the face of such problems. The party's leading media advisers used to hold occasional dinners at the Carlton Club to which cabinet ministers would be invited and questions of image and presentation discussed. She arrived at her dinner wearing a string of pearls, which Denis had given her on the day that the twins were born. The necklace, along with the rapidly abandoned hats, had been seized on as symbols of Conservative middle-class suburbia. She asked angrily why she shouldn't wear what she liked. The media men were impressed: close-up she was very much more charismatic and persuasive than her public appearances had led them to believe.

Her views on education then and ten years later make an intriguing comparison. She still appears to be uncertain about her overall philosophy; a voucher scheme took a long time to emerge and then did so only very tentatively. Although after she became Prime Minister there was little Cabinet discussion of general education policy, she occasionally intervened on a highly detailed matter being dealt with by the minister. She surprised colleagues by remembering recondite details of staffing levels which had been true when she had been minister but which had changed in the intervening years. She occasionally sympathised with Joseph's predecessor Mark Carlisle, complaining of the obstructionism which she had encountered from senior officials; Carlisle replied by pointing out that most of the ones she had worked with had retired. As one cabinet minister observed of these exchanges, 'She doesn't like local government, she doesn't like the civil service and she doesn't like teachers – so education isn't a very good job to have.' She made it clear that she thought that the necessary changes were fundamental and were still to be made. In autumn 1982 she revisited her old twelfth floor office on one of a series of Whitehall visits and delivered a familiar plaint to the ministers and officials she lunched with: why have we spent so much on education and achieved so little? She did not appear impressed by the answers. A few months later she was addressing a gathering of forty or so junior ministers on budget strategy and election timing when she was asked what the government was planning to do about education. 'It's a disaster,' she replied, adding, 'Is there anyone here from education?' There wasn't.

She did not leave those who came into contact with her between 1970 and 1974 with the idea that she would one day be Prime Minister. One civil servant, not in her department, but who dealt with her from time to time, quoted Tacitus: 'She reversed his aphorism "*Omnium consensu capax imperii nisi imperasset*" (generally understood to be a man capable of ruling so long as that capacity is never tested); if she hadn't been put to the test of leading her party, you would never have thought her capable of leading it.' One of the members of Heath's Cabinet said: 'If you had told me in 1973 that she was going to be the next leader of the party, I would have said that you needed your head examined.' But it had clearly been a formative experience for an impressionable politician; or, as Thatcher herself put it much later, 'Iron entered my soul.'

CHAPTER SEVEN

Leader

Thatcher became the leader of the Conservative Party through a succession of accidents. Many of those taking part in the leadership election did not realise the significance of her election for the direction of Party policy. Her success in the election against Edward Heath was a surprise to her supporters, even to herself. Many of those who voted for her did not want her to become the leader and discovered too late that their tactical votes, designed merely to dislodge an isolated and electorally unattractive leader, were part of an elaborate scheme to do something more. The rightwards shift which her election as leader announced was supported neither by the large majority of Conservative MPs, the Conservative peers, nor the Conservative party workers.

In the nine years that Heath had been leader, he had completed the transformation of the Party's image from one which appeared, above all, to protect the interests of the wealthy, the landowning, the titled and the businessman to that of a meritocratic party which encouraged market forces so long as they did not radically change the balance of the mixed economy or the welfare state: in short, the post-war consensus. Heath and his colleagues enjoyed a reputation for their managerial competence, committed to keeping the size of the public sector under control, the clear commitment of the meeting of the Shadow Cabinet at the Selsdon Park Hotel in 1969. They were committed to an expansion, as rapid as was feasible, of the British economy. Anthony Barber, the Chancellor of the Exchequer, led the adventurous policy of expansion until, in 1972, it was halted by the massive increases in the international price of oil by the oil producing and exporting companies which dented the buoyancy of world economic activity. Heath and his Cabinet swallowed their words and decided to protect the very industries which, under their aggressive growth policy, were most likely to falter. Where 'lame duck' industries would have been allowed to go under, Heath and Barber, with their Industry Minister, John Davies, sanctioned rescue programmes with large amounts of public money. The most notorious rescue was Rolls Royce, which became the symbol of Heath's U-turn, demonstrating that the preservation of the nation's industrial assets was considered more important than his desire to force British industry to be more competitive by ignoring painful bankruptcies.

By February 1974, Heath had become embroiled in a large-scale dispute between the National Coal Board and the National Union of Mineworkers. His policy had led to Government intervention in most significant economic decisions, including the determination of prices and incomes norms. A long-running dispute between the NCB and the NUM had finally involved first the Government, then the Prime Minister. It became established in the minds of many ministers that to defy the will of the Government, even during the pursuit of an industrial dispute, was to challenge the authority of the Government and thereby the legitimacy of parliamentary democracy. Heath called an election upon the issue, 'Who Governs Britain?', but found that during the campaign, this central issue became diminished as the Labour and Liberal opposition opened up the debate. By the quirks of the constituency boundaries, Heath won a popular victory, winning more votes than the Labour Party. But he had secured a smaller number of seats. Using this evident unfairness in the electoral system as justification, he had refused to admit defeat until he had invited the leader of the Liberal Party, Jeremy Thorpe, to Downing Street for talks about the possibility of forming a Conservative/Liberal coalition, combining to form a majority over the Labour Party, which, although the largest party in the Commons, still held less than half of the seats. The Liberals declined, Heath resigned and Harold Wilson returned to Downing Street, the victor of three out of four elections.

There was a good deal of private grumbling against Heath among Conservative MPs and, to a lesser extent, among party workers. The Tory Party is unhappy out of power and still considered itself to be the natural party of government. There was also a feeling that Heath was largely to blame for the defeat and that another leader should be found before long. However, there were few who doubted Heath's policy line. The Party had backed his Selsdon approach to the economy wholeheartedly and had similarly understood and agreed with his 1972 about-turn. They had happily followed Heath as he took them into government intervention in the economy. Heath's prices and incomes policy was thought by most Conservatives to be appropriate, to be fair and to be inevitable as a means of managing the economy.

Among the few who, after the election, disagreed with this point of view were Sir Keith Joseph and Margaret Thatcher, who had sat in the Cabinet from 1970-74. Their attitude to the election defeat was more complicated than those loyal to Heath's understanding of events. Although they were responsible through the notion of Cabinet collective responsibility, they thought the troubles of 1972-74 were unnecessary and the Government's reaction unnecessary. They thought the election had been fought on an issue which never should have arisen and that the Government had no place interfering in the market between employer and employee.

To Thatcher and Joseph, therefore, the election of February 1974 had been fought over an issue which should never have been raised, and had caused the defeat of the Government. Edward Heath was guilty of surrendering the reigns of power needlessly. There was, however, no prospect of an immediate change of leader. The election had been fought over the authority of Heath as Prime Minister and all sections of the Party had become too used to defending him against all comers to suddenly turn on him. It was evident, also, that another general election was in the offing. It was plain that Wilson would try to repeat the trick he performed in 1966, when he secured a working majority after scraping in in 1964. It would be an act of folly to dispose of Heath before that second election took place. None the less, many who were close to Heath – among them, Whitelaw and Carrington – thought that he should offer himself for re-election, knowing full well that the 1922 Committee — the Tory backbench committee — would not dare to oust him with an election impending. At the same time, they argued, it would quell the grumblers who blamed the defeat upon him. Heath stood firm. He deceived himself that he knew the state of the economy better than anyone else and was confident that, as the year wore on, the Government's economic position would worsen rapidly and the electorate would recognise its mistake and vote him and his Party back in. A leadership election would be unnecessary and only invite mishap. The confidence of Heath and those around him made open talk of changing the leader not merely disloyal but also defeatist.

The February defeat had, however, caused a shockwave through many sections of the party, particularly those on the right who had never trusted the social democratic tendencies of Heath and the tight-knit group which surrounded him. Unlike Macmillan, Heath had no time for those who disagreed with him and he kept them well away from the Cabinet and other positions of power. Heath considered the Tory right wing to be wrong-headed, mean-minded, ignorant of the complications of a modern political economy and, above all, quite the wrong image for a modern Conservative Party and liable to lose the Party votes. There was little to give the right any grounds for hope about the future. Heath was secure, for the time being, and there was little doubt that even if he were to be dislodged, then another member of the Party's centre to left would succeed him. The ruling section of the Party appeared to have a monopoly of potential leadership talent and of organisational ability. The right took some satisfaction, however, in Keith Joseph, a senior member of the Shadow Cabinet, who was now publicly questioning the wisdom of the Heath years. Joseph, a baronet and former chairman of Bovis, the building company, was an intelligent, conscientious, and intellectually curious man, sometimes visibly pained by the furious opposition generated by the practical consequences of his theoretical prescriptions. The fundamental shift in Conservative economic policy and the ramifications it had for all aspects of policy after 1972 had deeply disturbed him. He thought that the change had been inconsistent, made purely from motives of expediency. He felt he needed to explore what had gone wrong by establishing the fundamentals of Conservative belief and he was convinced that only through self-confession would an honest approach be found to the way forward.

Thatcher was a great admirer of Joseph. She was a regular visitor to the *Spectator* offices for lunch and had impressed Patrick Cosgrave and the others there as being an intelligent, forthright, determined woman of the true right, untainted by Heath's ideological corruption. Cosgrave wrote an article soon after the February election defeat postulating a Heath defeat and a Thatcher succession. Thatcher was embarrassed and insisted that as long as Joseph was available, she would most certainly not stand, nor even consider the possibility. It was her view at that stage that Joseph was the preeminent choice for leader, combining a rare intellectual capacity with a sense of resolution. She was also realistic about her own prospects. It was unheard of for someone to become the Conservative leader without experiencing the major offices of state. Feminism may have been making progress during the sixties and seventies, but for a woman to become the leader of one of the principal political parties still appeared a distant prospect. And, the Conservative Party being what it was, a bastion of male chauvinism, the prospect of a woman becoming its leader in the foreseeable future was laughable. In June 1974, she was asked about this by a reporter from the Liverpool *Daily Post* and replied, 'It will be years before a woman either leads the Party or becomes Prime Minister. I don't see it happening in my time.' Most Conservative MPs would have agreed with her and, with such a wide choice of able men at the top of the Party, few took seriously the *Spectator*'s suggestion.

She was, however, ambitious and hoped that she might become the Chancellor of the Exchequer. It was a feasible ambition if Joseph became leader. In the meanwhile, she continued to consolidate her reputation for being able to master a complicated brief on economic matters. She had chaired a committee for the Shadow Cabinet which would determine an attractive policy for mortgage holders and it reported to Heath in June 1974. Against her instincts for sticking to the market equilibrium interest rate, the committee had come up with a plan for pinning mortgage interest rates to a maximum $9\frac{1}{2}$ per cent, using subsidies from the public purse. It was a policy manufactured solely to win votes for the impending general election and she showed no enthusiasm for it in private. Heath had tried to encourage her to pin the mortgage rate lower, at 8 per cent, but she fiercely resisted his interference, arguing that it would prove far too costly. Such a commitment to further intervention to alter market forces established her, to those on the right, as unreliable on sound money policies, and confirmed to those on the left that, whatever she was known to think in private, she could be relied upon to toe the Heath line.

It was Keith Joseph who was making the running. During the summer he had let it be known that he would try to explain where successive governments had gone wrong, including the Heath government, admit his part in supporting the policy at the time, and suggest what should be done next. A large number of economic commentators were encouraged to help him construct his public confession, including Peter Jay, the monetarist-inclined but Labour-voting economics editor of *The Times*, and Sam Brittan, who held a similar post on the *Financial Times*. The line finally agreed by Joseph, to be delivered in a speech at Preston in September, which was circulated in draft form in advance for comments which he incorporated in the final text, was that inflation was government-made and that successive 'cures' had only made inflation worse. In particular, he criticised the notion that full employment could be guaranteed by governments by simply expanding domestic demand, irrespective of all other factors. Printing money, he argued, inevitably weakens the economy, slows growth, damages the social services and increases unemployment. His solution was to offer monetary restraint, which was a prerequisite for tackling the other serious economic problems, but which would cause more unemployment in the short run. However, he stressed that close control of the money supply was not enough on its own. It was an implicit criticism of the Barber years, during which the supply of money in the economy had been unchecked, and demand had outstripped supply, fuelling a high and damaging inflation. Although Labour leaders strenuously attacked Joseph's prescription, particularly because of its tendency to increase unemployment, the speech caused little obvious anguish to the Heath leadership or personal embarrassment for Joseph from within the Tory ranks.

As the year wore on, it became obvious that Wilson would most likely call a snap election in October. Heath was therefore safe from attack until afterwards. In any case, the number of Tory MPs who like Joseph wanted to display public guilt was very small. Joseph's second dose of mea culpa was due to be delivered in the middle of October at Edgbaston and was to concentrate on social policy. As expected, Harold Wilson called a general election for 10 October. One of the most incongruous meetings, in hindsight, was a meeting of all MPs, parliamentary candidates and agents at the Europa Hotel on 12 September, at which Edward du Cann, Chairman of the 1922 Committee, representing Conservative backbench opinion, testified to Heath's fitness to lead the Party and to resume his premiership. 'You do not only lead but command our Party,' he said. 'You command more than men and women. It is an army which is fighting with unshakeable confidence and purpose. We are a wholly loyal and united Party. You must be proud to be here today at this great meeting of the 1922 Committee as they are happy to welcome you. There is no one here who does not fully reflect your own devotion to our cause and above all your integrity. If you attack you need never look behind. We follow closely in support at your right hand. We are most grateful to you for having so clearly and cogently explained the theme on which you will fight the election. There is one more point to be remembered from this meeting; we know we can count abundantly on you and you equally know that you can rely on us.' Everyone in the room knew that Heath could only rely on them if he won the election. Within three months of that speech, Du Cann was considering offers from rebels to stand as their candidate against Heath.

Heath entered the election floating the possibility of a government of national unity. His failure to discuss this drastic action angered many Conservative MPs. What many Tory candidates found as they were canvassing was that Heath himself was proving an electoral liability. His public image had become one of a stubborn, power-hungry man. What is worse, his image and that of the Party worsened as it went northwards. Heath's form of Conservatism, as demonstrated by the subsequent election results, proved to be popular only in the south of England. Far from attracting a national vote, Heath had forced the Party back into its southern heartland. 164 out of the 276 Tory seats were south of a line between the Wash and the Severn. In Scotland the Party had been reduced to 16 seats and in Wales there were only eight Tory seats. The question uppermost in most Tory minds over the weekend of 12 and 13 October, immediately following the election, was whether Heath should be allowed to continue as leader. There was no obvious way of dislodging him if he did not want to go. The rules hastily worked out to find a successor to Alec Douglas-Home only defined the method of electing a leader. There was no regular vote of confidence, nor, in a Party which had always depended upon mystery for its decision-making, was there a mechanism for ousting an unpopular leader who was reluctant to leave. Even *voting* for a leader was a relative innovation.

On Sunday 13 October, there was a small gathering of right-wing Conservative MPs at the flat of Nicholas Ridley in Warwick Square, Pimlico. They were certain that sooner or later Heath would have to offer himself for re-election, even though there was no constitutional need for him to do so, and that they should find a candidate who would offer a real alternative to the Conservatism which Heath represented. Those who met were the direct descendants of the right wing rump which had been isolated from the upper echelons of the Party since Macmillan had routed them by taking some into his Cabinet, where he could keep an eye on them, and leaving others stranded on the back benches. The

Ridley group saw the coming leadership election as an ideological crossroads and they did not want to be caught unprepared. What they feared most was that Willie Whitelaw, who was universally popular in the Party but firmly of the centre and left, would be slipped in as a replacement to Heath. Whitelaw would have proven a formidable opponent in an open election and the Tory liberal establishment would persist. For Ridley and his fellow conspirators, the only obvious candidate was Joseph. A decade of Heath, following on from the benign regimes of Macmillan and Home, had put the right at a disadvantage. They had little choice as a candidate. Enoch Powell, who would have suited their purposes exactly — intelligent, articulate, imaginative and electorally popular — was no longer a member of the Party. Edward du Cann was available. Margaret Thatcher was barely considered. Joseph was telephoned that evening and he made his position clear: 'I am a candidate for the leadership and will be a candidate whenever the election takes place. You have my authority to tell that to anybody who asks.' Joseph had thrown his hat in the ring even though no election had been advertised.

The right thought it important to force Heath's hand. At least they knew that, with Joseph warming up in the dressing room, they would not have to stand by while Whitelaw was substituted for Heath. An election would have a serious candidate from the right. But no election was due. The following morning, Monday 14 October, the Executive of the 1922 Committee met at the home of its chairman, Edward du Cann, in Lord North Street. The 1922 Committee acts as a forum for all Tory MPs and, although it holds no formal power in the Party constitution, when united, its views are ignored by the Leader at his peril. It had been decided at the Europa Hotel on 12 September that a meeting should be called swiftly after the general election in order to avert what had happened the previous February, when it had proved difficult to advise Heath of the 1922 Committee's views on the proposed coalition with the Liberals because the members of the Executive were spread far and wide. The meeting would also arrange for elections of a new Executive and of the twenty-odd policy committees. It was inevitable, however, that the leadership should be discussed and not just because of the Ridley cabal. Members of the Executive which represented a broad range of views in the parliamentary party, from left as well as right, had been canvassed by back-bench MPs, peers and party workers over the weekend, as the election result had sunk in, and the overwhelming view was that something had to be done about the evident antipathy towards Heath discovered during the election even among traditional Conservative voters. The press, too, were conscious that the leadership issue would be raised and reporters and photographers greeted the eighteen members of the Executive as they arrived at Du Cann's home. They sat in a horseshoe in his drawing room and he asked them in turn to speak briefly about what they thought should be done. The unanimous view was that an election for the leadership should be held and Du Cann was deputed to inform Heath that that was their collective view.

Du Cann asked to see Heath that afternoon and was granted an audience. The meeting was brief and ill-tempered. Du Cann relayed the message from the 1922 Executive, but there was little subsequent discussion. Heath and Du Cann had always disliked each other, stemming from a lack of enthusiasm by Du Cann over EEC membership, and they had fallen out seriously when Heath dismissed Du Cann as Chairman of the Party, shortly after becoming Leader. Du Cann had not been given office between 1970-74 and had remained a brooding presence presiding over the 1922 Committee.

The next morning, the Executive agreed to meet again to hear Heath's response. To avoid the newspaper speculation which would be caused by them meeting twice in two days, they had decided to assemble secretly in the City offices of Du Cann's merchant bank, Keyser Ullmann, in Milk Street. It proved to be a politically inept plan. The venue of the meeting was leaked to the press, who turned up before the meeting and photographed various members of the Executive as they came out. The inevitable conclusion reached by the journalists was that the Executive were plotting the downfall of their leader – which they were – and that the plot was being arranged through the good offices of Edward Du Cann, who stood to gain by Heath's political demise. There has been a subsequent hue and cry about who exactly leaked the information – some blaming Heath's aides, others a wife of one of the Executive – but whoever was the cause of the press arriving in Milk Street is unimportant: the story proved to be advantageous for Heath, an honourable man apparently being undermined by sly men meeting in secret. At this time, almost every political reporter, leader writer and commentator was sympathetic to Heath and his policies and they had few contacts of worth in other parts of the Party, in particular the right.

Du Cann told the Executive in Milk Street – dubbed the 'Milk Street Mafia' – that Heath had given their request short shrift. William Whitelaw, the Party Chairman, and Humphrey Atkins, the Chief Whip, had also been told of the Executive's demand for an election. It was decided that Heath should be sent a letter explaining exactly the weight of feeling in favour of an election, with Heath as one of the candidates, so that Heath could not misinterpret the intentions of the Executive, as had plainly happened when Du Cann had delivered the news to him. A letter was drafted and, after reading it over the telephone to Atkins, who suggested a minor amendment which was incorporated, it was sent to Heath. It invited him to address the first meeting of the full Committee in the new Parliament. Heath declined and published his reasons. It was his understanding, he said, that the October election had made it necessary for new elections to take place for the Executive of the 1922 and that when these elections had taken place, he would be glad to take advice from the new Executive. There is little doubt that Heath's understanding of the constitution of the 1922 Committee was wrong. The historian of the Committee, Philip Goodhart, MP for Beckenham, made this clear in a letter to *The Times* the following week. Although the election of the Executive takes place each October at the beginning of the parliamentary year, the writ of the chairman and executive runs from election to election, undisturbed by intervening recesses and general elections.

Such a snub to the Committee officers was a dangerous gamble. His leadership had not been known for its encouragement of backbenchers – indeed those who were invited to join either the Cabinet or the front bench team during the period of opposition were predominantly from Heath's section of the Party. There was little attempt to emulate the leadership of Macmillan, who drew in disparate strands of the Party to the centre of decision making. Heath's personality also counted against him when dealing with backbenchers. He was reserved with strangers, unable to remember faces or names well, impossible at small talk and only capable of talking at dinner or lunch tables about his own obsessions, usually politics but now and then music or sailing. He was never seen around the Commons bars or the smoking room. He was incapable of mixing with people for the sake of it and felt awkward at a social gathering which did not have a deliberate purpose. A combination of this lack of social grace and an illiberal approach to promotion from the ranks had encouraged a reputation for being cool and aloof. If he had to stand before the 1922 Committee and seek re-election, which seemed inevitable, it would have been worthwhile respecting the traditions of the Committee. The new Parliament assembled on 22 October. Between 22 October and the first meeting of the main 1922 Committee, three meetings of the Executive were held, which discussed how best to handle the inevitable leadership questions which would be raised.

Du Cann decided upon the traditional parliamentary procedure of calling each member in turn, as they caught the chairman's eye, and this he followed impeccably at the main committee meeting on 1 November, allowing the meeting to continue until everyone who wanted to speak had had his say. There were newspaper stories the following Sunday that the meeting had been fixed to call anti-Heath speakers, but this was not the case. There was, however, a common theme among most of the members: that an election was important and urgent. Kenneth Lewis highlighted the constitutional difficulty which the Party found itself in when he asked whether the leadership, which had been in one man's hands for a decade, was a freehold or a leasehold? A week later, on 7 November, there was further bad news for Heath. The Conservative MPs acted in unison, as if to underline the snub which Heath had delivered the 1922 Executive, by re-electing the whole of the Executive intact – the first time that such a thing had happened. In particular, Du Cann's unopposed election as Chairman brought spontaneous applause, confirming that his handling of the leadership crisis was considered entirely appropriate by the majority of MPs. The Executive once again invited Heath to address the main Committee and asked that the question of his continued leadership be settled with a new election. Heath replied with a suggestion that he was willing for there to be an election, but that it was time that the system of election was overhauled and that he would be establishing a rules committee to determine how best these should be conducted in the future.

As he told the 1922 Committee at its meeting of 14 November: 'It is perfectly natural that after the election you should want to discuss the leadership. What the Party asks is that it should be done reasonably and with restraint and dignity. The Chairman of the 1922 Committee has reported the view of the Committee to me. As I understand it, they wish to have a review of procedure. This seems to be perfectly reasonable ... There is no reason why there should be any delay. I would wish to get on with it at once and any recommendations which the Review Committee made would naturally return to this Committee for discussion.' Heath was confident and saw the demand for an election as a little local difficulty. He was convinced, as he was after the February election, that soon the country's economy would precipitate a full-scale crisis which would either lead to another election or the fall of the Government and the formation of a national coalition which, after his campaign of October for 'national unity', he would be best fitted to lead. He was being over-optimistic and many of those around him argued differently. Several, including Pym, Prior and Gilmour, had dared suggest to him that he stand down and put himself up for re-election. Had this advice been followed immediately after the October election, he might well have been returned on the nod. If he had failed, the Heath men argued, then Whitelaw could have been drafted and could have taken over. The longer Heath stayed on, the more organised would be the opposition. At that time, before Christmas 1974, few Conservative MPs were discussing the ousting of Heath in ideological terms. They did not see the failure of the Party in the two 1974 elections as a failure of the policies but as a two-fold rejection of Heath. As the winter drew on, the opposition to Heath hardened and the delay in the election for the revision of the rules was widely interpreted as Heath's obstinacy, dragging his feet and putting off the contest.

While opposition to Heath steadily grew, the finding of a replacement from outside the centre-left was proving difficult. Keith Joseph had been continuing his process of self-criticism and on 19 October had delivered a speech on Conservative social policy which had caused a furore. Unlike the economic speech, this was principally the work of one man, Alfred Sherman, a former communist who went to fight for the Republican International Brigade during the Spanish Civil War, had started helping Joseph with speeches in 1969 and 1970 and had remained in contact with him during the Heath Government. After the February 1974 election defeat, Joseph had asked Ted Heath's permission to establish the Centre for Policy Studies, financed by subscriptions from mostly business sources, radically to reassess where things had gone wrong. Heath saw it as no threat; more as a means of preserving Joseph's frail balance of mind intact. He had nominated Adam Ridley, an economist from Central Office, to represent his interest on the CPS board. Joseph chose Sherman to instigate and inspire the work at the centre and had depended upon him for much of the work which led to his 1974 keynote speeches. The Edgbaston speech was an extraordinary assessment of British life and where Conservatives had gone wrong in maintaining its traditional character. It bemoaned the growing dependence of individuals upon the state. When the texts were sent in advance to the press, one section in particular raised eyebrows even in the ideologically sympathetic quarters of the *Telegraph* leader writers. It was a suggestion that, because social classes C and D – the working class – were least able to bring up their children without resort to the state, there should be a concerted effort to encourage them to have less of them and that contraception techniques could easily be enlisted for this purpose. To most journalists, the telling phrase advocated heartless social engineering and the storm broke even before Joseph delivered the speech. To those who had hoped that Joseph would lead the leadership fight against Heath, the speech was a grave disappointment. Leaving aside the wisdom of the words used – enough, in themselves, to send shivers through most Conservative MPs – the fact that Joseph did not recognise such a passage to be inflammable and had written it himself – against the express advice of Sherman, who had removed similar lines from several Joseph speeches – only confirmed their worst suspicions: Joseph would be a liability as a leader.

Other things dogged the hapless Joseph. It was a badly kept secret that his marriage was increasingly shaky – he finally divorced his wife, Helen, in 1978 – and that one of his three daughters was suffering from a mental illness. It was a combination of these family pressures which led him to decide on 21 November that he would withdraw from the leadership election. That afternoon he visited Thatcher, his close colleague, to tell her of his decision. Now the way was clear for her. She telephoned to Heath's office and asked for a brief audience with him that afternoon. She walked into Heath's room, the Leader of the Opposition's room, then a short way behind the Speaker's chair, and, remaining standing, announced her intention of running against him. The interview took barely two minutes and Heath dealt with her in a matter-of-fact way, barely breaking off from the paper work he was doing. She had no organisation to help her, nor did she establish one. And that is the way it remained for a long time. She was kept very busy as the second spokesman on Treasury matters, supporting Robert Carr. In retrospect, this seems a most unwise appointment. Heath had admired her performance as Education Secretary, had appointed her shadow environment spokesman after the February defeat and had toyed with making her the Chairman of the Party during the summer of 1974. She was satisfied with the more junior but more mainstream role of Treasury spokesman. She had ambitions of becoming the first woman Chancellor and did not want to be sidetracked. Her appointment to the Treasury bench, however, turned out to be a decision which rebounded on Heath. It was an unparalleled platform upon which she could prove her parliamentary ability and quickness of mind.

Even in November, with Joseph out of the race, Thatcher's candidature was not taken seriously by many Conservative MPs, because it was not thought that she would prove successful. If she was considered seriously at all, she was then dismissed as a political lightweight, with little administrative experience, with no mastery of the House of Commons and no strength of popularity among backbench MPs, with whom she rarely mixed. Nor did she have a great reputation outside of Parliament, among Party workers. What little was known of her reputation in the country was that she was unpopular, a leftover from her Education days, and that she could prove an electoral disaster. She epitomised to many the shrill, Home Counties Tory woman. In addition, the single fact which prevented her candidature from being taken seriously by many Conservative MPs was that she was a woman, and while it might have entered their minds that a woman might one day lead a major political party, it was generally assumed that she would emerge among the ranks of the Labour Party who, in Barbara Castle and Shirley Williams, had offered two women active in senior politics who might be expected to achieve the ultimate position.

The man whom most opponents of Heath looked to for leadership was Edward du Cann. He was a well-liked Chairman of the 1922 Committee and had been a leading figure in the Party for many years, having been elected to Parliament in 1956 and quickly promoted by Harold Macmillan to first the Treasury, then the Board of Trade. He had a solid reputation for his work on a number of Commons select committees and had spent two years as Chairman of the Conservative Party Organisation until his dismissal by Edward Heath in 1967. This antagonism towards Heath also encouraged Du Cann's supporters into believing that he would be willing to stand. He had been involved in founding one of the first British unit trust companies, and he was active in both insurance and merchant banking. It was his business interests which caused concern for those who were encouraging him to stand. It was thought that Du Cann might not be prepared to sacrifice his flourishing business career for the leadership of the Party and there was some concern about his City dealings, particularly with respect to Keyser Ullmann Holdings, of which he was chairman. On 22 October, Nigel Fisher invited six or seven colleagues, known to be in favour of Du Cann as a candidate for the leadership, to his home for a drink and it was agreed that he should be approached. Du Cann told Fisher that he was flattered, but needed to be shown wider support for his candidature if he was to stand down as Chairman of the 1922 Committee and throw his hat in the ring. During the course of November, a number of meetings of the Du Cann Group, as it became known, were held and their number reached over twenty-five in number.

Du Cann was a reluctant candidate, but the prospect of his challenging Heath was being taken most seriously, not least by the Heath faction, who were not worried at all by Thatcher's candidature. By what many thought a curious coincidence, Du Cann was approached by Heath and invited to join the Shadow Cabinet – the first approach of such a kind for eight years. Du Cann declined. As December progressed, the details of the shape of the contest became known. Lord Home's committee, charged with improving the leadership rules, delivered their report to Heath on time and it was distributed to the 1922 Committee members for their perusal over the Christmas recess. It stuck closely to the balloting arrangements agreed in 1965. However, three changes were recommended: it was thought that an annual election should take place, thereby removing the leader's discretion to stay on at will; second, the rule which said that a victorious candidate should have a majority of fifteen per cent of those who had voted over the nearest rival was altered to fifteen per cent of the eligible electorate; third, it was suggested that the informal means of consulting non-parliamentary sections of the party should be made more formal, although it did not broaden the electoral college to include Tory peers or constituency members. This in particular disappointed Sir John Taylor, who had hoped that both sections of the party, the peers and the National Union, would be given a small share of the votes available. The peers held back from recommending this change to the Home committee and Taylor felt he could press no further. The only change which was expected to affect the imminent contest was the fifteen per cent rule, instantly known as 'Alec's Revenge', which Heath supporters thought would force a second ballot, at which new candidates could stand, even if the leader was only moderately popular, therefore dragging out a contest which might, eventually, prove to have been unnecessary.

The common perception of the new rules was that a successor to Heath, who was known to be unpopular among Tory MPs and likely to be defeated, would be found in the second ballot. This allowed the essential element of Conservative loyalty to remain intact, while displacing an electorally unpopular leader. Most MPs at that time saw the leadership election as a method of finding a replacement for Heath, not an important ideological battle, although there was expected to be an element of that in the second ballot. Those of Heath's persuasion, most importantly Willie Whitelaw, who were being encouraged to stand were inhibited by their personal loyalty to Heath and felt that they could not challenge him while he remained leader. Whitelaw had the added embarrassment of being Chairman of the Party, installed in Central Office, which under the constitution was the leader's private office, and appointed by Heath. For him to stand in the first ballot, he would have to resign that position. As for the right, Du Cann made it clear that he was not prepared to stand — which would entail his resigning from the chairmanship of the 1922 — unless there was a good chance of his beating Heath on the first ballot, which was uncertain. It was, then, commonly assumed that this would be a two-stage affair. The first ballot would so undermine Heath's position that he would resign and then, in the second ballot, the real battle would commence without embarrassment: a more or less straight fight between left and right, between the old guard under Whitelaw and the right under Du Cann, with a few ambitious men putting down markers for subsequent contests. All that was expected of Thatcher was that she should be a stalking horse, allowing MPs to show their dissatisfaction to such an extent that Heath would not receive the important fifteen per cent majority and would therefore resign, leaving the way open for the rest.

To ensure that Thatcher was able to attract the necessary total of votes, it was decided that only one serious candidate should stand and, to this end, Du Cann stitched up a deal with her. The persistent lobbying of Du Cann by Nigel Fisher and Peter Tapsell, MP for Horncastle, on behalf of the Fisher group had led to a letter, drafted at a meeting in the Commons on 19 December, which praised him for his obvious qualities, asked him to consider most seriously his decision over the Christmas recess and hoped that he would be prepared to put himself forward for the first ballot. Du Cann, however, had already had a meeting with Thatcher, at his request, at which they agreed that as long as she remained a candidate, he would not stand, although she made it clear that if he were wanting to stand, she would withdraw in his favour.

Neave was, by this time, showing interest in Thatcher as a candidate. In December he held a party at his flat in Westminster Gardens at which she was carefully introduced to new MPs. Neave was hoping Du Cann would stand, but seemed to be holding Thatcher in reserve. Neave's own political stance was to the centre-left of the Party, and suspecting that Du Cann might not last the course, he approached Whitelaw at the beginning of November, encouraging him to stand against Heath and offering to run his campaign. Whitelaw refused. Even by December, Thatcher's function was merely to be a name on the ballot paper around which dissidence could form. She had not taken the task of campaigning very seriously, having established only a flimsy organisation under Fergus

Montgomery, her PPS at Education, and William Shelton, who also admired her for her time at Education. The fact that she was standing was widely considered as an act of bravery and there were considerable risks attached. If Heath were to trounce her unexpectedly on the first ballot, he would show no mercy. Her Shadow Cabinet career would end forthwith, as Heath did not have a forgiving nature. If, however, there was a new leader, her unsuccessful candidacy might act in her favour.

Her position was transformed by the arrival into her campaign of Airey Neave. He had been one of the Du Cann group and had urged him to stand. But on 15 January a meeting of the group had heard from Fisher that Du Cann would not stand at the first ballot. The reasons he had given to Fisher also gave the impression that he would not be available to become a candidate at the second ballot, either. Du Cann had been dissuaded forcefully by his wife, Sallie, who had reservations about his political career. She preferred their Somerset life to the political life of Westminster and their home in Lord North Street. During his time as a minister, as Chairman of the Party and the subsequent unpleasantness with Heath, she had disliked the publicity. She also had reservations about the effect of her husband being leader and likely Prime Minister would have upon their three children and had particular worries about security. Although she had assured him that she would stand by his decision, she had made her position clear. Du Cann also had responsibilities to his business associates which he could not lightly forget. The Labour policies of 1974 had caused a serious dip in the property market, which had put great pressure on his company, Keyser Ullman, which had already attracted uncomfortable attention for its previous lending policies. All this convinced Neave that Du Cann could not be counted upon to stand in the second ballot and that, even if Heath were to resign after a poor showing in the first ballot, there would be a pro-Heath victory at the second, probably in the guise of Whitelaw. He then determined to back Margaret Thatcher.

Neave had several good reasons for being vehemently opposed to Heath. His distinguished war record, in which he had escaped from Colditz and subsequently organised a chain of escape for others through occupied France, had led him to a safe Conservative seat, for Abingdon, in 1953. His prominence as a barrister, who had served indictments on Goering and other major Nazi war criminals, and as an author, of several books about his war adventures, had helped his governmental career and he had held several junior posts until 1959. In that year, he suffered a heart attack and had reported it to his Chief Whip at the time, Edward Heath, who is reported to have informed him charmlessly, 'Well, that's the end of your political career, then.' Neave subsequently developed a serious drink problem and, although he overcame this, was never promoted by Heath. Neave was a quiet, secretive character who acted for the Party like an unofficial whip. A former MP remembered, 'He had a lot of intelligence even the whips didn't discover. He never imparted a piece of bum information. His power lay there.' Few knew as much about the way opinion was moving than Neave, a natural spy who had learnt his trade in MI9, which had advised members of the wartime forces how best to avoid, or escape from, enemy capture. During December 1974, Neave had been using his contacts to make Thatcher better known and a number whose votes were critical were invited for drinks at his home to meet her. When Du Cann finally let it be known that he would not stand in the first ballot, Neave decided that the only chance of ensuring Heath's defeat was to run Thatcher as a genuine leadership candidate, which entailed a great deal of hard work. He was a prominent member of the Du Cann group and, at their 15 January meeting, suggested, in the light of Du Cann's position, that the whole group of twenty-five turn itself over to the Thatcher cause. Fifteen of them agreed there and then, although Fisher declined the invitation to become the group's chairman as he felt that, although he would certainly vote for Thatcher in the first ballot, he might still prefer Du Cann or someone else in the second.

Neave found that the Thatcher campaign barely existed. One of the two mainstays, Fergus Montgomery, was about to leave on an extended visit to South Africa, returning to

Britain after the first ballot had taken place, which hardly displayed to Neave the commitment to Thatcher or to hard work that was needed. Neave and Shelton saw as their main enemy a concerted, undercover smear campaign against Thatcher orchestrated by Central Office and extended by Heath's friends in the press. Although Heath knew nothing about it and such a campaign has been strenuously denied since, Neave suspected that a full-scale dirty tricks campaign was being mounted as a last-ditch attempt to save Heath from defeat. An interview, given the previous summer to a small-circulation magazine, *Pre-Retirement Choice*, was published in mid-November and had been given a wide circulation. In it, Thatcher had suggested to pensioners that while inflation continued at a high rate, they should stockpile high-protein food in tins as she did herself. The press jumped on the interview, interpreting it as an encouragement to panic buying. The 'milk snatcher' campaign, which had proved so painful to Thatcher, was revived. There were allegations from MPs that Central Office was putting pressure on people to remain loyal to their leader. Much of this alleged dirty-tricks campaign was unsubstantiated and remains so, yet the effect was important at the time, for the belief that Heath's supporters were fighting a dirty election further distanced him from their sympathies and invoked a wave of support for Thatcher, the under-dog.

As the leader, Heath was unable to do much campaigning himself. He was encouraged to visit the Commons bars, but his uneasy manner only counted against him. More purposeful were a series of often lavish lunches, dinners and drinks parties at which backbenchers who had been ignored for years were invited to meet the leader at the home of Sir Timothy Kitson, Heath's PPS. Again, the very artificiality of such a gathering counted against Heath, who was, in any case, unable to play the game of making idle but charming chit-chat. Meanwhile, Neave was trying to introduce Thatcher to as many MPs as quickly as possible. In contrast to the Heath gatherings, Thatcher held a series of purposeful meetings in the room of Robert Cooke, which was much larger than most, at which she answered questions about her views. She avoided making promises and, as far as possible, practised being a good listener. The reward for those who attended was a modest glass of claret, which contrasted well with the free-flowing drinks of the Heath campaign. Neave's advice to her was to avoid making clear statements on policy, but, where possible, to encourage those who thought that Heath's view on any line had been wrong. In particular, she maintained an ambivalent position on Britain's EEC membership, which caused a number of Conservative MPs, who had either been opposed to Britain's membership or who thought that Heath's Euro-fanaticism did not allow enough criticism of the Common Market and its institutions, to vote in her favour on that issue alone. Although her views on many issues, such as her support for capital punishment and her belated criticisms of the 1972 U-turn, were well known, she made no attempt to spell out a clear programme which she would like to follow. Her more obviously right-wing attitudes were consciously played down. Neave encouraged her to keep the principal issue of the leadership election one about the quality of leadership, not ideology, and to indicate that she was to represent a leadership that would listen to backbenchers. It was a skilful ruse on Neave's part to maximise the numbers who felt that voting for her in order to oust Heath was not a distasteful tactical vote for someone whose views were objectionable.

Parliament resumed on 13 January and on the Wednesday the Du Cann group heard that their chosen candidate would not stand. Neave promptly converted as many as possible to the Thatcher cause. On the sixteenth, the 1922 Committee considered the Home proposals on the leadership election and approved them. The next Sunday, the nineteenth, was the first of what was to be a regular Sunday night series of Thatcher campaign meetings at her Flood Street home. Only four active members would be present: Thatcher, Neave, Shelton and Joseph. The immediate decision was to maximise the methods of publicising her campaign in the following week. On Tuesday the twenty-first, she was to address the Parliamentary Press Gallery after lunch. For many reporters, this was the first time that they would have the chance to judge her since it had emerged that she was the main instrument for winkling out the Tory leader. The speech turned out to be the first set-piece engagement of the leadership campaign. She delivered a resume of her beliefs, then impressed the journalists with a question and answer session. She had shown that she was far more than the cliché Tory woman with right-wing views that the Gallery had so often painted. She had the added confidence of knowing that the canvass of Tory MPs' voting intentions by Neave and Shelton gave her a lead of sixty-nine to Heath's forty-three.

That evening, she performed in the Commons chamber, summing up the Opposition case against the Government in the Committee Stage of the Finance Bill. Her opponent on the Government front bench was Denis Healey, perhaps the most formidable parliamentary speaker available to the Labour side, combining Wilson's fine wit and turn of phrase with a steam-rollering, bullying style which no Conservative could counter effectively. That evening she put up a respectable case, but the true battle was not to take place until the next and final day of the debate. Healey laid into her, dubbing her 'La Passionara of Privilege'. He could not enjoy his glory for long. Thatcher mounted a withering attack. She had hoped to be able to say that he had done himself less than justice, yet he had done himself ample justice. She continued, 'Some Chancellors are micro-economic. Some Chancellors are fiscal. This one is just plain cheap.' And she went on, 'If this Chancellor can be Chancellor, anyone in the House of Commons can be Chancellor. I had hoped that the Right Honourable Gentleman had learnt a lot from this debate. Clearly he has learnt nothing ... He might at least address himself to the practical effects, because it will affect everyone, including people born as I was, with no privilege at all.'

The counter-attack was a considerable success and had not only proved her ability in the Commons, but had shown up the inadequacy of Heath's sedate, uninspired attacks on the Government. Neither he nor any of his supporters were good Commons performers, which had counted against them. She played to the crowd behind her and they enjoyed it, as does every backbencher who sees his principal opponent beaten on his own ground.

The debate had certainly improved her canvass figures for the leadership. Neave and Shelton reported that she now had a promise of support from ninety-five MPs, compared to sixty-four for Heath. There were also nine for a new candidate in the leadership, Hugh Fraser, the member for Stafford and Stone and a Scots aristocrat, who announced a platform of traditional Tory values. Although he was from the right and therefore a potential danger to Thatcher, he was considered too eccentric to be taken seriously and he made no attempt to campaign on his own behalf or attract supporters to his cause.

The following day, Thursday 24 January, Heath announced that he would accept Lord Home's proposals for reform of the leadership election machinery and he announced the date of the election: nominations would close on the following Thursday, 30 January, and the election would be held on Tuesday 4 February. The race was on in earnest and the Sunday Flood Street meeting of the twenty-sixth was an urgent affair. The Thatcher campaign was desperately short on organisation and manpower. By contrast, the Heath men were able to use the plentiful supply of help and secretarial assistance provided by Heath's Private Office. Thatcher could only depend upon her own secretary, Susan Shields, working in a pool of secretaries off Westminster Hall. That Sunday morning, Neave had phoned Joan Hall, formerly the Tory MP for Keighley from 1970-74, who was known to be a strong Thatcher supporter. She agreed to come down from Yorkshire to act as Thatcher's personal assistant, and began work the following Tuesday in Airey Neave's room in the Commons during the week and at Flood Street at the weekends. She was to do everything, from taking phone calls to acting as chauffeuse.

On Monday the twenty-seventh, Thatcher addressed her campaign team, explaining how the MPs canvassing on her behalf should answer questions about where she stood on various issues. From the canvass returns which Neave and Shelton were compiling, it was now known roughly which

MPs were certain to vote for which candidates and which were undecided or likely to switch. It was decided only to canvass those who were known not to have definitely plumped for Heath, starting, where possible, with close parliamentary colleagues of the campaign committee. Neave and Shelton stood at a decided advantage over Heath's campaign team of Kitson, Peter Walker, Nicholas Scott and Kenneth Baker. As Heath was leader and therefore the purveyor of patronage, few Tory MPs would wish either to be seen to be disloyal or to be so lacking in ambition as to tell their true intentions to the Heath camp. This would explain the optimistic canvass figures which were being reported to Heath and the confidence of his team. Neave's campaign was altogether more realistic and far more sophisticated than it appeared. While Thatcher made herself available for audiences to groups of interested MPs, often brought together because they shared a common interest, and Shelton operated out of the Commons library, Neave was often impossible to find. Only the four who attended the Sunday night Flood Street meetings were privy to the canvass results and, meanwhile, Neave would continue going the rounds, sampling opinion and often relaying the black propaganda that Margaret was doing well, but nowhere near well enough to guarantee that Heath would fall and that a second ballot would come about. In particular, this logic impressed a group of sixteen anti-Heath MPs of the centre left, led by Sir John Rodgers, who at first had intended to abstain, then switched their votes to Thatcher because they thought that, otherwise, Heath would achieve the fifteen per cent lead needed to remain as leader.

On Thursday 30 January, the day that nominations closed, it was Thatcher's turn to explain about the Tory Party she would like to see in an article in the *Daily Telegraph*, one of a series of pieces in which the contenders were invited to express their views. It was part of a three-pronged final push to consolidate her position as a serious candidate, worthy of winning the first ballot, which had been decided upon at the previous Sunday's campaign planning meeting. The *Telegraph* article was to be followed by a speech in Finchley the following day and by an open letter to her Finchley constituency chairman, to be released on the eve of poll.

She followed Keith Joseph's line of accepting that the Heath Administration had failed the electorate and the Tory supporters in the country: 'To deny that we failed the people is futile, as well as arrogant. Successful Governments win elections. So do parties with broadly acceptable policies. We lost.'

She continued by defining the two lessons of the Heath Government, the first that rapid inflation in the long run was the worst enemy and must be brought under control, the second that a preoccupation with economics should not blind the party to 'the day-to-day problems of ordinary people'. Both lessons were the ones popularly accepted by Tory MPs and Tory voters as the reason for the general election defeat, although most members of the Heath Government would have argued that it was a concern for reducing destructive inflation which had led the Government to become so embroiled in the macroeconomics which Thatcher was dismissing.

She then confronted the main personal issue which many had determined would be the principal worry for any MP thinking of voting for her: that her image was too middle-class and would prove an electoral liability. She made the middle-class image appear an asset: 'If "middle-class values" include the encouragement of variety and individual choice, the provision of fair incentives and rewards for skill and hard work, the maintenance of effective barriers against the excessive power of the State and a belief in the wide distribution of individual private property, then they are certainly what I am trying to defend.'

The argument did not impress Ian Gilmour, the former Secretary for Defence in Heath's Government, who, that night, in warning the Tory Party to be careful of 'digging our trenches further to the right', also said they should beware not to 'retire behind a privet hedge' – a reference to Thatcher's suburban image which ran counter to the traditional Conservative appeal to one nation.

The following night, in Finchley, she pointed out to her

constituents, and through reports of the speech to Tory MPs, that the leader had enormous patronage, in the Shadow Cabinet and in Central Office, which could only be questioned by an election of the leader. It was a reminder to every Tory MP who had been sacked or not preferred by Heath that it was worthwhile trying again with a new leader. And she played down what little ideological differences the election represented: 'You can forget all the nonsense about "defence of privilege" — I had precious little "privilege" in my early years — and the suggestion that all my supporters are reactionary right-wingers ... This is not a confrontation between "left" and "right".' And she restated her concern for: 'compassion and concern for the individual and his freedom; opposition to excessive state power; the right of the enterprising, the hard-working and the thrifty to succeed and to reap the rewards of success and pass some of them on to their children; encouragement of that infinite diversity of choice that is an essential freedom; the defence of widely distributed private property against the Socialist state; the right of a man to work without oppression by either employer or trade union boss.'

It was a fundamentalist, populist speech given in the confidence that canvass returns were improving. Before the speech was published, the latest figures showed 120 votes for Thatcher, 84 for Heath and 9 for Fraser. Heath needed a 42 vote lead to retain the leadership and this had already disappeared. But what Neave and Shelton wanted was for Thatcher to maintain her lead over Heath so that, by the time of the second ballot, when Heath's supporters would feel free to enter the contest, she looked an unbeatable second-ballot candidate. The Sunday papers reported Neave as saying that his candidate was leading Heath, though he did not report the figures. Walker and Baker were reported as being confident that Heath would win and remain leader — which was just what Neave hoped. The next day, he toured the Commons, saying that although Thatcher would do well, she might not quite do well enough to defeat Heath and that the conflicting canvass reports made it all the more important for the anti-Heath vote to back Thatcher. An abstention would not be enough.

The next day, Monday, the papers were full of Lord Home's decision, announced in a radio interview at the weekend, to back Heath. Although universally considered a poor prime minister, even by his own side, Alec Douglas Home, now Lord Home of the Hirsel, was one of the most popular figures in the Party and he represented the best of patrician Conservative feelings. The rest of the peers agreed with him. At 2.30 in the afternoon, their representative, Michael St Aldwyn — the Lords leader, Peter Carrington, was abroad — told the Executive of the 1922 Committee that, in a write-in poll among the members of the Upper House, there had been a large majority for Heath to remain leader. Sir John Taylor followed, representing the National Union in England and Wales, and reported that 70 per cent of constituents backed Heath, although 80 per cent had said that they would have preferred a wider choice of candidate. Similar messages came from Scotland and Northern Ireland. Even if Thatcher was going to win, she would have immediately to convince her peers and her party workers of her worth. It seemed, too, that parliamentary opinion was moving in Heath's favour.

In the Thatcher campaign committee's eve-of-poll meeting, the final canvass reports were collected and there was a nervousness. The early lead was plainly diminishing. When Neave and Shelton retired to Neave's room, the figures confirmed the disquiet. There were now 122 MPs for Heath, 122 for Thatcher and the usual 9 for Fraser. There were 23 whose views could not be ascertained or who said they were abstaining. It was decided not to tell Thatcher until the following morning. The word was deliberately passed around the Commons by Thatcher supporters that night that Thatcher would poll no more than 70 votes. It was done in a last ditch attempt to persuade the undecided and the waverers.

On the morning of Tuesday 4 February, Margaret Thatcher was up at seven, being photographed cooking Denis's breakfast. At eight, Shelton telephoned her and told her of the previous night's canvass. At nine she arrived at the Commons and spent the morning in committee on the Finance Bill. At noon, voting commenced in Committee

Room 14. The first to vote was Nicholas Fairbairn, MP for Kinross and West Perthshire, who boasted that he was voting for Thatcher. Just before one, Thatcher voted for herself, then went to lunch in the City, to discuss aspects of the Finance Bill. She returned to the committee; then, as voting came to a close at 3.30, she went to Neave's room. Heath voted shortly before the poll was closed, for himself. He had been told by Peter Walker that he could expect between 138 and 144 votes – 139 was a sufficient figure to keep the leadership. Kitson was more doubtful. His indications showed that there would be 129 Heath certainties and up to 17 hopefuls. He expected Heath to poll between 125 and 135 and, after Heath had voted, Kitson bet Shelton a pound that Heath would attract more than 130 votes. Shelton responded with a pound that Thatcher would poll more than 110. At 3.30 the polls closed and by four, the votes had been counted and Du Cann came out to greet the eighty or so MPs. Shelton was expressionless; Kitson was visibly shocked. The result was:

Thatcher	130
Heath	119
Fraser	16

Shelton told Neave who went straight to his room to tell Thatcher. He said, 'It's good news. You're ahead in the poll. There will be a second ballot. You got 130 votes.' She was elated. When Sir Nigel Fisher came into the room shortly afterwards, she rushed forwards and kissed him. 'Isn't it exciting?' A champagne celebration in Neave's flat was planned for that night, with the television cameras invited.

Meanwhile, in the Leader of the Opposition's room, Heath was being told the news. Kitson arrived, looking ill. Passing through the small ante-room where Willie Whitelaw, John Peyton, Jim Prior, Kenneth Baker and Maurice Trowbridge, from Heath's Private Office, were waiting, he said, 'It is no good.' Heath received the news without emotion. 'So, we got it all wrong,' was his comment. Lord Aldington, Heath's closest friend and confidant, was summoned from his office in the City and they promptly set about writing a letter of resignation and making arrangements for an interim leader. It was established that Robert Carr was not intending to stand in the second ballot and, as he was a well-respected senior Commons figure, he was approached and accepted the temporary post. Heath remained in reasonably good spirits. A line of people came to pay their condolences. Hugh Fraser arrived, in tears, saying that he had not intended to contribute to Heath's overthrow. Lord Hailsham arrived, also weeping. The Heath men were in disarray. Heath had never considered his succession, because he had not expected it to be necessary for at least another ten years. In as much as he favoured a successor in that time-scale, it was Francis Pym. But, as for the new circumstances, Heath was reluctant to become involved. That evening, Whitelaw, Prior and Peyton argued about who should stand; none would give way. Whitelaw concluded that if the others stood, he would stand little chance. The following day, Heath slept late at his Wilton Street home and spent a long time getting up, wandering around in bare feet and a large Chinese silk dressing gown. He discussed the engagements that he was committed to with a sense of mischief. He was due to go to the Young Conservatives conference in Eastbourne. 'I think I'll go,' he said. 'That will upset them.'

The second ballot was fixed for a week after the first, Tuesday 11 February. Nominations were to close on Thursday the sixth. The most obvious new candidate to declare himself, and the most danger to a Thatcher success, was Willie Whitelaw. He had been inhibited as Chairman of the Party from entering in the first place and had remained loyal to Heath. Had he stood at the first ballot, it is likely that he would have been the main attraction for anti-Heath votes and that Thatcher would have been left with only a small group of ideological dissenters. By the evening of the first ballot, however, when Sir Paul Bryan called a meeting of Whitelaw's twelve most prominent supporters — which included Christopher Tugendhat and David Howell — they had no illusions about the size of the task. Thatcher, who many had considered merely a stalking horse, had been transformed by Neave into the front runner, not merely denting Heath so that he would resign, but beating him in a straight fight. She would prove difficult to stop and many of the centre-left establishment, including Heath, thought there was little or no chance of reversing her fortunes. Certainly Whitelaw was not the obvious man to do it. He appeared like a member of the old guard, a roly-poly Cumberland farmer of the old Tory patrician school. There was no better candidate, however. Heath had not arranged for a dynamic heir apparent, nor any plausible plan for his succession.

Whitelaw's campaign was a well-intentioned shambles. His secretary was away and he felt that he could not borrow one from Central Office without first asking permission from Thatcher, which she gave immediately. He recruited Michael Mates, a former colonel who had only just entered the Commons and had never met Whitelaw before, to be his ADC. There was an air of amateurism about the whole Whitelaw campaign, which encouraged Neave and Shelton. However, they were not home and dry.

Neave reassembled the Thatcher campaign committee on Wednesday 5 February and they were in buoyant mood. Loud cheers greeted Keith Joseph when he entered the room, as they did Norman St John Stevas, an avowed Heath supporter jumping on the bandwagon. By Neave and Shelton's calculations, which they kept to themselves, at least forty MPs who had voted for Thatcher the first time had done so in order to vote for someone else in the second ballot – and Whitelaw was the most likely beneficiary. And three other candidates had declared: John Peyton, a solid Heath man, who was likely to take votes from Whitelaw; Jim Prior, a young, ambitious Heath man, who would, in putting down a marker for a later leadership election, take votes from Whitelaw; and Geoffrey Howe, a recent Commons member who could depend upon the Bow Group and members like Anthony Buck, Ian Gow, Kenneth Clarke and David Walder. He had been openly rethinking the Conservative philosophy and therefore looked a danger to some of the Thatcher supporters who might prefer his softer approach on social issues. Julian Amery, who might have taken a few crucial votes from Thatcher, declared he would not stand, as did Maurice Macmillan. In the first ballot, Thatcher had received 130 votes, 40 of which were going to move on. She needed 139 to win the leadership outright – anything less would cause a third ballot and a transferable vote system which would work against her. She therefore needed to attract 49 votes from the ranks of Hugh Fraser, who had withdrawn, and Heath. On that Wednesday night, Neave and Shelton's figures showed: Thatcher 99; Whitelaw 41; Peyton 8; Howe 7; Prior 5. People were keeping their options open. The following day, when nominations closed and the National Union and Tory peers were asked once again for their opinion, the figures had improved: Thatcher 106; Whitelaw 46; Howe 11; Peyton 8; Prior 6. She looked unstoppable.

All during this time, Thatcher was the only candidate who was seen to be going about proper Opposition business. Her leadership campaign was run in parallel with the gruelling sittings of the committee stage of the Finance Bill and each night – often well into the early hours – she was leading the Conservative attack and showing no signs of wear. This answered many of the doubts that the Conservative male chauvinists had raised about her stamina and concentration. Heath's appointment of her to lead the assault against the Treasury continued to work against the Conservative tradition which Heath represented. Neave was doubtful about one aspect of the Thatcher image – her attitude to the Common Market. Harold Wilson had called a national referendum on his renegotiated terms and the EEC was therefore a very live issue. The lukewarm enthusiasm which she showed during the first ballot meetings looked as if it could count against her if she wanted to win a substantial number of Heath's supporters to her side. On Friday 7 February, it was planned that she should issue a pro-Europe statement. She gave Heath the credit for his foresight in taking Britain into the EEC and continued, 'This torch must be picked up and carried by whoever is chosen by the party to succeed him. The commitment to European partnership is one which I fully share.' The following day, both Thatcher and Whitelaw were due to speak at the Young Conservatives' rally at Eastbourne, a body which was known to be more left wing than the party at large. A truce was agreed between

Thatcher and Whitelaw that this event should not be used for the leadership election and that they should speak on their original subjects. Whitelaw duly spoke on devolution, one of the dullest subjects available. Thatcher, however, steamed into a rousing reappraisal of Conservative ideals, encouraging a standing ovation, television coverage and the headlines in the Sunday papers. The Whitelaw camp felt cheated. Whitelaw had also, through bad advice, been encouraged to perform in press stunts which counted against him. At Eastbourne he was asked by a photographer to kiss Thatcher, which he did, adding a gushing comment that he had often kissed her. He did not look like a leader. A further indignity was when he agreed to a photographer's request to put on a pinny and stick his hands in a washing-up bowl. Whitelaw was undermining his own position by squandering one of his main assets: that, as an experienced senior Conservative of the old school and a male, he looked a natural leader. By contrast, Thatcher was already, with the encouragement of Neave, acting as if she had won. That weekend, another significant decision was made by the Thatcher camp. The BBC flagship current affairs programme, Panorama, had invited all of the candidates to present their alternative views of the party they would like to lead. After a short, snappy telephone conversation, Thatcher had refused to take part. What the BBC did not know was that she had, instead, cooperated in the making of a World in Action documentary about herself, which would be shown simultaneously on the commercial network. Not only was she seen to be separate, the candidate to beat, but, in order to see Thatcher, Conservative MPs would have to miss at least half of Panorama. At the regular Sunday night Flood Street strategy meeting, it was clear that the campaign was working well. The next evening brought the news that both the National Union and the peers were now substantially in favour of Thatcher and wanted an early end to the contest. That evening, Neave and Shelton telephoned to Thatcher their final eve-of-poll canvass results. She led with 137; Whitelaw had 78; Howe 19; Prior 11; Peyton 9. A further nine were wavering, but quite likely to vote for her. Thirteen others were totally unknown.

The day of the poll was like the previous Tuesday. She left in the morning for the Commons and more work on the Finance Bill. Voting began at noon and closed at 3.30. She went to Neave's room to await the result. At four, Du Cann declared the result:

Thatcher	146
Whitelaw	79
Howe	19
Prior	19
Peyton	11

Neave returned to tell her, 'It's all right. You're Leader of the Opposition.' She telephoned Denis, who had already heard the news. Then, while those around her popped champagne, she drafted the statement to be read at the press conference which, to allow the non-parliamentary press to attend, was held in the Grand Committee Room off Westminster Hall. She said, 'To me it is like a dream that the next name in the list after Harold Macmillan, Sir Alec Douglas Home and Edward Heath is Margaret Thatcher. Each has brought his own style of leadership and stamp of greatness to his task.' And she went on, 'It is important to me that this prize has been won in open electoral contest with four other potential leaders. I know they will be disappointed, but I hope we shall soon be back working together as colleagues for the things in which we all believe.'

CHAPTER EIGHT

Opposition

The Heath men took a long time to take Thatcher seriously. She appeared naive, badly advised, inexperienced and unlikely to appeal to enough voters to win elections. They thought that it was only a matter of time. Her impulses would derail her and they had only to wait to resume their control of the Party. They were wrong: the Thatcher image was cultivated with a calculation which assessed the mood of the electorate more shrewdly than the men who were still shell-shocked by the defeat of February 1974. The issues which caused the greatest strains at the top of the Party changed in her favour. The Party hierarchy was subtly moulded to reduce the influence of the old guard.

'I can still remember that first Shadow Cabinet meeting,' said one man present, 'the long faces and people stumbling into the room ... There was a desperate feeling that the Conservative party had met a calamitous fate.' Far from feeling assured as decisive victors, the Thatcher team felt insecure, most particularly in the company of the party's most senior figures. 'Edward Heath had a loyal Cabinet and a wobbly party,' one observer was to say later. 'Margaret Thatcher was the other way round: she had a loyal party and a wobbly Shadow Cabinet.' She was duly lauded by a party meeting in the Europa Hotel in London after Edward Heath had flown to Malaga for a holiday. But if the peasantry were easily won over, the barons were slow to swear fealty.

Thatcher was the focus of two sharply conflicting forces. She was closeted with a team of friends and admirers who for several months were to see counter-revolutionary conspiracies and backsliding under every chair at Westminster, and under many in Central Office. Her caution and gut-sense, however, advised against any wholesale purge. Neave, on whom she continued to rely heavily, suggested the same: the wave she had ridden had been an anti-Heath feeling – it did not necessarily extend to all his works or to all his lieutenants. There were few home-grown replacements for men who, after all, knew how to conduct the business of Opposition. Any over-reaching could be dangerous: on Neave's count, no more than four or five of the 20-strong Shadow Cabinet for which they eventually settled, had voted for her in the second ballot. Neave realised also that she had been pitchforked into a job that she did not fully understand.

William Whitelaw was being advised by at least one close colleague and his wife Cecilia that he should refuse any offer made to him and resist any temptation to become too closely tied to the peculiar new regime. It might go off the rails at any moment. Whitelaw rejected the suggestion – he accepted the deputy leadership and spokesmanship on devolution, refrained from comment on Mrs Thatcher and much later said that he thought her victory was what the party had indeed wanted and was therefore right. But the suggestion accurately reflected the combination of shock and disdain which prevailed among the displaced. Whitelaw has kept to that original decision to be loyal to his Leader, underpinning her authority which would have been in jeopardy without it. One was even rescued and reinstated. Thatcher commissioned Sir Michael Havers QC, who sat in the Shadow Cabinet supervising legal matters, to discover if the Poulson investigation had finally finished looking into Reginald Maudling's affairs; the investigation had precipitated his resignation as Home Secretary in 1972. Maudling himself assured her that it was over and when this was confirmed he became shadow Foreign Affairs spokesman. 'I've been rediscovered,' Maudling told people wryly. Pressure was also brought to bear by Whitelaw and others against Thatcher's first instinct to make Sir Keith Joseph shadow Chancellor; she was persuaded against it and gave him instead what was awkwardly titled 'overall responsibility for policy and research.' Opponents of the Thatcher-Joseph camp who thought that this represented a significant defeat for the new leader underestimated the importance Joseph attached to the business of changing the climate of opinion. His new post allowed him to continue the work he had begun alongside the CPS in 1974 by making another series of speeches revising post-war economic and social policy.

Thatcher's insecurity showed in her aggression: she appeared at the same time contemptuous and slightly afraid of most of her Shadow Cabinet colleagues. Some of them were also afraid of her. She talked a great deal at the meetings every Wednesday afternoon, although the stream of words abated as time went on. Relations between her and James Prior were especially poor. She is remembered once saying, after an argument and out of his hearing, 'He can't talk, he only got 19 votes.' When Michael Wolff, who had been very close to Edward Heath as one of his principal speech-writers, was dismissed from his job as director-general of Central Office, Prior failed to turn up for a vote on the Finance Bill. Some time later, when the Thatcher team had relaxed slightly, she asked a party official close to Prior why her employment spokesman was so rude to her. Because of the way you treat him, came the reply. She treated Prior more carefully thereafter and relations thawed slightly.

Her inexperience was painfully obvious to her senior colleagues and also clear to Harold Wilson. 'Some of us are rather old hands at these matters,' he said with lordly patronage as he brushed aside her first intervention from the other side of the Despatch Box.

Relations with Edward Heath were even less friendly. After his resignation, he had retired to his house in Wilton Street, Pimlico, which he used to refer to modestly as 'my house in Victoria'. Shortly after the second ballot for the leadership, Thatcher was driven to Wilton Street by Joan Hall in her white Mini. (Heath had been using the official Leader of the Opposition's car, waiting for a successor to claim it from him.) Press men were waiting outside. The only other person in the house was Kitson, who left the two of them alone. They drank some coffee.

What then passed between them has always been a mystery. Heath was certainly in no mood to be persuaded to join the Shadow Cabinet. He was profoundly hurt, not because he had lost the leadership, but because Thatcher and Joseph had so criticised his period of government. The version of the conversation which Kitson told Heath's friends he had heard from the kitchen, next to the downstairs office where Heath and Thatcher met, was that Thatcher asked Heath, 'What are you going to do now?' He replied, 'Stay on as a member of the House.' She continued, 'What are you going to do about the referendum?' He answered, 'I shall play my full part in the campaign.' Then came the important question from her: 'Don't you think that would be done better from the front bench?' Heath replied, 'No, I do not want to get bogged down in organisation. I want to be out in front as a campaigner.' After making some awkward small talk, Thatcher left. There was an agreement between the two of them that neither side would issue a statement. However, at five o'clock that afternoon, Humphrey Atkins issued a statement through Central Office containing a reference which suggested that Heath had been offered a Shadow Cabinet post and had refused it.

A parallel version of the Heath/Thatcher encounter was then fed to journalists, a full version of which appeared, eventually, in Ernle Money's biography of Thatcher published the same year. In this account, Thatcher explained that she wished Heath to continue to serve with her. 'Shan't,' came the reply. She asked him what he would like to do. 'Won't,' was his response. 'What can I say?' she asked. 'There is nothing to say,' he is reported to have replied. Within five minutes, she was back in the hallway and she and Kitson then filled in the time, avoiding the inevitable questions from the press about why the interview should have been so short. This version of the events at Wilton Street has since been denied by Kitson. Whatever happened behind those closed doors in Heath's small office in Wilton Street, it soon became clear that the intensity of the antipathy between the two of them made it impossible for Heath to serve under Thatcher.

Thus began an extraordinary period of frozen relations between them. Heath had sent a formal congratulations message to her on her success in the second ballot: 'Grave

The Thatcher wedding, 1951, at Wesley's Chapel, City Road. The bride wore a blue velvet dress, later turned into an evening gown. *(Camera Press)*

The twins in 1953. They had been delivered by Caesarian section. *(Camera Press)*

The Iron Lady, as seen by Luck and Flaw, November 1976. *(Luck and Flaw)*

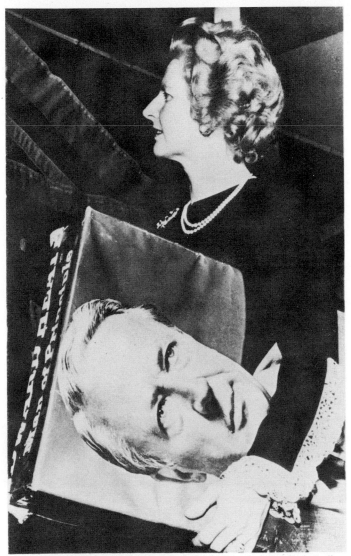
Things to come: Thatcher tucks Heath under her arm at a party meeting in Dudley, Worcestershire, in 1973. *(Keystone)*

Heath takes the economic policy to task at the Conservative Conference in Blackpool, 1981. Thatcher and Howe look on. *(Press Association)*

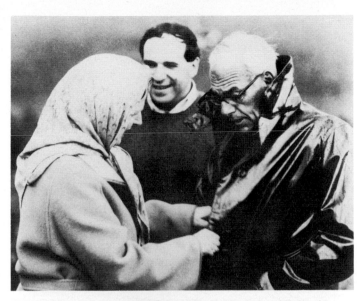

December 1979: Keeping
Denis buttoned up. Leon
Brittan stands behind.
*(Scottish Daily Record/
Ian Torrance)*

Hair ruffled and in Army
combat uniform, she made
a surprise visit to the British
troops in South Armagh in
August 1979.
(Press Association)

Mark Thatcher, beaming, on returning to Britain after being lost in the Sahara. She had been told he had been found dead.
(Associated Press)

Walking with President Reagan in the garden of the US Ambassador in Paris before the June 1982 Versailles summit.
(Associated Press)

At the Conservative Conference at Brighton, October 1982.
(The Times/Brian Harris)

The Argentine magazine *Tal Cual's* spoof cover during the Falklands War. The headline reads: 'Thatcher is crazy. She thinks she's Wonder Woman'. *(Associated Press)*

The Thatchers visit the Falklands and stand with the civil governor, Rex Hunt, and his wife outside their residence in Port Stanley. *(Press Association)*

At the Falklands service in St Paul's. *(The Times)*

Remembrance Sunday 1982. From the left Callaghan, Heath, Steel, Foot, Thatcher. *(The Times/Bill Warhurst)*

problems face us as a nation and as a party, which will not
be overcome simply or easily, and which will need both skill
and determination for their solution. Margaret Thatcher has
both, and I sincerely wish her well.' And that was the last
kind word he had to say for her for years.

Kitson advised Heath with eloquence and force that it
was in his interests to make an early peace; he argued that if
such a truce was not struck, everything that he said inside
or outside the House of Commons would be read only for
its significance in relation to her, and that by not
establishing a basis on which he could disagree with her
from time to time he would lay his old colleagues still inside
the Shadow Cabinet open to charges of divided loyalties
and undermine the party's unity. But, although both
predictions were richly fulfilled, Heath would not make the
move. 'He was,' said one man close to him at the time, 'just
too dazed and proud to give ground.' He took up his place
in the Commons, below the aisle, and would gaze sourly
across at Thatcher and her front bench team. It became a
favourite Labour joke, to point out the glowering presence.
At Tory conferences, Heath's entrances brought applause
from his loyal supporters and a great deal of embarrassment
as Leader and former Prime Minister tried to avoid meeting
one another. He was even unable to speak her name in
public. He became a persistent critic of her policies
particularly her economic policy.

As time has gone by, his obvious resentment has worked
in her favour. His behaviour has been understood as
ungenerous and ungentlemanly. One explanation, however,
has been underestimated. For the latter part of his
government and throughout 1974 and 1975, Heath had been
seriously ill with a thyroid complaint, which he had kept to
himself. It became well known that he would doze off in the
middle of conversations or at dinner and it was considered a
quaint, if rude, habit which went along with his inability to
interest himself in subjects that he knew nothing about. It
was not until a close friend mentioned it to him that Heath
admitted that he was unwell. He underwent a full medical
check and it was discovered that, at one time, his thyroid
gland had stopped working altogether. His condition had

resulted in permanent discomfort and an apparent ill humour and had lasted throughout the leadership campaign. By the time that Heath had recovered from his illness and rediscovered a public smile, Thatcher had learnt to live without him.

Shortly before the general election in 1979, Heath had worked himself around to being willing to be considered for a Cabinet post. He sent her a congratulatory telegram on her victory. In an act of omission which appeared deliberate because of her known compulsion about thank-you letters, Thatcher did not reply, nor did she thank Heath for his help in the 1979 campaign. Nor did she give him a Cabinet post. Since then, there have been various attempts to bring him back into the fold by Whitelaw, although Thatcher has never approached him herself.

The election of the first woman leader of a party hardly noted for its lack of sexism or snobbery, exposed the Thatcher family and lifestyle to the full rigours of Fleet Street's eagerness to promote the new heroine. On becoming leader, as one writer put it, she lost three things: sleep, weight and privacy. As Thatcher herself explained to friends and the more sympathetic interviewers, a woman leader not only has to be a politician, she has to look smart as well. Thatcher was clearly never disposed to risk breaching this convention in the way that Shirley Williams had, by frequently ignoring the traditional womanly virtues of make-up, hairdos and smart clothes. The compulsion to look smart did not only come from the Fleet Street women's editors and her own party; Thatcher considered that it was part of the job. Jean Rook of the *Daily Express*, starting an interview at ten to nine in the morning at the House of Commons wrote, 'She was fresh – in fact dewy – off a plane from Northumberland. Pale orange linen suit still crisp. Skin petal soft. Spun-gold hair fluffy as a dandelion clock. Even the orchid from last night's dinner in her buttonhole looked newly plucked.'

The key to survival of the ordeal was an extraordinary self-control. Clive Limpkin, then working as a staff photographer for the *Daily Mail*, was detailed in early 1976 to specialise for a few months on the new lady leader, to get his face known, to know her habits and to forge the kind of relationship which picture editors hope will squeeze a photograph just a little bit different from the usual run. For the first time in his considerable experience, Limpkin was defeated. 'I can't,' he said, 'think of any politician with that much control. If you go on a foreign trip with the queen for eleven days to Papua New Guinea, you get a heel coming off a shoe, you get a yawn and you get her rolling her eyes. She's been behaving herself in front of photographers for thirty years and still you end up with something. Mrs Thatcher: not once.' On the weekend before a party conference speech, Limpkin was sent to Flood Street with instructions to return with a picture of her preparing the speech; his familiarity was enough for her to let him into the house for two quick posed shots. Having counted the clicks, she showed him out and accompanied him down the short path to tell the policeman on duty that there were to be no more callers. There was a bang behind them; she explained to Limpkin that she was now locked out without a key and there was no one else in the house. She remained quite cool and persuaded him to leave; he discovered later that he had missed his picture: she had had to climb in through the kitchen window. 'I was watching her at that conference,' he said, 'and waiting for an interesting facial expression and I suddenly realised that she was yawning with her mouth shut; at that point I knew I'd been beaten.'

Readers learnt where and how she bought her clothes. Her secretary would call Mansfield Originals in Great Tichfield Street and the shop's stock in her size (14) would be gathered on a rail and she would make a brief evening visit to choose and buy. There was a short-lived experiment with a one-man band — who himself wore gold chains and shirts open to the waist — recommended to her by her Flood Street neighbour Susan Masterforte, but who talked too much about the designs he had been asked to try out for the trip to the United States in September 1975.

She read *The Times*, *Daily Mail* and *Daily Telegraph*; she liked Alistair Cooke's *America*, Maigret and André Previn on television; she did not share Harold Macmillan's taste for the political Palliser novels by Trollope, but read

Solzhenitsyn, Arthur Hailey, Hammond Innes and Alistair Maclean. The leadership had deprived her of 'flop days, which keep me going' when she had relaxed by sorting towels into different colours. The party was keen to make her better known and more sympathetically received. For once, the leader was worth turning to electoral advantage. A number of loyal biographies followed.

In the edgy months immediately after the leadership battle, Thatcher gathered around herself a small, protective group, principally chosen for its loyalty and capacity for providing emotional support. It attracted a great deal of back-biting within the party for its siege defence of the leader's privacy, its paranoia about counter-coups and its lack of a dominating political figure equivalent to the position which Douglas Hurd had occupied in Edward Heath's inner counsels. Airey Neave, most members of the Shadow Cabinet were surprised to learn, was to continue as head of her private office as well as being spokesman on Northern Ireland; both were extremely demanding jobs. Her first Parliamentary Private Secretaries were Fergus Montgomery and William Shelton, rewarded for their close support during the leadership campaign. Neither were effective, although Thatcher was loyal to both men until yielding to persuasion that they should be replaced by John Stanley and Adam Butler. Her two other principal assistants were Richard Ryder and Caroline Stephens; she retained the Press Secretary she had inherited from Heath, Derek Howe. For the first three months, Whitelaw found himself almost completely removed from the leader's presence. Long delays occurred before he was given appointments and their conversations were spare. An ally of Whitelaw's lunched one day with two of the MPs belonging to the Thatcher circle and mentioned this. A weekly half-hour for leader and deputy was duly instituted.

The twice weekly briefings for Prime Minister's questions, which under Heath had lasted no more than a few minutes before the Tuesday and Thursday sessions at 3.15 p.m, became major operations. She wanted vast quantities of facts and statistics marshalled for every possible eventuality and supplementary. In the early days, these briefings would be conducted by a panel based around a nucleus of Central Office officials, together with Montgomery and Shelton. The panel would be asked to write out supplementary questions. 'It was rather like writing out a hundred lines at school,' said one participant. The cast list for these sessions gradually expanded, particularly on the appearance of what became nicknamed the 'gang of four'. The phrase had originally been coined for the four senior figures alleged to be moving the party to the right: Thatcher, Neave, George Gardiner the ex-journalist and Norman Tebbit.

Gardiner and Tebbit became regular attenders. Neave, Howe, and two sympathetic back-benchers, Nigel Lawson and Geoffrey Pattie, also came frequently. These processes opened a gap between the policy-making process of the Shadow Cabinet and those of the Leader. Members of the Shadow Cabinet could never be completely confident that their portfolio was not to be reanalysed from first principles by a 'study group' or 'policy working party' which did not form part of the Shadow Cabinet's committee structure. Eighty 'policy groups', composed of MPs and outsiders dealing with subjects from superpowers to water-meters were formed. The fierce rivalry between the Conservative Research Department, the main source of intellectual energy during the Heath years, headed by Christopher Patten, and the CPS complicated matters still further. Alfred Sherman made no secret of his belief that the department should have been far more vigorously de-Heathed than it had been. CPS literature and memoranda continued to arrive in copious quantities.

The rivalries and suspicions perhaps reached their height at the first party conference which Thatcher addressed as Leader. There was an epidemic of rumours of plots and counter-plots which bore little relation to reality; the Thatcher leadership was more secure than many of the individuals around her. The Thatcher team continued to angle for a public reconciliation with Heath, which Heath continued to deny them. The particular form of reconciliation which Howe wanted to organise was a photograph of them together. Heath took the view that he could not win either way: if he agreed, it would be interpreted as his final humiliation and would make speaking out on the 'major issues of the day' harder; if he refused, it would be interpreted as a snub.

The Heath team, which arrived in Blackpool a day after Thatcher, spent some of its time worrying that they were about to be ambushed by Thatcher and a photographer who would snatch off pictures of the moment when she graciously offered him her hand. Heath arrived in the hall to massive applause and made his way to his seat without going past her; later that evening he walked straight past her table in the restaurant of the Imperial Hotel without acknowledgement. He made an ineffectual denial after newspapers had reported him as denouncing Thatcher and Joseph as traitors and fanatics. Her speech at the rally was, in the event, received with normal rapture.

If there was one trauma, one issue which dominated the Party's life from 1975 to 1979, it was trade unions. In 1975, the defeat at the hands of the miners was still a fresh memory and by 1979, government-union relationships were again at the forefront of voters' minds, both Labour and Conservative. The Party's approach to unions could not be disentangled from the debate over incomes policy. These related issues were to account for a high proportion of the most active debates in the Shadow Cabinet. Its members increasingly came to feel that they were no longer the principal policy-making body. Prior in particular strongly objected to Thatcher's tendency to announce changes without reference to the Shadow Cabinet.

However successful a 'holding operation' the party's liberal wing thought that they were performing there could be no mistaking the change in style. The managerial Heath, some felt, had been at heart a civil servant; Thatcher was emphatically a politician. Some were embarrassed by her lack of guile or cynicism; whatever agreements or disagreements any colleagues had over specific policies, it was quickly obvious to those who had not known her before that she believed completely that she was engaged in a crusade. Even Neave, to whom she was so close personally, worked gently and firmly to convince his protegée that there were constraints on waging war on the trade unions or over the Public Sector Borrowing Requirement. He was impressed by the strength of her vision, but wanted to pull her gently towards the centre. To others, he would explain it by saying that she was a truly sincere politician, something of a romantic. At first people found such novel things difficult to cope with.

He was not the only one working to bring her towards the centre. Any Conservative Shadow Cabinet of that time would have faced a problem. As some policy-makers assessed the scene, they faced a public in an inconsistent mood: they apparently wanted inflation brought down, but at the same time wanted the freedom of collective bargaining. Clearly the approach to the unions which had been tried by the 1970-74 government had not survived the confrontation with the miners. James Prior, who was to speak for the Party on employment for seven years, and Ian Gilmour felt strongly that their party had to work with the union grain and not against it. 'The voters,' Gilmour wrote, 'do not want perpetual confrontation between government and unions, any more than they want the unions to be the effective government.' Nor was a hard line thought to be helpful to the small numbers of overtly Conservative trade unionists working in major industries or to the background helpfulness of one or two union leaders who were thought to be sympathetic. No Conservative Opposition can ignore the fact that it cannot regain power without the right number of working-class votes. Central Office's psephologists calculated that at general elections which the Conservatives had won, more than fifty per cent of their vote was working class; when they lost it was always less. Similarly, victorious Conservative elections turned out to have been the ones in which 40-45% of trade unionists voted Conservative; defeats coincided with the figure reduced to 30-35%.

Thatcher regarded such arguments as 'appeasement'; she reserved a special contempt for the middle class who did not have the courage of their convictions, something she had always clearly held against Sir Edward Boyle. Although her instincts were clearly anti-union and fiercely expressed, it quickly became clear, as the Party debated its stance, that the new leader was more complicated than she looked. She was emotional and despised 'fearful' politicians, but her intelligence and tactical instincts drew her to move only cautiously. This analysis did not entirely comfort the liberals. Whatever the real state of party policy, Thatcher's style seemed to be calculated to be as abrasive as possible, sometimes creating a 'right-wing' image when the substance was nothing like it. Alfred Sherman's editorials in the *Daily Telegraph* had a tendency to interpret statements drafted as careful compromises in the most extreme sense possible.

She turned constantly to Keith Joseph and defended him fiercely against his critics. 'Instead of criticising someone else's ideas,' she stormed at one of her colleagues one day, 'why don't you have some yourself?' They both argued at one point that the closed shop should be made illegal. Most of her colleagues, led by Prior and Pym, objected that in the name of freedom they would be seriously inconveniencing employers who were already operating satisfactory closed shops. The compromise which emerged was a commitment to modify the closed shop. Some of the sharpest duels between her and James Prior came over the prolonged strike and picket over unionisation at the Grunwick film processing laboratories in North London.

Formal policy documents such as *The Right Approach*, published in 1977, attempted to phrase compromises which would disguise these tensions and which could be supported in public by those who were carrying on ferocious disagreements in private. A draft of the document was shown to Edward Heath and Peter Walker to ensure that they would not repudiate it when it appeared. But behind this facade, the hard-liners were consolidating their forces. There is no better example of the ability of some complete outsiders to rise swiftly within the party than the arrival of John Hoskyns. In the early 1970s, Hoskyns, who had been an army officer and executive with IBM, sold the computer consultancy which had made him a millionaire. He had flirted briefly with politics in 1971 by helping with Dick Taverne's independent stand against Labour but had not found any further outlet for his political interests until he met Alfred Sherman in 1975. Sherman introduced him to

Joseph, but he did not become involved in the making of party policy until 1977, after another 18 months of reflection on the causes and cures of Britain's decline. Joseph invited him to attend a strategy meeting of senior politicians and Central Office officials. As a result of his criticisms of what he heard, he was asked to write a paper for Thatcher, Joseph and Howe. Working with a Unilever marketing executive, Norman Strauss, he argued that the conventional wisdom about trade union reform – that the toughest action will have the most expensive cost in votes lost – should be turned upside down. Rather, people now wanted measures tougher than the prescriptions on offer.

The battle over the Party's trade union stance became a long-running siege of Prior's position by Hoskyns. Hoskyns and Strauss were invited to set up several groups studying key priorities in party policy. The participants were sworn to secrecy and the subjects which they were supposed to be studying were not divided along conventional lines. One looked at policy and communications: how to promote policies in a hostile environment. Another was called Policy Search. The studies aimed to identify economic and political factors which had helped governments to miss their economic targets in the past: public sector pay, indexed benefits and allowances, nationalised industries. Essentially, they were aimed at Prior and the union line. They were called Stepping Stones – as in the footsteps to the revival of Britain and its industry.

One group consisted of Hoskyns, Strauss, Prior, a Priorite MP interested in labour affairs Barney Hayhoe, the Central Office employment researcher Robert Shepherd, and a retired industrialist who had helped draft the Heath government's industrial relations legislation. Hoskyns and Strauss would present their ideas; Prior and Hayhoe would counter-attack. Hoskyns and Strauss would return the next week and the argument would go round much the same circle again.

The Stepping Stones exercise reported to an inner group of the Shadow Cabinet which had been established in November 1977. They did not make much headway in changing the balance of power inside it until the winter of 1978-79 made the changes for them. John Biffen converted to the tough line during the winter of discontent, significantly altering the atmosphere. Shortly before the conference in October 1978, Hoskyns had urged Mrs Thatcher to reshuffle Prior away from a job which should be controlled by a loyalist. She rejected the suggestion.

When Prior became the Employment minister, the siege continued, with variations. Organisations loyal to the Thatcherite wing of the party kept up well-orchestrated pressure to fulfil manifesto commitments which had been strengthened during the winter of discontent. Prior had resisted their inclusion as specific legislative proposals until the last moment. Prior moved as slowly as he could, pursued particularly by the lobbyists of the Institute of Directors, the voice of businessmen who disliked the corporatism of past governments, and of the Confederation of British Industry. Its director, Walter Goldsmith, was a member of the monthly lunches at the Soho restaurant L'Escargot also attended by Thatcher advisers like Alfred Sherman, Alan Walters and Michael Ivens. The group became known as the Argonauts. By the time Prior had been replaced by Norman Tebbit at the Department of Employment, the IoD was working very closely with Downing Street on the fine print of new union law in the pipeline.

At this stage in her career Thatcher presents a clear picture of the conflict in her personality between being an evangelist and a tactician. She herself was aware, and told colleagues, that political leadership was more than articulating visions. Fondly as she might speak of Keith Joseph, she distinguished between his ideas and his political judgement, and she was critical of his tendency to get carried away by the jargon of whatever he was studying at the time. That was the essence of her criticism of the speech referring to 'social classes C and D' – not wrong in itself, but a tactical misjudgment. She herself was heard to say that the art of political leadership was the timing of an idea. Float an idea five years ahead of its time and it will be killed off; float it two years ahead and, if it takes off, it will be thanks to true political leadership.

Her technique is to watch the public's mood and opinions, push out a hitherto controversial idea and then draw back to observe the results. A private poll of voter attitudes conducted in October 1977 showed a majority of voters in favour of the Labour Government's handling of inflation, unemployment and the unions. But on non-economic issues, the Conservatives were ahead. At a meeting of senior Conservatives over the 1977 Christmas recess, a decision was taken that for the first five months of 1978, the party would concentrate on social issues. The decision was influenced by two further factors: Keith Joseph was increasingly turning his attention away from economics towards these topics and the past year had seen some striking rises in votes for the National Front on immigration and social issues previously regarded as natural Conservative territory.

On 30 January, two nights after a disturbance involving crowds of black and white youths in the centre of Wolverhampton, Thatcher was interviewed by Granada Television's World in Action. Noting statistical estimates which suggested that Britain's black population would rise to four million by the end of the century, she said, 'Now that is an awful lot and I think it means that people are really rather afraid that this country might be rather swamped by people with a different culture. And, you know, the British character has done so much for democracy, for law and done so much throughout the world, that if there is any fear that it might be swamped, people are going to react and be rather hostile to those coming in. So, if you want good race relations, you have got to allay people's fears on numbers.' She agreed that the National Front was seen by some as 'at least … talking about some of the problems.' Not, apparently, giving much time to the worries of the black viewers, she said that 'we are not in politics to ignore people's worries, we are in politics to deal with them.' One of the first things which her many and vociferous critics pointed out was that a significant proportion of the projected four million would not be immigrants at all, but blacks born and bred in Britain.

During the tumultuous row which followed, political correspondents were told that she had a habit of saying what she was thinking and that she sometimes ended up making policy as she went along. But any implication that the use of the word 'swamp' was spontaneous was untrue. It had been discussed with, and opposed by, at least one party official. She had used the word during Shadow Cabinet discussions.

She had broken the unwritten code among senior Conservatives (excepting, notoriously, Enoch Powell) that there are certain things you will not do to please the party's rank and file. Even worse, it looked as if she believed what she was saying. Edward Heath commented that she had caused an 'unnecessary national row'. Callaghan told his colleagues that his true contempt for Mrs Thatcher dated from that interview and at Question Time proposed a three-party meeting on immigration which Thatcher declined. 'The British public – and this is not a nation of racialists – ARE worried about further immigration,' said *The Sun*. Within two weeks of the interview, one opinion poll took the Conservatives from two points behind to eleven points ahead. Around 10,000 people wrote to Thatcher after the broadcast. An analysis by her staff disclosed a striking number of Labour voters among the overwhelming majority who supported what she had said. On 2 March, the Conservatives won the Ilford North by-election with a 12% lead, after a campaign dominated by the National Front and its marches. Roughly 6000 voters who had been Labour in 1974 had crossed over and one election-day poll claimed that more than half had changed because of the Conservative position on immigration. So confident did Thatcher feel of the impact in the country, if not among her colleagues, that she repeated the assertion in a slightly less noticeable form three months before the general election campaign. An interviewer suggested that she had modified her statement: 'I *never* modified it! I stood by it one hundred per cent. Some people have felt swamped by immigrants. They've seen the whole character of their neighbourhood change ... Of course people can feel they are being swamped.'

Jonathan Aitken MP had been dining in Beirut during the final stages of the party leadership contest. His fellow guests, Lebanese bankers, had plagued him with questions on what line Thatcher would take on various sophisticated Middle Eastern questions. 'Look,' Aitken eventually said in exasperation, 'she doesn't have any views on the Middle East. She probably thinks that Sinai is the plural of sinus.' The thrust of the story is correct although the Jewish vote in Finchley has ensured that the Middle East was one of the few areas of the world which Thatcher did know something about.

Thatcher policy-making in foreign affairs was perhaps a more disjointed process than in any other area. She began with an energetic programme of foreign visits, a plan which did not impress Harold Macmillan, when he heard about it. He felt that she still needed some instruction from the life of the Tory Prime Minister who was to become the 'One Nation' talisman of the anti-Thatcher liberals. 'She would do much better,' he said, 'to stay at home in her garden – has she got a garden? – and read Moneypenny and Buckle's life of Disraeli.'

The fascination of a future woman Prime Minister held her in good stead on her first visit to the United States in September 1975. She was visibly annoyed to be asked so many questions about women's liberation and feminism. Did she owe her position to women's liberation? 'Some of us were making it long before women's lib was ever thought of.' Was she 'Mrs' or 'Ms'? 'I am not sure I fully understand the significance of your question,' she said primly. 'I am just Margaret Thatcher. You must take me as I am.'

She had decided from the start to mount a major series of speeches on the Soviet Union, detente and human rights. The third, delivered in the summer of 1976, was sufficiently tough to earn an immediate invitation from the Chinese, which she took up the following spring along with stops in Hong Kong and Japan. She admired Hong Kong's market economy and delivered herself of the view that 'the spark of human spirit' would eventually spell the end of Chinese collectivism. She invited her entourage to a bottle party in her rooms in one of the provincial cities on the tour and outlasted most of the weary travellers; 'she bounces from one group to the next, her enthusiasms ranging over the cleaning of Chinese silk paintings, comparative living standards in China and India, the beauty of Chairman Hua's hands.' Well after midnight, she was found to be wandering up and down a corridor looking for Carol. 'Carol, dear, are you there?' Carol, recently qualified as a solicitor, was about to make her first trip to Australia in search of some life away from the family. The changes of the last two years had been too much and she was tired, she told someone on that trip, of being 'somebody's appendage'.

That autumn Thatcher made a second journey to the United States. A few weeks earlier, Francois Mitterand had been declined a White House meeting with President Jimmy Carter on the grounds that such contacts were restricted to heads of state. She, however, was received. Carter, who was in the process of forging a close rapport with James Callaghan, may have regretted the exception by the end. Carter asked whether a Conservative government could get along with the unions. 'Let me put it the way I put it in my campaign speeches,' she said and proceeded to give him edited highlights from a speech on the theme.

During the 1979 election there was some discussion inside Carter's National Security Council of whether the President should make a public statement in favour of Callaghan – an unwelcome possibility which worried Central Office. Nothing came of the idea, which was closely connected to the American interest in missile purchase and deployment negotiations then under way between Washington and London, but it also reflected Carter's marked preference for Callaghan.

'The broad stream of British foreign policy,' Reginald Maudling wrote in *The Times* in the summer of 1975, 'should not be sharply diverted with every change of government, for the national interest does not change, much as it needs to adapt to external circumstances.' It was hardly the sort of approach likely to appeal to the new leader, even in an area where she was only beginning to amass briefing material in the shape of heavily underlined cuttings and books. The previous month, she had made a little-reported speech to Chelsea Conservatives staking out a sceptical position on detente in general and the forthcoming Helsinki conference in particular. During the autumn she began a series of conversations – in a pattern to be expanded and repeated in the future – with the hawkish commentator on Soviet affairs, Robert Conquest. She planned a widely spaced series of major speeches on East-West relations, which were to be one of the principal jobs of the author and journalist Patrick Cosgrave who joined her staff on a part-time writing contract that year.

She returned to these themes at Kensington Town Hall in January 1976 with the speech which first led to the coining of the 'Iron Lady' nickname in the Soviet papers. Again, although scorn was poured on her, she was chiming – and she knew it – with the burgeoning fashion for an escalation of cold war rhetoric based on new assessments of Soviet military strength. Robert Conquest, by this time studying in Washington, kept her staff aware of the currents of opinion inside the American defence and foreign policy establishments.

Maudling was growing increasingly disenchanted with his inability to influence the content of her speeches. The difficulties grew worse with the preparation of the third speech in the series. The Thatcher line was broadly supported by the defence spokesman, Ian Gilmour, but not by Maudling. When the final draft was shown to him two days before the speech was due to be delivered, he despatched an angry letter complaining that he had had no idea that she was due to deliver a speech, let alone what it was going to say and that he regarded helping with speeches as a major part of his job. 'I understand,' he wrote, 'that the draft was produced by Lord Chalfont and Mr Patrick Cosgrave. I have no idea of their views on foreign policy, or their reasons for them..

'No doubt a violent and sustained attack upon the Soviet government may have some political advantage within our own ranks,' he went on. 'But I am doubtful as to what long-term purpose it is intended to serve, not only in Opposition, but more important, in Government.' He added that the speech implied a commitment to 'immediate and massive rearmament', and said, 'Maybe we should adopt this as a policy, but I do think we should consider it carefully and at length in the Shadow Cabinet before we do.' He submitted a draft of his own speech which lacked the moral fervour of the Thatcher series – it described the events of the first year since the Helsinki Declaration as a 'profound disappointment' – which was wholly ignored and her speech was duly delivered without concession to his complaints.

Maudling's memoirs record the following scene later that year. 'Without beating about the bush, she told me, in the most charming manner, that she must ask me to relinquish my responsibilities ... She said that there had been a lot of pressure from Central Office because I was not making enough speeches for the party. I must admit it was rather a shock, after more than twenty years on the front bench in one capacity or another, as Senior Privy Councillor on the Conservative side of the House, and with an experience of government and a record of service to the party much longer than Mrs Thatcher's, to be summoned and dismissed without any prior criticism or warning from her of any sort whatsoever ... There we are.'

It is dubious whether Maudling's leisurely temperament would have taken easily to the Thatcher style of speech-writing which was becoming a testing obstacle course for those caught up in it. She is a voracious reader with a long memory; people borrowing books from her find them heavily underscored – and that includes dictionaries of quotations. Once, when preparing a speech on science, she asked to see a speech on the subject by Winston Churchill. She was asked why it was important and replied that she could recall it being highly recommended by her father.

Her speech-writing sessions may spread over weeks and will last at least several days, often spilling into the small hours of the morning. Those who have been through this mill say that she is curiously indecisive over the texts of speeches, pays close attention to them line by line and is seldom satisfied before she has introduced extra writers to the circle. She is not, left to herself, an exciting stylist and has long relied on others for expressive words; the appeal 'give me a phrase' regularly punctuates these meetings.

She inherited from Heath the playwright Ronald Millar, who had been writing occasional scripts and speeches unpaid. The leader of the party had been due to make a radio broadcast within days of the second ballot and Millar turned up with his script. He explained that what was right for Heath would not be right for her; she asked him if he would try a version for her. During rehearsals for 'The Case in Question', adapted by Millar from C.P. Snow, he sat in the stalls of the Haymarket Theatre and rewrote. She approved the new version and turned out to be an amenable pupil to Millar's methods, which included advice on delivery as well as a script. Millar has become known as the author of the jokes (he was responsible for 'U-turn if you want to — the lady's not for turning'), but his principal skill was and is playing director to the leading lady, a combination of firm steering mixed with reassurance. He became a close friend of the Thatchers.

The injection of jokes (or 'Ronniefication' as it was known when Millar was about) was important, however: speech-writers quickly discovered that their new leader had little sense of humour. Peter Jay, Callaghan's son-in-law, had recently been sent to Washington as ambassador and had made a speech comparing his father-in-law to Moses. A speech in preparation at the time made several jokes on this theme, including the daft line, 'So my message to Moses is, keep taking the tablets.' Thatcher was worried that the audience wouldn't laugh: Millar and Christopher Patten just as frequently urged her to trust them and believe that it would. The line was put in and taken out of the speech several times. In the middle of the night, she returned to the subject and announced that she had thought of a better line: 'So my message to Moses is: keep taking the pill.' In stunned silence the team realised that she had never understood the joke.

Until the election, the three most heavily used speech-writers were Patten, Millar and Adam Ridley, an economic expert at Central Office who was also on the board of the CPS. Sherman, Jock Bruce-Gardyne, an economic hard-liner who was working at the CPS between losing his Commons seat in 1974 and finding another just before May

1979, and Cosgrave also wrote drafts. As the election neared, the *Daily Telegraph* leader-writer T.E. Utley and historian (now Lord) Hugh Thomas contributed ideas and themes. From 1977 until the election, the American-born political philosopher Shirley Letwin wrote one or two papers on her interpretation of English conservatism and occasionally talked her ideas through with Mrs Thatcher; she did not take to the less academic work of speech-writing.

Letwin's brief was to try to produce an intellectual framework for what otherwise sometimes appeared to be an uncoordinated set of instincts and values; Keith Joseph in particular was keen to establish coherent grounds for opposition to socialism which went further than simply pointing to the fact that it was inefficient. Letwin argued (and later expanded the theses in a book published in 1982) that the party should broaden its reappraisal to look at the moral arguments which lay behind economic theory. Her ideas were not easily digested by those exposed to them, for Letwin admitted that the collectivist position was simpler to express and had been put vigorously for some time. Thatcher, however, wanted the issues, no matter how abstract and theoretical, debated. 'She wanted to find out what she believed and she wanted her party to think it all out,' said one observer of these sessions. 'It's rare to find a party doing that so thoroughly and the fact that it was done was due to her energy.'

Her style of assembling a speech suggested to some that her vigour and certainty of delivery were not matched by an equal intellectual self-confidence. She marshalled huge quantities of statistics with the strict logic of the lawyer and chemist, but seemed to fail to translate the impulsive, romantic streak, only occasionally revealed to close associates, into ideas and words which would fire the imagination of an audience.

During a long session in her room at the House of Commons, (the menu was Marks and Spencer's ocean pie washed down with whisky) she announced that she had an idea to illustrate the moral superiority of West over East for a speech to be delivered in the United States at the end of

1978. What would really make the speech good, she said, is not just a mention of dissidents, but to name all of them in the paragraph under discussion. She briskly announced to the gathering that the party's research department should get a list, and she took some persuading, after the giggles had died down, that producing and reading out the list might be more complicated and laborious than she imagined.

By June 1978, it was common wisdom that there would be an election in October. The Lib-Lab pact had exhausted itself and David Steel confirmed during the summer recess that it would not be renewed. Callaghan began his final speech of the session, by quoting Dryden's 'Absalom and Achitophel' at his opposite number:

'Stiff in opinions,
Always in the wrong,
Was everything by starts and nothing long;
But in the course of one revolving moon,
Was chemist, fiddler, statesman and buffoon.'

Thatcher packed up her office for the recess in the expectation of moving to Downing Street before the next session of Parliament. She took, and cut short, a brief sailing holiday. By the end of August, Saatchi and Saatchi's posters were on hoardings all over the country. At the last moment, Callaghan announced that he would carry on. Thatcher, he sang, had been left 'waiting at the church'.

It was a sour autumn until it became clear in the new year that Callaghan's final phase of pay restraint would not command union support. Thatcher's advisers thought with hindsight that if there was a single speech or broadcast which consolidated their advantage, it was a party political broadcast that January, scripted again by Patten and Millar. Millar made one crucial late change by advising against the clothes she was thinking of wearing and recommending something less formal and suggestive of a governess. The result avoided the shrill, domineering tone which her media advisers had worked to tone down and hit a note of firm friendliness which appeared to get through. She was generous and patronising towards Callaghan: move over and let Mummy do it because you've got yourself in a pickle, was the tone.

Licensed by the brief spasm of public anger at the behaviour of the unions, which even Callaghan was forced to admit to be justified ('the trade union movement must operate within the parameters of public opinion'), the manifesto was toughened on industrial relations generally and secondary picketing in particular. Twice during January, Callaghan fended off what amounted to confidence votes, although the margin dwindled: on 16 January his majority was 24 and on the 26th (after Callaghan had made the unusual observation for a Labour Prime Minister that picket lines were not 'sacred objects') it was down to 16. A brief recovery was followed shortly afterwards by the decisive defeats on the devolution proposals, which had occupied so much Parliamentary time and energy. Thatcher herself had taken relatively little interest and relied heavily for advice on William Whitelaw and Francis Pym.

After two weeks of inconclusive negotiations with the minority parties, Callaghan faced a no-confidence motion on the night of 28 March. Northern Ireland MPs had been offering their votes in exchange for promises of a gas pipeline to the mainland; there was furious speculation over whether an elderly and ill Labour MP, Sir Alfred Broughton, could be brought to Parliament and nodded through the division lobbies. In the end he did not arrive, although his presence would have tied the vote and saved the government. But Callaghan's heart did not appear to be in an all-out effort to hang on. Just after 10 p.m. a packed House heard that the motion had been lost by 311-310, the first government defeat on a confidence motion since 1924.

The morning after, Thatcher slept late and enjoyed the unusual treat of breakfast in bed. She knew that her campaign would start later than Labour's, but her advisers were confident that it had been better planned. It was, someone remarked afterwards, a static campaign: minutely prepared and consisting of several set pieces, designed to remind the voting public of well-rehearsed themes. Most strategists in both the major parties knew that it had already been won or lost.

CHAPTER NINE

Election

The rehearsals were over and the performance about to begin. With a solid lead in the polls, Thatcher found herself in the position of tightrope walker: her task was simple to plan but nerve-racking to execute. If she went forwards in a straight line and avoided falling off, she would take the prize on the other side. Many of those below, some of them in her own party, were waiting for her to slip.

'The only thing that can defeat us is ourselves,' Denis Healey had told Labour's 1977 conference. In the end it was the unions which delivered a Labour government, with a popular leader who had managed the country's problems well in the voters' eyes for several years, into the hands of the Conservatives. Callaghan's forced conversion to monetary restraint at the bidding of the IMF in that year meant that both major parties were seen to be offering a monetarist base to economic policy. Callaghan the calm helmsman was, Tory strategists well knew, a formidable personality to campaign against. But the early Shadow Cabinet battles over incomes policy and union legislation during 1976 and 1977 left Thatcher with a reasonably solid truce from which she could launch an offensive. Labour's claim to be the only party able to work with the unions unravelled in the face of the damaging images of the discontented winter: pickets at the gates of Liverpudlian cemeteries, hospitals and dockyards stacked with deteriorating food.

One Thatcher instinct on which the Shadow Cabinet had been able to agree without difficulty had been the size of the manifesto. Her eye had been caught by a piece in *New Society* in 1975 by Professor Sam Finer surveying the word-inflation in manifestoes: between 1945 and 1974, he noted, Conservative manifestoes had doubled in size. The pendulum now swung back with agreement that the Heath

manifestoes had burdened themselves with too many
detailed commitments. Lord Fraser (formerly Sir Michael
Fraser and the party's senior deputy chairman) had once
boasted to her that between 1966 and 1974, the party had
produced at least 1000 policy proposals. 'What use is that,'
she replied, 'when we didn't win the argument?' The new
1979 draft of the manifesto was still not written by Thatcher
loyalists, although the final editing was done by Angus
Maude. The authors were again Christopher Patten and
Adam Ridley, assisted by a Central Office official who was
also a confidant of Gilmour's, Dermot Gleason. The ground
had shifted under the advocates of a conciliatory policy
towards the unions: commitments to legislation on
picketing, the closed shop and secret ballots were not only
made for the first time, but promoted to the front of the
document.

Thatcher was also to benefit from deeper and longer-term
trends than the spasm of discontent with the unions which
so dominated public life during the first few weeks of the
year. Some of these had been clearly seen by Thatcher's
strategists and matched to promises.

Starting in 1963 and unregarded by most economists and
social scientists, the Institute for Economic Affairs had
compiled surveys on attitudes to taxation and welfare. The
full results were not published until 1979, but much of the
material had been made available in the interim. In one
sense, the results provided strong evidence that there was a
slowly but steadily building resentment against the size and
style of government social provision which might be
answered by a libertarian appeal to greater individual
choice; looked at in another way, the statistics provided a
persuasive tactical guide to the points at which the Labour
vote might be at its 'softest' and most vulnerable to a
change of emphasis from the Conservatives.

The surveys found, unsurprisingly, that many people
wished to reduce the levels of taxation. Surprisingly,
however, Labour voters were as keen on the proposition as
Conservatives. More surprisingly still, social classes C2, D
and E were markedly more in favour than the higher end of
the scale, social groups A, B and C1. The most powerful

support was to be found in occupational class C2, the skilled working class. Taxes were apparently most harshly felt by those whose incomes had recently risen most steeply. The trend of these findings was echoed once the manifestoes had been digested. There was heavy support for lower taxation coupled with greater choice in the purchase of health and education services which would not be state monopolies.

The other subject on which an even more striking majority of trade unionists (58/22 per cent) preferred Conservative policies was law and order. The Conservative image on the question appeared powerfully attractive. The actual wording of the party's manifesto reveals a relatively restrained stand (it pointed out, for example that longer sentences do not necessarily bring down crime rates); but Thatcher performed the characteristic feat of suggesting a tougher face on the problem than the party was committed to (or than it in fact has shown in government). Each party leader appeared, towards the end of the campaign, in front of the 'Granada 500', a cross-section of voters from the 'weather-vane' constituency of Bolton East (a marginal which regularly changed hands with each swing). The loudest applause for any reply to any question by any of the three leaders was for Thatcher's ringing support for capital punishment. Callaghan was canvassing an elderly working-class couple in his own Cardiff constituency when the husband mentioned that he had been at the confrontation between miners and troops at Tonypandy in 1910. Callaghan slipped fluently into a brief speech of assurance delivered to obviously friendly voters when he was interrupted by the wife. 'Now, when are you going to do something about these vandals, then?' she demanded, jabbing him in the chest. It was highly characteristic of that election, that the stress on crime should have been from the wife of a traditional Labour voter. Law and order was the issue on which Conservatives had succeeded in effecting the largest change in voters' attitudes: both during the campaign itself ($9\frac{1}{2}$% advantage, according to MORI figures) and over the period from the previous summer (21%).

Thatcher was approaching an election which she would be unlikely to survive as leader if she lost. But two subterranean changes were working in her favour. The strength of voters' commitment to established political parties has been gradually weakening since the war and voting patterns have been steadily more volatile. There is a more and more attractive premium to be won by parties which can successfully present themselves as radical in idef . These tendencies are partly connected to the long-term attenuation of class loyalties; fewer and fewer people think of themselves as belonging to a particular social class. Those tendencies would not automatically have helped Thatcher, although it appears she did successfully make them work for her.

The 1981 census figures revealed that, whatever people's view of their class, a massive expansion of the middle class had taken place in the previous decade. The change is to the long-term advantage of the Conservatives (and now also the Alliance) and to the disadvantage of Labour.

Conservative election efforts had begun in earnest as 1978 opened. Gordon Reece agreed at the turn of the year to take up a job in Central Office as head of publicity, charged with the simple job specification of winning the election, whenever it might come. His relations with Thorneycroft were never easy. Particularly offensive to Thorneycroft was Reece's extravagance. He always seemed to be popping champagne corks. Reece's relations with Mrs Thatcher and her family (he is one of the favoured circle of Christmas day guests at Chequers) were closer and he made little attempt to conceal his contempt for some Central Office bureaucrats. (He returned from America in 1983 to mastermind the next campaign.) He began by settling the question of the advertising agency. He was intrigued by the fact that Saatchi and Saatchi, a medium-sized agency run by a pair of Iraqi Sephardic Jews, had originally refused to pitch for the account. Reece liked their ideas and they recommended themselves by being the right size: large enough to take the strain but not so big that the work disappeared into a giant machine. After some tussles inside Central Office, their brief covered all advertising and all sound and television broadcasting. Saatchi's managing director, Tim Bell, began with market research of his own, unimpressed by the statistical rigidity of Central Office's work. He thought that Thatcher would be difficult to sell. She looked and sounded like a Tory wife and she needed to be sold as the leader of the country. The early research, however, showed some promising lines. Labour was better supported on subjects connected with the state while the Conservatives polled better on subjects to do with individuals. Saatchi's first strategy document stressed broad abstract concepts. The ideal themes seemed to be choice, freedom and minimum state interference. Dissatisfaction with the government would be crucial.

As the strategy evolved in the spring of 1978, special target voters were identified: first-timers, women in council houses and Labour households and the C2 social group of skilled manual workers. The approach thrashed out by Reece, Bell and Thorneycraft, and agreed to by Mrs Thatcher, was to concentrate – in a way that the Conservatives had never done before – on these groups in order to persuade them either to come off the fence or to switch from their traditional loyalties. The idea carried some risks: advertising at particular groups can stress elements of policy or appeal which will turn off other groups or the party's traditional voters. Bell felt that the risk was worth it, if only on the grounds that traditional Conservative voters were unlikely to be so offended as to actually vote for other parties. Thatcher was known to be popular with women in general, and with women in the north in particular, but she was unpopular with middle class women in the south-east.

The difficulty Reece had with his leader was that modern politicians need two styles: one for broadcasting and one for the House of Commons. Words that may sound calm and rational on television or radio will not be heard by a soul in the House of Commons at Question Time. A full-blast Commons speech can sound like raving hysteria in a broadcasting studio. The broadcasting of the Commons (which happened to coincide with Reece's arrival) caused him special problems. He was heard to remark that the selling of Margaret Thatcher had been put back two years by the mass broadcasting of Prime Minister's Question Time as she had to be at her shrillest to be heard over the din.

Thatcher had already worked on the problem of shrillness; on the advice of Ronald Millar, she had done humming exercises to lower her voice under the guidance of a woman voice trainer who worked for the National Theatre. Millar had also taught her that lowering the voice brought the speed of the words down to a steadier rate. He advised holding to a steady and equable tone at Question Time which would eventually drive through, not over or under, the noise. Reece advised that on television, which made her nervous and consequently aggressive with producers and interviewers, she should pay attention to simplicity — as little jewellery as possible and no complicated hairdos.

By far the most important element of his broadcasting strategy was selection. Before the campaign began, the private office used to assemble, at the close of each week, a list of applicants for interviews. Thatcher would tick the ones that she was ready to do and take advice on the advisability or otherwise of her choices. Reece became the principal source of advice. With his target voters in mind, he tried to confine her appearances as far as possible to programmes which reached predominantly female audiences: mid-morning radio shows with Jimmy Young, Jimmy Saville and Gerald Harper. During the election, Radio 4's morning Election Call fitted this tactic; he tried to create whatever the leading picture of the day's campaigning was to be, in time for early evening national news bulletins and the 6 p.m. local television news magazines which are watched by families. That promptness also helped meet the earlier deadlines of the national popular papers, particularly *The Sun*.

The entire programme was ready to run for an election called in October 1978. Saatchi and Saatchi's poster campaign was designed to take advantage of the summer recess. They scored an immediate hit with the 'Labour Isn't Working' poster showing a long dole queue (consisting of Hendon Young Conservatives) snaking across the poster.

The row was eventually reckoned to have generated millions of pounds worth of free publicity. It was followed by other equally bouncy offerings. Bell was not over-scrupulous about his use of statistics. In his own words: 'We then ran an advertisement on law and order, reporting the increase in crime: "Mugging up 240%" and so forth. Many critics claimed exactly the same thing had happened under the last Conservative government. I must confess I didn't myself see how this negated the point of our advertisement.'

Reece was especially close to the editors of *The Sun*, Larry Lamb, and of the *Daily Mail*, David English (who were both knighted by Thatcher, Lamb in 1980, English in 1982). *The Sun* ran a sizeable series of spreads on the rise in crime in the early autumn of 1978 which appeared to have been coordinated with a likely election. The *Mail*'s most striking contribution to the election campaign was the front page of 26 April. Under the headline 'Labour's Dirty Dozen', it listed twelve Labour 'lies' about the Conservative post-election plans as if it were a *Mail* story. It was in fact a Conservative campaign gimmick which was subsequently published as a party handout. Reece was unrepentant about his lack of interest in the quality media. It did not reach the floating or detachable voters in which he was interested.

Reece did not neglect an element in publicity planning sometimes overlooked by metropolitan pundits: that the vast majority of people receive the information and images which form their important impressions about politicians from short television news slots, both national and local, and from local evening newspapers. Local newspapers usually provide politicians with detailed and uncritical coverage, providing the event itself is sufficiently interesting. It usually was – and Thatcher was professional at seizing unplanned opportunities. There was a fierce debate in the Thatcher camp over London Weekend Television's invitation to a debate with Callaghan, which the Prime Minister had promptly accepted. Thatcher herself was strongly in favour and reluctant to be seen as ducking out; Reece was just as strongly against the idea, but had to argue his point hard and long. He felt that with a solid lead in the polls, the debate would not have influenced floating voters and that it would have been preceded by a massive amount of speculation about arrangements for the broadcast which would have been a distraction. The only other supporter of her appearance was Christopher Patten. Reece was supported by Janet Young, Thorneycroft, and Whitelaw, and their view prevailed. Reece also continued his policy of not allowing his leader to be interviewed by Lew Gardner, who was suspected of left-wing sympathies, and Thames were forced to substitute Denis Tuohy instead. The policy of avoiding hostile interviewers who were likely to increase Thatcher's stridency had been followed since the time of her election as leader.

Election tactics were enshrined in a loose-leaf binder known in Central Office as the 'war book'. It had been prepared over eighteen months by a committee chaired by Janet Young and serviced by Thorneycroft's personal assistant, Alan Howarth. Much like her speeches, the three thousand mile leader's itinerary went through a large number of drafts, since it took some time for Thatcher to stop sending it back for revision. Tactical considerations did not overlook the smallest details: company schedules were scrutinised to see in advance if there were any embarrassingly huge profits due during the campaign; there was considerable worry that the observers watching the Rhodesian elections would arrive back in Britain before polling day and open up a potentially damaging issue which Conservative tacticians hoped would be left in the background until the poll was over.

Saatchi's party political broadcasts during the campaign were not judged a success by the Conservative leadership. It was thought that they should have varied the themes from the ones which had already been hammered home during the previous few months. Saatchi's film-makers were impressed by Thatcher. She was cooperative and practised characteristic self-control: she would repeat a script for 45 minutes, making perhaps only one fluff, but keep doing it until the director was satisfied. 'Was the tone right?' she would frequently ask. Saatchi's had also prepared a series of one-line slogans for her to use, but the occasion never arose and they ended the campaign unused.

Four major speeches had been prepared for the previous October and they were cannibalised and reconstructed for the campaign. Patten, Ridley, Millar, Sherman and Hoskyns were the principal authors; T.E. Utley could not be released from the *Daily Telegraph* for a second spell, so he and Hugh Thomas contributed to morning ideas sessions. Thorneycroft's doctor had mistakenly advised him that he would be fit to do the duties of Chairman of the Party. In fact he had been unwell for several extended periods. Nonetheless he worked exceptionally long days holding the organisation together. He occasionally intervened in long phone calls late at night to intercept what he saw as extreme statements which might find their way into speech texts, particularly on industrial relations. He had been asked to do the job of chairman by his cousin William Whitelaw, and Thatcher approved of him on the grounds that she wanted a chairman without personal ambitions. He had provided gratefully received fatherly support in her early days as leader. Latterly she had shown some signs of wanting to be more independent of his guidance – in opposition she had usually attended at least one meeting a week at Central Office – and his normal composure had begun to desert him when he approached his appointments with her.

On the afternoon of Friday 30 March, the day after the election was announced, Thatcher arrived by car in Finchley, where she was making a brief stop before recording a broadcast replying to Callaghan's opening shot of the night before. As she stepped out of the car in front of the cameras which were to pursue her until polling day, she was intercepted by Derek Howe. There had been an explosion that afternoon at the House of Commons. It was feared that the victim was Neave, her closest political confidant. The broadcast was cancelled and Thatcher returned to the Commons. It was soon confirmed that just before three o'clock Neave's Vauxhall Cavalier had been reaching the top of the car park ramp which emerges into New Palace Yard when the bomb exploded. He had been trapped in the shattered car for half an hour before being rushed to Westminster Hospital. He had died eight minutes after arriving and before his wife, Diana, could reach him. It appeared that the Irish National Liberation Army, the offshoot of the Official IRA, which claimed responsibility, had evaded the closed-circuit cameras in the House of Commons car park by planting the device under the car while it had been parked outside the block of flats in Westminster Gardens where Neave lived. It had been fitted with a tilt switch which delayed the explosion until the car was on a steep slope.

'What a good thing it is,' Thatcher said as she re-entered her office in the Commons, 'that when we wake up in the morning we don't know what will have come by night time.' She disappeared into her room to write a statement in tribute, telling Ronnie Millar that she wanted him to wait and give his opinion on her words. Millar approved the text with only a reservation about the use of the word 'hero', which he felt Neave himself would not have liked. The word was removed. With her emotions apparently under control, she released the statement, which described Neave as a 'gentle, brave and unassuming man' and 'one of freedom's warriors'. She went on BBC Television's Nationwide to say: 'Some devil has got him. They must never, never, never be allowed to triumph. They must never prevail.'

Security arrangements were immediately tightened. Speeches to be delivered by Thatcher, Whitelaw and Pym were made all-ticket events, at the request of the police, and searches of the audiences were organised at the entrances. The itinerary was unaffected. A Saatchi and Saatchi newspaper advertisement and poster which had been due to run that weekend was cancelled on grounds of bad taste and never used. Over a picture of a liner, the caption asked voters whether they would buy tickets for another cruise from a captain who had driven his ship onto the rocks and sunk it.

The travelling circus, nicknamed 'Thatchertours' by the accompanying journalists, went on the road. The journalists found themselves comfortably travelled but frustrated in their search for hard news. The Thatcher team was constantly on duty and consisted of Janet Young and David Wolfson, who were in overall charge and in touch with

Central Office, Derek Howe, David Boddy in charge of the press corps, and two Central Office officials, Roger Boaden (who had run Heath's election tours in 1970 and 1974) and Michael Dobbs, who looked after details of timing and briefing. On nights when the team returned to London so that Thatcher could be at the headquarters press conference the following morning, there would be late-night tactics sessions ranging from discussions with Guinevere Tilney on the next day's clothes to marathon speech-writing conferences. Mornings would start with meetings coordinated by another Central Office official, Michael Portillo, to brief Thatcher and that day's selection of ministers for the morning press conference or on any issues requiring immediate reply which had arisen the previous evening or in that morning's papers. The Conservative press conferences were very much better attended than the Labour version a few yards away in Smith Square, although the difference in numbers was largely accounted for by the number of foreign journalists who wanted to see the first woman likely to be Prime Minister. She put on an aggressive display, at one moment in an early conference imploring the audience to ask Whitelaw a question and then proceeding to answer it herself.

The selection of tour stops had been chosen with news pictures, both moving and still, in mind. In contrast to Callaghan's diffidence when presented with garlands of pound notes, bunches of flowers and invitations to play snooker, the opportunity to *do* things suited Thatcher. It also provided a wide selection of newsworthy images. At Eye in Suffolk, the entourage came across a calf which had been born the night before: Thatcher posed for almost 15 minutes with the animal, satisfying the photographers. 'You're going to have a dead calf on your hands in a minute,' Denis murmured. She was photographed using a sewing machine, sweeping a floor and rushing round a chocolate factory. She used her proven ability at the walkabout to good effect, although in her case it is really a talkabout. She has a consistent ability to relax a conversation by talking as if the entire hubbub roundabout is not happening, and by the deft use of inverterate curiosity about domestic detail.

The first major speech of the campaign was held until the end of the second week in April and delivered to a packed audience in Cardiff Town Hall, which Callaghan failed to fill a few days later. It was preceded by the routine agonies and indecisions of speech-writing, which persisted until the last moment. Millar, as always, was the most effective calmer of fears: he persuaded his leading lady, who was convinced until almost the moment that she rose to deliver it that it 'wasn't quite me', that indeed it was. The speech went after 'soft' moderate Labour voters and tried to link Callaghan's 'steady as you go' approach with remorseless decline and mediocrity. The peroration concluded: 'The Old Testament prophets did not say "Brothers, I want a consensus." They said: "This is my faith, This is what I passionately believe. If you believe it too, then come with me".'

Callaghan was a formidable opponent, for all his unenergetic campaigning and the feeling that he radiated that he had already lost unless his opponent committed electoral suicide. Briefed by the head of his Downing Street policy unit, Bernard Donoughue, he relentlessly repeated three questions on the Conservative manifesto: how many jobs would their policies lose? where was the money to come from for tax cuts? how were prices to be kept down? Private polls taken during the campaign by both parties suggested that these had been an effective approach and that Callaghan's ruthless control of the Labour manifesto and election machine stilled Labour's doctrinal tensions long enough so that they did not show to disadvantage. Voices in the Labour camp had pressed for a gloves-off campaign aimed largely at Thatcher herself, although Callaghan rejected the idea; Tory tacticians were surprised by the end of the campaign that Labour had not chosen to make more of their leader's inexperience.

Both sides, and particularly the Conservatives, felt vulnerable to the Liberals. The Central Office private polls contained some clues which pointed to the long-dreaded Liberal 'revival' which would take more from the Conservatives than from Labour. Personal relations between Thatcher and Callaghan had always been courteous but she had always been frosty towards David Steel. She regularly refused to countenance discussion on any possibility of pacts with the Liberals. In opposition, papers had been written analysing the options for a party after a hung election, but they had not been shown to her for fear of the consequences. She was hostile to Steel (who describes a Privy Council ceremony in late 1977 at which she greeted him with 'forced icy charm' and they exchanged 'meaningless pleasantries about the Christmas recess') because there was no tactical reason to conceal her ideological distaste. 'Not only does she hate socialists,' one of her Shadow Cabinet colleagues said, 'which I do too, but she hates social democrats as well. She thinks they are all the same. Thatcher made no secret of the fact that she thought Steel and Pardoe social democrats — ergo collectivist, ergo enemies.'

There were campaign panics. The election had barely begun when the *Daily Telegraph* carried a piece by Jock Bruce-Gardyne spelling out in painful detail exactly what cutting public expenditure would mean. Thatcher, advised quite exaggeratedly that it could 'cost her the election', was furious: 'After all we've done for him!' she was heard to explode. The article had in fact been written before the confidence vote had been called; the damage was healed after the election. (There was a subsequent rift and reconciliation when a private letter from Bruce-Gardyne to his ex-colleague Samuel Brittan at the *Financial Times* was leaked during the Falklands. He was dismissive about whether governments go to war over principles.)

The other early fluff was more eagerly seized on by Labour, which printed a huge number of leaflets on the subject and built it into the standard speech notes for party election meetings. A Mrs Evelyn Collingwood, living ironically enough, in Erith, Kent, where Denis Thatcher used to work, wrote a 'chatty' note to Thatcher to let her know what ordinary people were thinking about her plan to sell council houses. Matthew Parris, concluding a reply on her behalf, wrote: 'I hope that you will not think me too blunt if I say that it may be well that your council accommodation is unsatisfactory, but considering the fact that you have been unable to buy your own accommodation, you are lucky to have been given something which the rest of us are paying for out of our taxes.' Once revealed, the letter was disowned by Thatcher, who apologised. Labour audiences heard it repeated throughout the campaign.

The tour managers faced two worries with Thatcher: that she would exhaust herself, and that her voice would go before the end of the campaign. She did not admit to tiredness and appeared to enjoy campaigning. Janet Young remarked to her one morning that she had been glad to get to sleep the night before, only to hear from Thatcher that she had been too excited to sleep and had read Aristotle for an hour. Her voice showed signs of failing on the last weekend, but just stayed the course. Thorneycroft banned smoking at meetings which she attended and tried to prevent her from talking while travelling between stops. Two late opinion polls created alarm: a MORI poll in the *Daily Express* gave the Conservatives a 3% lead and NOP poll in the *Daily Mail* gave Labour a 0.7% lead. Both front pages caused unpleasant shocks: the MORI poll was in some ways worse, because it was more plausible and might have suggested a falling Conservative lead at a time when Callaghan appeared to be making up ground. The NOP poll, which Saatchi's quickly advised had been taken over a weekend and was therefore liable to greater inaccuracy than usual, was harder to believe.

In the end, the lead over Labour was 7.2% and its decisive margin was obvious from early in the evening of 3 May. The Thatcher family spent a rare evening together before driving to Finchley at about 10 p.m. She nearly doubled her majority, but failed to reach the five-figure margin she had been hoping for. She drove to Central Office, where the media had been equipped with 800 cans of beer to sit out the night, to find the Australian Prime Minister Malcolm Fraser on the phone, wanting to deliver congratulations. She thanked him, but cautiously. She left at 5 a.m. and returned to Flood Street, which was by now under siege from crowds and cameras. The crowd sang the

Conservative campaign song 'Blue is the colour, Maggie's the name.' At dawn, she announced, 'I feel a sense of change and an aura of calm.' Shortly afterwards, the Conservative seat total passed the crucial majority figure of 318. At 2.45 in the afternoon, she and Denis went to Buckingham Palace. Denis remained downstairs while his wife went to the first floor audience room where the kissing hands ceremony is held. At the same time, Callaghan was saying at Transport House, 'For a woman to occupy that office is a tremendous moment in our history.'

Ronald Millar had recommended St Francis to bring the right magnanimous touch to the proceedings as she entered Downing Street. Asked the inevitable and obvious questions by the massed ranks behind the crush barriers, she delivered the lines:

'Where there is discord, may we bring harmony.
Where there is error, may we bring truth.
Where there is doubt, may we bring faith.
Where there is despair, may we bring hope.'

As it happened, when political scientists began analysing the full results, it became clear that the election had accented regional and sectional differences as never before. The Conservatives had hit most of the targets they had aimed for: skilled manual workers had defected to the Conservatives, and especially heavily in the West Midlands (much of that vote was to travel back towards the centre in the form of the newly-founded SDP two years later). Their 43-seat majority had been won by a highly concentrated vote. Their 43.9% share of the vote was the smallest for a majority party since 1922, although Labour's share, down to 37.7%, had fallen to its lowest since 1931.

The archetypal Thatcher voter was white, lived in the south-east, belonged — in the widest sense of the word — to the middle class, worked in a professional or skilled manual job and did not live in an area of high unemployment or an inner city. A constituency like Streatham would be heartland where a Thatcher-led party would expect to do outstandingly well. The Conservative vote has risen higher there since the 1979 election than anywhere else in Britain.

Another seat in this mould which showed a pronounced Conservative swing was Basildon — until 1979 a safe Labour seat. Harvey Proctor, the Conservative candidate, turned a Labour majority of 10,000 into a Conservative majority of over 5,000. The explanation may have been connected with the fact that he held hard-line racist views on immigration and that owner-occupancy had been increasing much faster there than in the rest of the country: in 1971, 39% of the housing was private and in 1981 53%. By contrast, seats with high immigrant or black populations showed pro-Labour swings.

Although she was later to confront what she saw as the problem of the civil service not being responsive enough to the wishes of their political masters, she turned herself over to the Cabinet Secretary from the moment she arrived through the door of Number Ten. She was eager to follow the traditional protocol and happy to accept the existing structure of administration surrounding the Prime Minister. Several of those close to her came to regret this compliance, hoping for a radical departure from the accepted pattern.

By the time that the Thatcher team set foot in Downing Street, the instant transitions behind the front door which effect a truly rapid transfer of power were already under way. Only two junior members of Callaghan's personal staff were left in the building, supervising the bagging and labelling of his papers which were later collected by John Lewis pantechnicons and taken to the Callaghan farm in Sussex. She was immediately introduced to her private office, headed by the grey-haired Principal Private Secretary, Ken Stowe, who had been due to move from Downing Street some months before, but had agreed to stay until the election period was over. She had already met the Cabinet Secretary, Sir John Hunt, who had made the routine call on the Leader of the Opposition paid by the Cabinet Secretary during an election to take guidance on what an incoming administration will want to do quickly in its first few days. Hunt had been startled to be told that she thought that the Cabinet Office was much too large and that when she was in office it would be required to confine itself to its proper role of taking the minutes at Cabinet meetings and at its committees. She added that she only wanted decisions recorded and not the debates themselves. Neither instruction was ultimately put into practice.

Cabinet appointments were the most urgent business of the weekend: her principal advisers were William Whitelaw and Humphrey Atkins. She had been under pressure from her more hawkish advisers to stack her team with loyalists or as she had put it the previous February: 'One way is to have in it people who represent all the different viewpoints within the party ... The other way is to have in it only the people who want to go in the direction in which every instinct tells me we have to go ... As Prime Minister, I couldn't waste time having any internal arguments.'

But this did not really describe her thinking, which was again ambivalent. She had, for example, thought for some time that Peter Walker should return to the Cabinet. His rudeness to and about her had excluded him from any chance of Shadow Cabinet membership, but he had approached her for a session on the party's position in late 1977 and she had listened to his reservations for two hours. A short time later, she had travelled to his home and constituency in Worcestershire and stayed the night while extending the discussion. He returned to the front bench as Minister of Agriculture.

The group of hard-liners around Thatcher were later to draw the moral from the selection of the Cabinet that at the height of her powers, when she had all the Prime Minister's patronage and public goodwill at her disposal, she missed her chance to design her government without the braking mechanism which the traditional liberals would represent. There appear to have been several reasons. She may have thought that the Cabinet would be as easy to by-pass as the Shadow Cabinet had become. She may have assessed the risks of leaving heavyweight dissidents on the back benches with time on their hands as too great. She must certainly have been influenced by the fact that with the exception of being able to staff the Treasury with like-minded economic specialists, those most loyal to her were short of experience. It was a problem which began to solve itself only during the life of the Government, with the promotion to Cabinet rank

of men like Norman Tebbit. Excepting Tebbit from this
generalisation, one minister appointed to the Cabinet that
weekend observed that Thatcher respects the ministers she
disagrees with and tends not to respect those who agree
with her. Her head and heart seem to have pulled in
opposite directions.

Although Thatcher and Heath had never been reconciled,
he let it be known before the election that he would be
prepared to serve under her. It was assumed that if she was
to offer him a post it would be as Foreign Secretary. After
the election, a despatch rider was sent to where he was
staying in the country telling him that Lord Carrington had
been appointed. Heath was disappointed but not surprised.
He told his friends: you were too optimistic. Heath was also
considered when Thatcher came to consider the
replacement for Peter Jay as ambassador in Washington,
but it came to nothing.

In Downing Street Bernard Donoughue was so confident
that his successor as head of the policy unit would be Adam
Ridley, that he left him a note and a bottle of whisky as he
moved out. Ridley himself was so confident that he began to
move his belongings, only to be suddenly translated to the
Treasury a few days later and replaced by John Hoskyns
who was accompanied by Norman Strauss. At the
Treasury, they were inspecting the figures, which were to
reveal some formidable difficulties in preparing an
immediate budget.

CHAPTER TEN

Economy

When Margaret Thatcher became Prime Minister, by far the most important issue which she had to deal with was the British economy. It was her belief that a determined approach to economic policy — the application of a rigorous monetary policy — would solve several problems at once. Few shared her faith in the new economics either inside the Treasury or, more importantly, inside the Cabinet. Overcoming their resistance to change would be time consuming and would need a unique approach to Cabinet government. Her opponents from within argued that her strict monetarism would lead to civil disorder as increasing numbers of people were put out of work. And, with the riots of summer 1981, the prophecy appeared to be coming true. They had guessed wrong. The public's appetite for austerity appeared to be closer to her own proscription than to the political judgment of her more liberal colleagues. However, it turned out that many of the bankruptcies and much of the unemployment endured had been unnecessary. Before the size of the error had been completely understood, she had purged her Cabinet of many of her opponents and found herself masterminding a military campaign in the South Atlantic.

On winning the general election, Thatcher was acutely aware of the experience of the previous Conservative administration. Like most political leaders, she was guided in her actions by a need to break away from the quality and tone of her immediate predecessor. As Callaghan wished to distance his Prime Ministership from what he understood to be the debilitating pragmatism and unashamed political gimmickry of Wilson, so Thatcher was intimidated by the memory of Edward Heath's 1970-74 Government, which she had so eagerly damned as soon as it came to an end.

It was economic policy which was to bring about the change in Britain she wished for. Thatcher is neither a trained economist, nor an original thinker, yet it was her ambition always to become the first Chancellor of the Exchequer. She had encouraged Heath to make her Shadow Chancellor in 1974 and had been content to deputize for Robert Carr. In her four brief contributions to the debate on the 1974 Budget in the Chamber she depended for the fine print of her tax expertise upon those who had made it their job to study and understand such matters – Nicholas Ridley, David Howell, Peter Rees and John Cope.

Although she was happy to support Heath's interventionist policies until the election defeat in 1974, her instincts were toward a set of policies which confounded the post-war Tory tradition and she found that the economic alternative offered in monetarism, notably by Professors F.A. Hayek and Milton Friedman, matched those political needs. She met – and impressed – both Hayek, in 1976, and Friedman, in 1977.

Post-war Conservatism was based upon the principle born of political pragmatism that many aspects of the post-war welfare state consensus should be embraced as Conservative policy because they were so popular with the electorate that any party which denied the need for such reforms or considered them to be undesirable would be so far from the wishes of the public as to exclude them from electoral success and, therefore, from government. This assumption had been the basis of 'Butskellism', the unwritten pact between the Labour and Conservative parties since the war which meant that the reforms mostly established in wartime, principally instigated by Lord Keynes and Lord Beveridge, should not be undermined. The parameters of party political debate in the post-war years had been fixed and the main differences between the parties had been restricted to defining exactly where the boundary line between private and state industry should lie in a mixed economy which was agreed by both sides. There had been some dissenters from this agreement, mostly on the Labour side, and it was from the Labour side that the threat to the consensus was usually perceived by Conservative politicians and political commentators. The Tories who rejected the consensus were a small group of burnt-out cases which had been discounted by every Conservative leader. The only exception to this in the mainstream of British politics was Enoch Powell, who had left the Conservative Party in 1974 and who had persistently tried to introduce a number of issues — most notably the limitation of immigration and the removal of the government from the regulation of the economy — which the leaders of both Labour and Conservative parties had declared off-limits.

In the reappraisal of her belief which her friendship with Keith Joseph and her association with the Centre for Policy Studies entailed, Thatcher came to understand that her convictions lay outside the consensus. 'Freedom and Reality', a collection of speeches delivered during the sixties by Enoch Powell, published in 1969, she considered to be her bible. In it, Powell considered the basis of political freedom and came to the conclusion that only a free market economy could provide true liberation. Nationalisation should be halted, then reversed. There had been a ratchet effect in operation which had meant that the state had become increasingly embroiled in commercial affairs in which it should hold no part. As a direct consequence, the state had become entwined in people's lives to an intrusive degree, to the extent of stifling freedom. The solution was denationalisation. Thatcher agreed, but was conscious that the Heath Government had become involved against its stated wishes in the running of the economy as a means of limiting price inflation. She also believed that the trade unions were too strong and had, by employing their monopoly provision of labour, increased British wage rates so that British industry was uncompetitive on the world market. Her instincts demanded that the state's influence in economic affairs be rolled back, that trade union power should be sharply diminished but, at the same time, that inflation should be reduced as a first priority. Under a conventional understanding of economics, the three wishes were incompatible.

There was an economic theory, however, which was

growing in fashionability during the seventies, that would allow all three to be granted simultaneously: monetarism. The quantity theory of money was primarily a nineteenth century economic dogma which had fallen into disuse as the twentieth century progressed and Keynesianism took root. After the Second World War, however, it reestablished itself in Chicago, led by Milton Friedman. Because of the economic turmoil in the capitalist world following the massive oil price rises in the early seventies, Friedman's proscriptions became popular among some economists, journalists and politicians. His theories seemed to answer many questions which confounded the Keynesian economists. His solutions were plausible. Above all – and without undervaluing the sophistication of thought which led to them – his theories were simple and could be simply understood by the layman. Friedman's notions could be understood by many newcomers to economics because little knowledge of conventional economics was necessary to understand them. Put simply – and there is no more complex way of explaining it – Friedman contended that: 'Inflation occurs when the quantity of money rises appreciably more rapidly than output, and the more rapid the rise in the quantity of money per unit of output, the greater the rate of inflation.' Although Denis Healey, Labour's Chancellor, after the advent of the International Monetary Fund loan to Britain in 1977 had applied a more strict control on the money supply, he considered it only part of the weaponry in his armoury and also depended upon more conventional fiscal measures, and political measures such as an incomes policy. But Friedman claimed more for his theory than the way it had been employed by Healey. He maintained that such things as incomes policies were irrelevant to reducing inflation and that keeping the money supply in order would reduce inflation on its own after a short time lag. Thereby, governments need not become involved in the miseries of wage control, which was, in any case, none of their business. Professor Hayek noted, however, that unions, through their monopoly supply of labour, might try to force governments to increase the money supply to offset unemployment.

Thatcher was convinced by the logic of monetarism, as was Keith Joseph. The roots of Thatcher's monetarism are mysterious. She was an admirer of Powell's and had noted the reasons that he gave for resigning with the Chancellor, Thorneycroft, in 1957: they had claimed that Macmillan was asking them to condone living above their means, which would be thoroughly irresponsible and would increase inflation, Powell had delivered in a speech at Halifax in December 1957, saying: 'How tempting to satisfy these ambitions (for increased government spending) at a greater rate than the nation was willing to make possible out of its production by taxation and savings! How simple and delightful to meet them by increasing the supply of money!' By 1968, Thatcher had become convinced of the importance of the money supply and had spoken of it in her Conservative Political Centre lecture in a curiously specific reference, for the fashion for monetarism which most commentators have associated with Thatcher and Joseph was that encouraged by Friedman and Hayek. Yet neither became popular until the seventies in Britain. It is more likely that their monetarism stemmed from an association with the maverick Powell. Indeed, in Joseph's rapid rise to ministerial prominence during the seventies, most described him as a Powellite in economic matters. Friedman, however, provided corroborative evidence. And there was another advantage. Friedman's solution answered many of their incompatible demands. The main means of reducing the supply of money in the economy – exactly what the money supply consists of or how you measure it were practical difficulties which would arise later – was to reduce the Public Sector Borrowing Requirement – the difference between the government's expenditure and revenue – by cutting public expenditure and restricting the amount that the banks could borrow. Thus there was a sound reason to reduce the state's contribution to a whole range of goods and services in which the government should, in any case, have no part. Here was a panacea, advertised by its founder as such, which combined two elusive goals: inflation could be beaten by withdrawing the state from people's lives, overcoming the creeping state socialism which had progressed steadily since the war. There was also a solid Conservative precedent: the resignations of Thorneycroft and Powell in 1957.

There were drawbacks to Thatcher's conversion to monetarism. First, belief in the theory was not shared by many of her senior colleagues. Indeed, many of them had made it clear that they thought it was nonsense. Second, there was a price for reducing the money supply and one which was easy to predict. A sharp restriction on bank lending and a sharp reduction in public spending would cause a severe economic recession, forcing bankruptcies and large-scale unemployment. She inherited in 1975 a party which was still committed to ensuring full employment. As the world economy shrank during the seventies, unemployment in Britain was already higher than at any time since the war. But the application of monetarism would send that figure soaring, which would endanger the Conservatives' electoral chances.

As Prime Minister, she was determined to try out monetarism — an experiment which no major nation had attempted. Such was the hostility from within the Shadow Cabinet, that she ensured in 1979 when forming her first real Cabinet that those opponents were kept well away from economic policy. She took for her Chancellor of the Exchequer Sir Geoffrey Howe, a man sympathetic to the arguments of monetarism and a lawyer, like herself, who would take a brief. This dramatic departure from the post-war consensus was so important to her that she would have to work with the Chancellor on her lap. Sir Geoffrey had the requisite doggedness and thick skin to endure both the battering that might occur as unemployment rose and the firm control of the Prime Minister to keep him on course. After that significant appointment, she needed a loyal, committed Treasury team, led by John Biffen. In the key position of Secretary of State for Industry, she placed Sir Keith Joseph, who would be expected to resist all requests from lame ducks for government aid. It was assumed that the tightening of money would force the most inefficient companies either to streamline their operation or go bankrupt. John Nott, another loyal believer, was made Secretary of State for Trade. The only doubter allowed near the sharp end of the economic policy was James Prior, the Employment Secretary, who would have to deal with the trade union reaction and the fast rising unemployment. It would not prove a comfortable position.

The rest of the Cabinet appointments kept at arms' length from Thatcher those who believed in government intervention in the economy. Sir Ian Gilmour, who was to prove the most vocal public critic, was Lord Privy Seal, acting as deputy to Lord Carrington, the Foreign Secretary, who also doubted the wisdom of monetarism. Peter Walker, a considerable opponent and an articulate critic, was effectively banished to Brussels, as the Agriculture Secretary, where he would monitor Britain's contribution to the Common Agricultural Policy. Francis Pym was at Defence; Michael Heseltine, like Pym, a loner, but with grave reservations about the economic policy, was at Environment. Lord Hailsham, a stalwart of the Butskellite Tory tradition, was Lord Chancellor. And there was Willie Whitelaw as Home Secretary. His patrician Tory notions put him among the Cabinet opponents to monetarism but his ignorance of economics of any kind left him unable to argue his case.

From the beginning, the Cabinet was divided. Although at first the divisions were concealed, it was clear to the interventionists that they were being excluded from formulating economic policy. They hoped that the force of circumstances would argue their case for them. Not only would the policy be seen not to work — it was based, they argued, on a falacious cure-all theory which made no sense — but the political consequences of the misery that would be caused would force the Prime Minister to return to conventional methods. Thatcher was open about her hostility to her internal opponents. Borrowing public school slang, she dismissed the bleeding hearts around her as 'wets'. She sharply divided in her mind those of her colleagues who were 'on my side' and those who were 'unreliable'. Her Parliamentary Private Secretary, Ian Gow, divided the Cabinet, and then the Party, between 'heroes' and 'reptiles' – a nomenclature snapped up by Denis Thatcher.

The first Budget was on 12 June, 1979. At the meeting which informed the Cabinet of what was in store there were a number of groans. Although Cabinets do not always discuss the general direction of economic policy, this time the omission was more serious, because the policy to be followed was so radical and contentious. What is more, the Prime Minister knew how much hostility there was to it. The Cabinet opponents expressed their displeasure, but there was nothing to be done, except coded speeches, Cabinet leaks and as much delay as ministerial authority allowed them. The convention of Cabinet collective responsibility meant that they could not express that displeasure publicly. Geoffrey Howe proposed a cut in public expenditure of £3,500 million, which went against his initial judgement. He had, at first, proposed a cut of only £500 million, but, when he had presented his package to Thatcher, she turned him round on his heel and told him to find more. This was unusual. Usually, a Chancellor will be trusted by a Prime Minister to recommend what is suitable within a shared understanding of what should be done. Thatcher was, from the first, determined to push harder and faster than Sir Geoffrey's more timid temperament would allow. The money would be found from: a sale of public assets, rolling back the public sector; a sharp cut in existing spending; and an unprecedented rise in the level of Value Added Tax to fifteen per cent. Under conventional economic logic, such an increase in VAT would not only be considered to be inflationary in itself, but would fuel wage demands, thus leading to higher inflation. By monetarist logic, this was not so. Only increasing the size of the money supply relative to the nation's output caused inflation. By reducing the amount of money in the economy by reducing public spending while, at the same time, encouraging the Bank of England to trim bank lending by pushing the minimum lending rate to fourteen per cent, inflation would actually be reduced. There was a small income tax cut – 'to encourage incentives to work' – and a maximum taxation level was fixed at 60 per cent.

Faith in the free market, which would establish a true equilibrium level for prices of goods and labour and a more. 'natural' level of unemployment, was further demonstrated by the swift ending of pay, price and dividend controls – imposed by the Labour Government to keep inflation figures down – and the lifting of all foreign exchange controls. Wage demands began to rise increasingly steeply, as did the exchange rate for the pound, bolstered by the inflow of foreign money eager to take advantage of the high interest rates. A high pound was making British goods more expensive and exporting companies began to feel the pinch. Thatcher was moving boldly and quickly: what she called a 'break for freedom'.

The boldness of her approach did not take into account the slowing effect of internal dissent, nor did her instinct for running things herself fit happily with the conventional operation of Cabinet government. Under the model of Prime Ministerial government established by Attlee, and followed, more or less, by every Prime Minister since, the Prime Minister is no more than primus inter pares and it has been assumed that it is necessary for him to carry a majority of the Cabinet with him on all major planks of policy. There are no votes in Cabinet, and Prime Ministers traditionally asked the opinion of each Minister in turn, then summed up the collective Cabinet view. This did not mean that every major issue was decided at the Cabinet table. Every Prime Minister has attempted to settle the major issues before a decision comes to Cabinet. But the Cabinet has remained the principal policy-endorsing body and any Prime Minister who did not carry the day in Cabinet would be considered to have lost the confidence of his colleagues. Sometimes, as in the Cabinet discussions over the 1977 IMF loan, Cabinet meetings have been essential policy-forging meetings in which genuine, substantial issues are decided. In Thatcher's Cabinet, the opposite was the case. With such a large majority of her Cabinet opposed to the dogma which governed her economic policy, she kept discussions as far away from the Cabinet as possible, never raising the central direction of the policy at Cabinet level.

The core of Cabinet government – that a majority of the Cabinet is needed to maintain the principal elements of the government's policy – was intentionally avoided.

She ignored the well-established precedents for Prime Ministerial chairing of Cabinet meetings in favour of a more dirigiste approach. She would sound the views of each colleague in turn, but would argue loudly with each who dare raise a dissenting voice. Although it is true that she enjoys an argument, she does not enjoy losing them, particularly at a full Cabinet meeting. The distance between the Cabinet and the Cabinet committee which formulate economic policy – the 'E' Committee, which used to meet each Tuesday – was substantial and there was considerable resentment among Cabinet ministers who had views on economic policy but who were excluded from the policy-making, decision-taking process. Many times the discussion of an unpopular measure would be batted by ministers one by one in succession around the Cabinet table until it gradually became clear that a majority of the Cabinet were opposed to the Prime Minister. Normally, the sounding process would stop at the half-way mark, at Lord Carrington, who rarely put up strong opposition to her in the full glare of a Cabinet meeting, preferring instead the behind-the-scene chats at which he would get his own way more effectively. In Cabinet, when the conversation stopped at him, on economic affairs, Lord Carrington would allow an old-fashioned look to make his point for him.

The direction of economic policy was discussed eventually by a back-door method when ministers resisting the public expenditure cuts imposed upon them by the Treasury brought their case to the full Cabinet as a means of appeal. Even so, this meant that the debate was still limited. First, only spending ministers were able to raise the subject. Many of the most vociferous opponents of the economic policies had no reason to raise the matter themselves as they did not master a large-spending department. The debate was limited, also, because the resistance to cuts meant arguing in favour of the threatened services or capital investment. The best line of defence of these threatened services was to point out how politically and, ultimately, electorally important they were. To question the logic of the whole framework of economic policy within which the cuts were needed was to be talking out of turn. It was always difficult to argue from the particular — the proposed cut — back to the general — the monetarist base of the economic policy. Questioning the foundations of that policy, the need to reduce the PSBR, seemed a far-fetched way of defending, say, nursery schools in the north.

However, despite the obvious irritation of the Prime Minister, the Cabinet did get to discuss the direction of economic policy. Perhaps the most vocal and passionate critic was James Prior, who, as Employment Secretary, was acutely aware of the effect of the policy in rapidly rising unemployment and the destruction of industries which depended upon a high level of borrowing. Peter Walker also argued strongly against the root of the policy and backed his arguments with a barrage of figures. Michael Heseltine was adept at resisting cuts, although he was not critical of the need for cuts per se. Mark Carlisle was in a difficult position. As Education Secretary, he was working in a department which Thatcher thought she knew well, although Shirley Williams, the Labour Education Secretary, had streamlined the department so that many of the figures which the Prime Minister quoted in Cabinet argument were no longer pertinent. Lord Carrington's methods were subtle and concealed. Although he had not made a pact with the Prime Minister that he would keep out of the economy if she would keep out of foreign affairs — a generally believed rumour — he brought his influence to bear in private, preferring to exert his easy charm to get his own way. All the same, it was as much as he could do to contain the wilful Prime Minister and, when others asked him to speak on their behalf, he pleaded with justification that he had his hands full converting her instincts about foreign affairs into a more practical form of foreign policy. Lord Soames was opposed to the policy, as was Lord Hailsham. Ian Gilmour was intellectually opposed to monetarism and well able, on paper, to oppose its logic. But he was hampered by not having a budget to defend — Lord Carrington defended the

Foreign Office from assault. He made his feelings felt nonetheless.

By February 1980, it became generally known that the Cabinet was divided. Gilmour made a speech in Cambridge which eloquently described the division between what he saw as true Conservatives, who had worked to build the welfare state, and those in the Government who were followers of economic liberalism, which he saw as a threat to political freedom because of its failure to create a sense of community. The views he held were not new; even the Prime Minister accused him of merely rehashing his old books. Yet it was evidence that a fundamental debate was taking place and that the two sides were far apart. In February, Milton Friedman and his wife, Rose, were in London and visited Thatcher at Downing Street for an hour, meeting there Sir Geoffrey Howe, John Biffen, Nigel Lawson of the Treasury, Patrick Jenkin, the Social Services Secretary, and Ian Gilmour.

The next month, March, Howe unveiled in his second budget his four-year strategy: the Medium-Term Financial Strategy. The money supply, as determined by M3, would be reduced progressively over the next four years. The main instrument would be to reduce the PSBR – meaning more public expenditure cuts – as a proportion of gross domestic product. It was to be easier said than done. The next three years were to provide a confusion of economic actions. One of the difficulties was that the measure taken as an indicator to live by – M3 – gradually lost its magic. As time went on, exactly what constituted the money supply was gradually widened from M3 – in itself a vague enough term, which fluctuated for no apparent reason – to a range of monetary indicators. Yet it was this measurement of money which was to guide the government's actions. Trade union leaders were meant to understand how much money could be expected by watching the increase – or decrease – in money in the economy and pitch a 'realistic' wage claim accordingly. Yet noone, not even the Chancellor, was able to say which indicators were apt, nor explain mysterious nature of their movement. Gradually it became clear, too, that constituents which made up the PSBR made it an inappropriate tool for calculating cuts in public expenditure. Many nationalised industries' investments were provided from that source, as were other elements of public spending which had little significance for determining wise reductions in the public sector. Also, each indicator was interlinked in a way which caused a spiral of recession. To reduce the supply of money, interest rates were held high, thus causing a curtailment in investment, the laying off of men from employment and the bankruptcy of firms, which, in turn, drastically reduced the GDP, thereby necessitating, by monetarist logic, a sharper cut in the PSBR so that the proportion of GDP which the PSBR represented was held low. Simultaneously, Britain had been overtaken by a world recession, thanks mainly to a doubling of the price of oil in 1979. This was to take a while to penetrate the world economy, and, it was argued, could help Britain, a net oil exporter. The strength of the pound, which had savagely affected British exports' competitivity, was thought by the Treasury to be due to the high price of British oil and they were divided as to what should be done about it. Also most significant was a wage explosion, caused by the indexation of wages in the public sector recommended by the Clegg Report, which Thatcher, before the general election, had promised to implement, whatever its findings. Many of her close advisers thought this was lunatic. David Howell said that it should be ignored, despite the promise. Sir John Hoskyns thought that she should come clean and admit that the promise had been an error and that the country could no longer afford the Report's findings. For both those reasons, Britain was plunged into recession. On top of this, Thatcher's policies of monetary containment were causing an added, deliberate level of recession. The speed of job loss and bankruptcies were unprecedented – and, as it was to turn out, quite unnecessary – and many in the Cabinet warned of electoral disaster and widespread civil disorder if the stern measures were continued.

Thatcher held firm. Despite criticism from all quarters, including the businessmen who traditionally funded the Conservatives and a large proportion of her Cabinet and back-benchers who passed on the anxiety expressed by party workers about the electoral chances for a party which had so proudly invited such apparent disaster, she appeared at the Conservative Party Conference at Brighton and declared her intention to resist the temptation to change her policy. Misquoting Christopher Fry in a speech whose most memorable line was penned by Ronald Millar, she said: 'The lady's not for turning'. She received her traditional standing ovation, yet many of her colleagues were contemplating how secure her position as leader was. The same month, October 1980, she recruited a personal economic adviser to keep her right about conflicting advice from the Treasury as to what should be done next. Professor Alan Walters, a British economist working at Johns Hopkins University, Maryland, was invited back to work in Downing Street, to counter what Thatcher suspected was treacherous advice coming from the Treasury and to bolster her argument.

When Parliament resumed, Cabinet meetings became increasingly fraught. The Treasury were proposing cuts worth £2000 million and there was fierce resistance from all outside the economic clique. There were weeks of fierce argument. Francis Pym was asked to cut £500 million from the Defence budget and refused, offering to tender his resignation rather than give way. (He was never to be forgiven.) He finally settled for cuts of £175 million. The Cabinet threw out a proposal to find a cut of £600 million by de-indexing social security benefits, including old-age pensions, which would mean a cut of three per cent in their value. Patrick Jenkin arrived at the Cabinet meeting with the text of a television interview, in which the Prime Minister had committed her Government never to cut old-age pensions. By mid-November, it became clear that only about half of the proposed cuts had been approved by Cabinet. Instead, the general view was that the money should be found from extra taxation, which ran counter to the Chancellor's attempt to master the money supply by cutting expenditure. His argument was that the price of protecting public spending was not only the taxation needed to support it, but the maintenance of a high interest rate, with the resulting damage to industry and employment that it entailed. Inflation would remain high. The rest of the Cabinet argued that if the proposed cuts were carried out, the Conservative Party would not win the second five-year term which the Prime Minister and the Chancellor had said was needed to turn the economy around, so that all the sacrifices would, in any case, be wasted.

The previous year, Thatcher had invented a new Cabinet committee, which quickly became known as the Star Chamber, to try to iron out the differences between the Treasury, demanding cuts, and the departmental ministers who must carry them out, before the proposals reached Cabinet. It was made up of two hard-line monetarists, Geoffrey Howe and John Biffen, and two moderates, Willie Whitelaw and Lord Soames. They met either at the Treasury or at Number 11, Downing Street and spending ministers would be summoned to make their case for exemptions. The committee would, occasionally, be bolstered by two further hardliners, Keith Joseph and John Nott. Towards the end of 1980, the committee had considered submissions from Francis Pym, resisting massive defence cuts; Patrick Jenkin, the Social Services Secretary; Mark Carlisle, at Education; and Michael Heseltine at Environment. It was the failure of this committee to provide a satisfactory compromise that meant that the Cabinet became the main forum for resisting the Treasury's demands.

At the end of November, the Chancellor announced a mini-budget – a particular tactical defeat for the Prime Minister, who had hoped to avoid the fine-tuning between traditional spring budgets which had been so much the trade mark of Denis Healey. It raised £3000 million: £1000 million from increased taxes on North Sea oil; £1000 million from National Insurance charge increases; and £1000 million – half of what the Treasury had hoped – from public spending cuts, including a one per cent cut in the real value of old-age pensions. Although the Government had carefully leaked the proposals, to minimise the reaction from their own backbenchers, there was widespread dissatisfaction among Conservatives. Edward Heath, who had kept his criticisms of Government economic policy outside Parliament, turned on the Prime Minister's monetarism. Cheered on by the Labour benches, he called for a complete change of course, lower interest rates and a devaluation of the pound. Thatcher and Howe sat expressionless on the Government front bench as Heath made his points. Enoch Powell then went on the attack. Their policies had been altogether too timorous and a further six or seven thousand million pounds would need to be raised from taxes to curb public spending, he said. Ian Gilmour delivered a second speech at Cambridge, openly attacking the passing fad of monetarism and appealing for a return of undivisive, national Conservatism. Norman St John Stevas, who had, throughout the Cabinet wrangling, combined a sceptical view of the miseries of monetarism with a running line of quips, maintained his usual flippancy. If the Government found itself squashed between Heath and Powell, then it must be on the right lines, he argued. He was not rewarded for his trouble.

Stevas had been an unlikely ally for Thatcher. Conspicuously defecting from the Heath camp during the leadership election, he had become a licensed fool to the Thatcherites, protected from the intolerance displayed by many right-wing Tory backbenchers who despised his dandyish, effete manner, by the lady herself, whom he nick-named the Leaderene. A string of similar nicknames followed for each of the Cabinet ministers. He was able to articulate his criticisms of monetarism through barbed wit. By the end of 1980, it was wearing thin. When it was reported to her that Stevas had described her, jokingly, as 'The Immaculate Misconception', he was a marked man. At the very beginning of the new year, 1981, Thatcher embarked on her first ministerial shuffle. Stevas was the most prominent victim. Angus Maude retired and was given a knighthood. Reg Prentice, the former Labour Cabinet minister, one of Thatcher's favourite converts, resigned through ill-health. There was nothing particularly ideological about the changes – any attempt to pick off the weaker members of the Cabinet opposition might have sparked off a full revolt – but she drew in reinforcements, in the shape of Leon Brittan, to the Treasury, a committed, articulate monetarist, brother to the *Financial Times* house monetarist, Sam Brittan; and Norman Fowler, the Thatcher loyalist, to Transport. Another important reason for Stevas's departure was to make way for Francis Pym, who was made Leader of the House in his place, so that John Nott could take over at Defence and deliver the cuts which Pym refused to implement.

There was still strong pressure on the tight group of Government ministers who ruled the economic policy. It was revealed that the crucial 'E' committee, chaired by the Prime Minister herself, which determined key economic policy decisions, was no longer being held each week on a Tuesday because of persistent leaks. No such meetings had been held for five weeks and policy was now discussed less formally behind closed doors in Downing Street. Francis Pym, who had proved so stubborn in beating off Treasury assaults upon the Defence budget, was given the uncomfortable job of promoting the economic policy to the nation. His first task was to explain a huge draught of money to prop up British Steel — a cash transfusion sanctioned by Keith Joseph, the non-interventionist Industry Secretary. Leyland had also been granted funds in the mini-budget, part of a package to nationalized industries of £620 million. At one stage, a delegation from the Institute of Directors went to see Pym to complain about the presentation of government policy. He told them that he had little faith in the economic policy. Free from Cabinet collective responsibility, St John Stevas urged the Government to reflate to reduce unemployment, before it went totally out of control. The Conservatives were feeling the pinch in more ways than one: the launch of the Social Democratic Party, under Roy Jenkins, was seen by many outside the Thatcher circle as an immediate electoral threat, unless the Government could be persuaded to change its economic policies.

A fierce debate broke out in the Cabinet over public pay. Although, in theory at least, there was no such thing as wage inflation, it became clear that, despite ministerial exhortations to workers to ask for less, the public spending targets were nonsensical so long as the trade unions in the public sector managed to maintain high annual wage

increases. Walters and Hoskyns did some simple
calculations and came to the conclusion that in order to
avoid the previous year's massive 20 per cent increase in
public sector pay, a realistically small pay increase should
be allowed. The previous year, an initial target figure of 14
per cent had been pushed up to 20. Walters and Hoskyns
came to the conclusion that, to remain within spending
targets, the total public sector wage bill could only rise by
six per cent. The Cabinet dissidents thought the figure
laughable and, instead, suggested a more modest decrease —
say to 13 per cent, with a little slippage. Walters and
Hoskyns held firm and convinced Howe and Thatcher, who
decided to stand firm at six per cent, whatever the outcome.
Thus started a series of painful public sector strikes, of
which perhaps the most anguished for the Cabinet was the
Civil Service dispute, which had extra repercussions on the
economy though the halting of tax revenues. Soames was
vehement from the very beginning against such a tight
public pay target, then said early on in the dispute that the
affair could be settled if he was allowed to relax by a half a
per cent. Thatcher and Howe would not have it and a
punishing dispute dragged on for months. Eventually the
Government was victorious, slipping only by Soames's half
a per cent, which allowed him to bemoan the Prime
Minister's stubbornness for pressing on with an unnecessary
and bitterly fought dispute. He was not to be forgiven for
being right about the half a per cent.

Even monetarists were beginning to worry about the
Government's difficulties. In order to find out what was
going wrong Alfred Sherman asked Alan Walters if there
was anyone who could help and, as a result, the Centre for
Policy Studies invited Professor Jurg Niehans, from Berne
University, whom Thatcher had visited in Switzerland the
previous summer, to come to Britain and inspect the figures
and tell them where the mistakes were being made. Niehans
came to a swift conclusion and, in February 1981, the
report was ready. It was a damning document which made
clear that Howe had got many things wrong and had been
encouraging quite unnecessary misery among British
companies and their dwindling work forces. Niehans said

that the monetary policy was excessively tight and the extraordinarily high interest rates were attracting 'hot' money into London and causing a high pound. He declared that North Sea oil was not the reason for the high level of sterling. The overtight monetary policy was thus causing unnecessary bankruptcies and unemployment. The CPS Niehans Report was so damning that it was declared too politically embarrassing to publish and it was kept secret. Alan Walters and John Hoskyns, Thatcher's chief policy adviser, agreed with Niehans. Howe, Terry Burns, the chief economic adviser to the Treasury, and others such as Alan Budd, Peter Middleton and Patrick Minford, did not. Hoskyns provided an abridged version of the Niehans Report for Thatcher and she, too, could not bring herself to agree with it and see that she was wrong. But the proof of his diagnosis was in subsequent action. First, despite opposition, Thatcher came round to Walters' view, suggested by Niehans, that too narrow a range of monetary measures was being used which ignored bank deposits and that a monetary base system would prove more effective. Second, a relaxation of the tight monetary control was coupled with a tightening of fiscal measures, which had been left lax because they were considered relatively unimportant.

The Niehans Report came at the time of preparations for the 1981 Budget and Howe was being given conflicting advice. Walters, Hoskyns and the CPS were anxious about the medium-term financial strategy, because there was little chance of the Government meeting its proscriptions. They suggested a massively deflationary Budget which would remove £6,000 million from the economy. They argued that if the (ill-named) strategy meant anything, then it must be stuck to, and there was no point in hoping for the best. It would be possible to relax the stringency if it was proved that they had been too gloomy. However, if Howe were to take the Treasury's advice to go easy and things turned out to be for the worst, then the whole policy of trying to rid the nation of unsound money – which they referred to among themselves as 'funny money' – would be killed off. And there would be political consequences within the Cabinet. If the strategy was seen to collapse, then Howe would, at best, have to be moved; at worst he would have to resign. The Prime Minister's authority would be undermined and the Cabinet dissidents might even push for her resignation. It was Howe's decision alone. Thatcher had told him that he must take the decision for them all. Despite Treasury cries of 'masochism', Howe took the strict but safe option, trimming the suggested amount to be removed from the economy by £2,000 million. (He was not to know that the Treasury recommendations would, just, scrape him home.)

A crisis point was reached between the two lines of Conservative thought on the morning of Budget day, Howe's third, 10 March, 1981. This might have been a turning point in the Thatcher Administration and almost caused a substantial rebellion in the Cabinet. It is not normal to tell Cabinets in advance what is to be in a budget – the need for secrecy of tax changes has always ruled out anything except a last minute briefing. But, considering the radical natural of the Thatcher/Howe economic strategy and the amount of dissent it was causing, it might have been wise to at least allow some proper discussion of the broad effect of the measures before the morning of the Tuesday on which Howe delivered his Budget speech. The Prime Minister's view was that to allow such a debate would slow down progress towards what she considered to be financial continence. Major opposition before the Budget might allow time for wide-scale, organised opposition within the Party which would demand a less stern approach upon threat that their stringent measures – which both she and the Chancellor thought necessary – would not get through the Commons. Her decision was to keep silent and announce the Budget measures as a fait accompli. There was bound to be a furore, in Cabinet, but by then it would be too late for the critics to do anything except resign. It was an open challenge to them to do so – and a risky tactic.

A Cabinet meeting was called for the morning of 10 March, to inform the Cabinet of the Budget proposals. It was a depressing package. There would be no increase in personal allowances or widening of tax bands. Excise duties were to be increased by double the amount needed to allow for inflation. Although the minimum lending rate was to be reduced, there was to be no relief for industry. In 1980, total output had fallen by $2\frac{1}{2}$ per cent and manufacturing industry by a staggering 9 per cent. The total effect of the Budget would be to take £4,300 million out of the economy – almost the total figure taken out in the previous two Budgets. The Chancellor had wrongly forecast the government borrowing requirement for the year and it was overshooting the estimate of £8,500 million by £5,000 million. The news came as a shock to most of the Cabinet. Two full years of stringency and cuts had led to this unprecedented package of deflationary measures. Because of resistance in November to more public spending cuts, the money had to be raised by taxation – and those tax increases would, in themselves, increase inflation by two per cent, keeping it in double figures.

Those particularly aghast were, of course, those who had been encouraging the Prime Minister and the Chancellor to reflate the economy by increasing public expenditure and relaxing the tax burden, thereby encouraging a demand-led recovery. Their views had been totally ignored and there was no evidence that their arguments on political grounds to ease up on the electorate were getting through. Three senior members of the Government made their total opposition clear to that Cabinet meeting: Jim Prior, Peter Walker and Ian Gilmour. Francis Pym and Lord Soames expressed their profound reservations. Mark Carlisle, George Younger and Nicholas Edwards also let their unease be known. Willie Whitelaw, while appearing to share their views, came down loyally on the side of the Chancellor.

For Pym, Walker and Gilmour, it was a critical time. The choice was open to them. Either they must stay and remain silent about an economic policy and a Budget which profoundly offended them, both on political and logical grounds, or they must resign and be free to mount an assault upon monetarism from outside the Cabinet. One thing was clear: it was too late to do anything about the 1981 Budget and, short of an imminent economic crisis, which they by no means ruled out, there would be little chance of forcing a change of policy until the following year, which seemed a long way off. They took advice, from each other, from Lord Carrington, from the others in the Cabinet who shared their views but who had not joined them in their vehement criticisms of the strategy. They also took their own counsel, for resignation in any party, but particularly the Conservative Party, is rarely forgiven quickly. That option might mean the beginning of a frustrating political career of internal opposition, waged from the back benches, or the end of a career altogether. If all three resigned at once and persuaded some others to join them, they would be able to form a significant rump around which opposition to the government's economic policy could be rallied. But that would be open rebellion against the Prime Minister. As she had guessed, they decided to stay. They felt impotent to change the Budget proposals, so no immediate good would come of resignations, and opposition from within the Cabinet was more effective — and more comfortable — than opposition from outside. It was a Thatcher victory and she celebrated it by sharing it: she allowed the extent of the dissent within the Cabinet to be conveyed to the press, in order to make the point that few Government ministers were opposed to the measures. At the same time, the leak looked as if it had come from the three principal critics, making them appear to be disloyal as well as defeated. It was a clever political coup.

But there were conditions for continued loyalty from the dissenters on economic policy. In exchange for their public loyalty, they demanded that they should be allowed to discuss the economic strategy in full Cabinet, on the agenda, without recourse to the back-door approach. Thatcher reluctantly agreed, but the fact that she agreed at all was because she was certain that the trauma of the 1981 Budget had permanently weakened their powers of opposition. She had chosen the ground for a final confrontation and had called their bluff. The fact that they had not resigned en masse meant that they could not implicitly threaten to depart again. And, by the time of the next Budget, there might not be as many of them in the Cabinet in any case. She agreed to a series of three Cabinet discussions on the economy. The first would be held in June and would concern the cut in public spending of five per cent across the board being demanded by the Treasury. The second would be in November, the traditional time for a mid financial year assessment of progress in the light of the Industry Act forecasts on inflation and output. The third and most crucial would be shortly before the following year's Budget, although she made clear that this would not allow specific measures to be announced in advance.

On the eve of the June Cabinet discussion, Thatcher addressed the Confederation of British Industry and made it clear to any Cabinet minister who read the report in the following day's paper, that she was in no mood to change her policies and embrace expansionist methods. And so it was. The principal critics each took their turn to suggest an alternative; and each was refused and rebutted. 'There is no alternative' was her main line of argument. The traditional Tories suffered from two main disabilities: they were not able to determine a common, clear, plausible alternative that would counter Thatcher and Howe on their own terms; and there was little obvious back-bench support for their efforts.

However, the summer was to bring useful if unwelcome evidence to be used by the Prime Minister's critics. Their main line of attack against the monetarist experiment had not only been that it did not work − and by the summer of 1981, the Chancellor could not even boast success in his own terms: he had not been able to keep his monetary targets, reduce the proportion of national income consumed by public spending or reduce taxation levels − but that the policy was politically suicidal. With such high levels of unemployment, they argued, it was only a matter of time before social disorder broke out on a large scale. That summer it did, in a spectacular and unprecedented series of riots in the large cities, often with racial overtones. Edward Heath, who had been keeping up his attacks upon Thatcher, had warned of the likelihood of crime and racial tension if unemployment remained high. Others joined in in what was a concerted effort to force Howe into a corner. At a July Cabinet meeting, the Chancellor came under strong pressure from a wider than usual spectrum of Cabinet opponents, attacking his latest proposed public expenditure cuts and demanding reflation. Some even hoped that, by the time of the annual conference in Blackpool, there would be an irresistible pressure from MPs and party workers for a U-turn on economic policy. Others hoped for a change of leader. Francis Pym, in charge of Government communications, gave a speech in Northumberland which offered a gloomy prognostication for the chances of an economic recovery. And Lord Thorneycroft, the Party Chairman and, because of his resignation on a sound money issue in 1957, one of Thatcher's economic heroes, attacked the notion that doctrinaire economic theories or single system solutions could lead to recovery. As Thatcher set out on her holiday in Cornwall, there were rumours that Thorneycroft would not be chairman for much longer.

He was not the only one to go. Three leading detractors of the Thatcher/Howe economic strategy were asked for their resignations in September. Thorneycroft could claim — and he did in his letter of resignation to her — that he was getting old and the Party needed a younger man. However, Ian Gilmour knew why he was asked to leave. His sacking was neither a surprise nor unwelcome. As he put it: 'It does no harm to throw the occasional man overboard, but it does not do much good if you are steering full speed ahead for the rocks.' Mark Carlisle left cordially, exchanging polite letters. But Lord Soames did not. His letter of resignation to the Prime Minister, by convention a polite document, was brutally short: 'You told me this morning that you wished to put someone in my place, so I hasten to place my office at your disposal. Yours sincerely, Christopher Soames.' When he delivered the letter there was, as with the others, a private secretary in the room. Thatcher asked them each if they minded the secretary being there. Only Soames objected, asking him to leave. He then spoke freely and bluntly to her. She found it most upsetting. Sacking people is not easy for her and she had not expected such an emotional response. She had picked off the weaker parts of the Cabinet opposition, knowing that none of them, either individually or united, would be able to cause very much dissent among backbench MPs.

The same could not be said for Prior, Walker or — at that time — Pym. Prior was a particular menace to her. He was a key irritant in the pivotal Cabinet economic committee, know as 'E'. She chaired it herself. Prior was the most vocal dissenter from the Thatcher line to penetrate 'E' and he jealously guarded his place. He argued forcefully against the direction of government policy from the very committee which was formulating it. Thatcher found this time-wasting and tiresome. The September reshuffle was to deal a blow to Prior. He was banished to Ulster, as Ulster Secretary. Although he was not excluded from the 'E' committee his permanent state of movement between Ulster and the mainland meant that he was unable to keep a grip on what the committee was deciding. Unlike Employment, Northern Ireland did not have its own economics section to prepare background papers for him. But, in any case, to avoid an open discussion of the policy, particularly when it was going wrong, the Prime Minister would use the inter-connecting door to Number 11 and would hold breakfast sessions with Howe, Nott and Biffen.

Banishment and exclusion was better than having Prior lead dissent from the back benches. But one backbencher was capable of causing trouble. A week before the party conference in Blackpool, Edward Heath launched a massive, comprehensive condemnation of Thatcher's economic policies and demanded a return to the post-war consensus. His timing was good, riding a wave of widespread dissent, in good time for the conference. In his speech to the Federation of Conservative Students in Manchester, he settled old scores, asking how anyone dare accuse him of printing money when they enjoyed the biggest budget deficit in history. Without referring to her by name, he accused Thatcher of jeopardising the Party's chances of electoral success by sticking to monetarism and causing massive unemployment. He spelt out an alternative for reflation. Thatcher, in Melbourne, Australia, replied with some hastily written ripostes: 'For me, consensus seems to be the process of abandoning all beliefs, principles, values and policies. So it is something in which noone believes and to which noone objects.'

That charge and counter charge were to be a trailer for the action in Blackpool. For once, the Tory Conference was a place of lively debate over real differences. Even the Prime Minister's set-piece in the Winter Gardens, usually a stage-managed affair, was interrupted by a demonstration by Tories. It was a confident speech which dealt first with economic policy and the challenges to her creed. On unemployment, she said, 'I learnt from childhood the dignity which comes from work, and, by contrast, the affront to self-esteem which comes from enforced idleness. For us, work was the only way of life we knew and we were brought up to believe that it was not only a necessity, but a virtue.'

And she took to task those who, like Heath, were invoking a pragmatic solution to the economy: 'If ever a Conservative government starts to do what it knows to be wrong because it is afraid to do what it is sure is right, then that's the time for the Tories to cry stop. You'll never need to do that while I am Prime Minister.' Her message was the same as the year before – she was not going to change her tack – although she was careful not to oversimplify it so that she appeared obstinate. What had seemed determination the previous year was beginning to look like inflexibility this. In fact there was growing evidence that the pressure on the Prime Minister's unrelenting attitude to the firmness of her policy was giving way to a more relaxed attitude to government spending. A series of Cabinet committee meetings had hammered out the difference between the public spending estimates for 1982-83 established the previous March by the Treasury and what the departments wished to spend. The March estimate was £110,000 million and the Departmental Secretaries had demanded a further £7,000 million. The Treasury team, who had hoped to claw back £3,500 million of this had to settle for a £2,000 million cut. Therefore, in December, the Chancellor announced a £5,000 million increase in estimated public expenditure for the year. The Cabinet agreed the figure, after two hours forty minutes without major discussions. Since the autumn reshuffle, Thatcher was enjoying a total change of atmosphere in Cabinet meetings. The liberal Tories in Cabinet had also made progress. Heath, in the Commons debate, taunted Howe that he was 'going beautifully around the curve'. However, there was a small backbench rebellion, led by Gilmour, mainly against a two per cent cut in unemployment pay. Thirteen MPs joined him in abstaining.

By the Budget of 9 March 1982, monetarism as it was envisaged at the beginning of the Thatcher administration had all but disappeared. The tight control of M3 had proved elusive and Geoffrey Howe was by now monitoring 'a range of indicators'. While maintaining reasonably strict cash limits, he was also indulging in a modest reflation, injecting £1,200 million into the economy. The opposition to blind monetarism had been right in retrospect, because, in the search for the elusive formula of government spending, defined imprecisely, as a proportion of domestic output, the economy had been hurled onto an adventurous experiment which resulted in a permamently damaged manufacturing industry, which would never be restored, and an enormous number of unemployed, which would take years to reduce – and at enormous cost. The trick was to play up the bright side – what little there was. The tight controls on public spending, high interest rates and a very high pound had caused a massive shedding of jobs and in some industries had caused a significant rise in productivity as a result. The inflation rate had been brought down to single figures, mainly because of the depth of the recession and the weakening of cost-push inflation caused by trade union wage bargaining. Unemployment had undermined union strength. The theory offered by the Government was that if and when the world economy were to recover, Britain's new-found productivity would be able to take advantage because it was newly competitive and it would take on workers as it captured orders to meet the demand. The main problem was that demand to increase output and thereby employment could either come from home, through an increase in public spending, which was not allowed under tight fiscal logic, or from abroad – but the strength of the pound made British goods unnaturally expensive.

If both were to be pursued, the economy could start to recover, but there was a reluctance by Thatcher, Howe and the Treasury team to do either. Their instinct was to wait for the American recovery to finally abandon its tight monetary restraints and to jump on the back of the expansion of the US recovery. The liberal wing of the Party, within and without the Cabinet, thought that there was no time to waste — unemployment was an outrage and politically damaging — so government-led expansion should begin right away, even if it were to cost an increase in inflation. Their pressure during the summer of 1981 had been successful and they expected that, to avoid a violent summer of 1982, they would make some substantial headway. All such assumptions changed when the Argentines invaded the Falklands in May 1982. First, the nation was preoccupied and gained confidence, which ruled out major social disorder. Second, and most importantly, the authority of Margaret Thatcher as a British leader first and Conservative leader second gave her an almost unassailable position. Instead of a defensive Prime Minister under pressure from internal dissidents, she was able to defy her opponents. The 1922 Committee considered her a heroine and her determination, which had once appeared a dislikeable obstinacy, was now considered resolution. Third, a key restraining force, Lord Carrington, resigned from the Government. The Falklands War gave her a free hand.

Opposition, however, did not cease. The Falklands War may have changed Thatcher's authority in the country, her party and the Cabinet, but the economic dilemmas remained the same. By August 1982, James Prior was making it clear that unemployment remained at an intolerable level and it was clear that he was supported by Patrick Jenkin, at Industry, George Younger, the Scottish Secretary, and Nicholas Edwards, the Welsh Secretary. Prior was arguing for selective help for industry, in response to an appeal by Sir Terence Beckett, director general of the Confederation of British Industry, once a group of industrialists which no Conservative Prime Minister could ignore. As the Falklands factor faded from the electorate's minds, an increasing number of Tory MPs were becoming anxious that any future general election would be fought on the one issue which successive opinion polls had recorded at the top of the list of anxieties: unemployment. At the

October Conference there was an unstated truce among Cabinet members to keep away from economic differences as it might be the last full-scale gathering before a general election. Unbound by such an agreement, Heath declined a seat on the platform and thundered again against the Government's policy of stagnation. Both Prior and Peter Walker chimed in, while addressing the Tory Reform Group, each demanding more stimulus to the economy. It became clear that however strong Thatcher had become personally, she would still have to endure a strong body of vocal opposition from within the Cabinet as long as Prior, Walker and Pym were there.

The promised discussions about the Budget went easily, because, although Howe had budgeted for a public sector borrowing requirement of £9,500 million, an unexpected increase in oil revenues had reduced that substantially, to about £7,500 million, and he was proposing that the difference be given away in aid to individual and industrial taxpayers. There would be no massive reflation, but, similarly, the windfall of unexpectedly large oil revenues was not being used to reduce more quickly public borrowing as a proportion of output. He offered a prudent, safe Budget which injected £1,700 million into the economy. The hard-line deflation was over – until after the election, at least. Monetary growth was being interpreted generously and he announced that an average of three key indicators was within the target which he had determined. Blind monetarism was at an end. Circumstances were changing. Inflation was low and only expected to rise slightly until the end of the year. But two other, more unpredictable, elements had entered the Chancellor's calculations. The pound had slumped to a record low level, anticipating the Opposition's plans to devalue, and the OPEC oil ministers had decided to cut oil prices and the price was expected to go even lower. This affected the price of North Sea oil, which was fixed outside the OPEC agreement, and upset the future plans for the economy. But one thing was clear. Howe had by now reduced public spending by as much as possible without changing the foundation of public spending itself: the extent of the welfare state. To make further advances in her policy of removing the state from the lives of individuals, Thatcher was now sanctioning widespread discussion within the Party so that a clear programme of public spending cuts could be included in the election manifesto. So far, the advice she had received, at her own request, on the feasibility of changing the basis of payment for health had caused uproar in Cabinet. Progress in the next five years would demand a more sympathetic set of colleagues.

CHAPTER ELEVEN

Style

What is Thatcher government? In opposition she displayed an unusual combination of cautious pragmatism and radical right-wing rhetoric. Her opponents inside the first Cabinet she appointed noted the contrast and confidently expected the pressures and responsibilities of government to modify the rhetoric and emphasise the pragmatism. As time began to run out on her first parliament, it was at least clear that they had been wrong. But it was still hard to describe – at least with the labels which commentators had used for Prime Ministers since the war – the kind of politician who was running the country.

'People know what I stand for and will judge me on that,' she said as the Falklands campaign neared its objective. Yet it was also clear that she felt dissatisfied with the results of those few years. She has clearly not been purely a 'conviction' politician – there have been too many examples of her convictions being reversed or suppressed for that to be of any value as a description. It may not describe her policies, but it did describe something of her style. One senior civil servant watched the crises of the Iranian embassy siege and the Belfast hunger strike unfold inside the Cabinet Office and said that every official, whatever they may have thought of the government's policies, was aware of a different kind of leadership being exercised from the top.

Or was that simply the behaviour of a self-confident reactionary? 'Just as the wets are old-fashioned, muddle-through pragmatists,' said one party official, 'so, underneath, she is just an old-fashioned reactionary.' In many ways, the government has been led by a right-wing Conservative, only restrained from giving full reign to her instincts by her Cabinet and some external circumstances.

But she is not a High Tory and is ready to embrace novelty, experiment and exploration if it will meet her definition of the country's interest. She is the first scientist to be Prime Minister and she has vigorously advocated the introduction of new technology in industry, and of communications technology in particular. She has little patience with aristocrats who do not share her view of the urgency or seriousness of politics. She has little more patience with many City financiers. She has, indeed, an instinctive suspicion of institutions of almost any kind.

She is fond of converts and introduced to Number Ten men like Alfred Sherman and John Hoskyns whose inclinations to 'think the unthinkable' are in many ways subversive of the association between the Conservatives and the preservation of the status quo. But she has been careful to keep her distance from even close advisers – she has so far had no one dominant 'guru' – and has worked to extend the range of advice available to her. While she has been careful about some ideas thrown up by the advisers (and time in government has slightly increased that caution), she seems to have little time for the idea that leadership is to tell your own followers difficult truths. It is hard to find an example during her government of a policy which she has been determined is right and which she has decided to sell to the country against the grain.

Unemployment, although persistently at the top of lists of voters' concerns, appears to be unpopular in that sense alone. Its cost in votes turned out to be far lower than most would have predicted in 1979 and when asked who they blamed for unemployment, few people blamed the government.

Thatcher's government has been dominated by the interplay between her emotions and her intellect. The tension between them has produced some of the inconsistencies which make the thread of Thatcher government hard to trace, although its rhetoric has been clear enough to follow. On policy questions such as Rhodesia, her intellect conquered her emotions. Over the civil service strike, which could have been ended with a pay rise of the same size six weeks before it was, her emotions beat her intellect. On a number of other issues – the row between Whitelaw and the Conservative right over new immigration rules or the row between Prior and the Conservative right and Northern Ireland Official Unionists over Ulster assembly legislation – the two seem more finely balanced. One of the hardest tasks for a minister or official advising Thatcher is to find out whether a policy question will start such a conflict and, if it does, which way it will go.

One point on which those who have worked with her disagree is the extent to which she has a vision in her mind of the kind of society she would like to see. Is there a blueprint or is it just a collection of intuitions and prejudices? 'She's very good at the here and now,' said one, 'but she has no New Jerusalem that she's trying to reach.' Another man, noting Thatcher's well-advertised ability for powerful concentration while she briefs herself on specific issues, said that after a time the separate areas began to 'join up' into an overall picture. 'She's good at the short term and the close-up,' said a third, 'at hacking through the undergrowth of detail and difficulty. And she does also have a horizon, a vision of what she wants to come about. But what she lacks is the middle ground. She often doesn't quite seem to know how to organise to get from the day to day to her vision.' The people charged with implementing the vision are civil servants.

Early in the life of Thatcher's government, a pair of her most senior civil servants went to see a retired mandarin who had worked for her during her years at Education. They had come, they explained, to seek help and guidance; relations between the Prime Minister and her senior officials were dreadful. She made little attempt to conceal her contempt and mistrust for their ineffectual and detached attitude to her priorities. She had recently held a dinner for Permanent Secretaries which had been a disaster: she had berated them all evening. Occasionally she had been heard to say that if only she had officials like the man they had come to see, things would be better. 'Can you tell us,' they asked, 'what your secret was?' He could not.

'She just wanted to put the fear of God into them,' said one loyalist. Few civil servants would claim that she had failed. Whitehall has suffered a systematic assault and its power to fight back has been negligible. The resentment has registered in some informal open government: as numbers and morale fell, the number of leaks went up. By the end of 1982, the Government was on target to bring the size of the public service down from 732,000 to 630,000 by April 1984 (although the methods of achieving a nominal reduction in numbers did not always reduce the cost to the government and the bulk of the cuts did not fall on central government administration), the Civil Service Department had been abolished, its head abruptly retired and the civil service had experienced the longest public sector strike (21 weeks) since the 1920s. After leaving 10 Downing Street, John Hoskyns delivered a lecture in which he told his audience that 'the first thing to realise about civil servants is that few, if any, believe that the country can be saved'; he suggested shortly afterwards that if he could make one single reform of British government, it would be to dispense with every civil servant over the age of 50 and start again. The speech, made to the Institute of Fiscal Studies in October 1982, was a remarkable testimony to the frustration which he had clearly felt; the answer lay, he said, in mixing political outsiders into the upper reaches of government departments.

It was tempting to think that this represented Thatcher's view, but her view was by then more complex. To the immediate disappointment of some who had been close to her before the election, Mrs Thatcher went to work at once with the Downing Street and Cabinet Office machine with every sign that she thought it excellent. She showed no sign of wanting to move towards the creation of a Prime Minister's Department to strengthen her hand against recalcitrant departmental ministers. The policy unit in Downing Street was kept very small; for two years it consisted only of Hoskyns, Strauss and one civil servant. Mrs Thatcher settled down well with Clive Whitmore, the unassuming-looking high flier from the Ministry of Defence who succeeded as Principal Private Secretary shortly after she arrived. Perhaps most important of all, she needed the major Whitehall power-brokers to help cut Cabinet opposition down to size. A Prime Minister exercises enormous power in the selection of the members of Cabinet committees; that influence over what reaches the Cabinet and in what form is extended by decisions on which committees will deal with which subjects, both in general terms and week by week. A weekly meeting of the Prime Minister, Cabinet Secretary, head of the policy unit (Hoskyns was succeeded in mid-1982 by the political columnist of the *Spectator*, Ferdinand Mount), the PPS and a handful of senior Cabinet Office officials decides what business will go before which committee.

'E' committee, although always large, contained a better proportion of her economic supporters than the full Cabinet – a strong incentive to keep as much economic decision-making as possible in the former rather than the latter. She has substantially streamlined the system by keeping down the proliferation of ad hoc groups and sub-committees. Whitelaw is worked hard in the committee network: he is chairman of several which tackle difficult questions of domestic policy; he chaired, for example, Misc 79, charged with designing a reformed rating system. By 1983 the committee's failure to solve the problem had led to a reshuffle and Thatcher replaced him in the chair. He has been chairman of Misc 62, known more familiarly as the 'Star Chamber', which brings together Treasury and spending ministers to hammer out expenditure cuts to be assembled for White Papers detailing spending plans.

It is hard for any Prime Minister, even one not temperamentally sympathetic to Whitehall clubbability, not to come to rely on her two closest advisers, the PPS and the Cabinet Secretary, for early warning, intelligence and guidance on matters which cannot be anticipated by any manifesto. They provide the machine which stems and sorts the endless flow of paper, tailoring the quantity and detail to the individual (in her early days, Mrs Thatcher issued instructions that she wanted more to read, not less); they schedule and reschedule every waking minute of the day. They will hold the options on political problems where wide or prolonged consultation is impossible. When the long-hidden story broke that Sir Anthony Blunt, art historian and ex-Keeper of the Queen's Pictures, had been a Soviet spy, Armstrong took charge and coordinated the advice. One of the Cabinet Secretary's most important functions is the preparation of short briefs for the Prime Minister giving tactical tips and advance warning to help the successful chairing of Cabinet and its committees.

Thatcher is ambivalent about Whitehall: some individuals and parts of the machine impress her, others enrage her. By coincidence, an unusually large number of permanent secretaries have retired during the life of her government. She has put effort and time into making sure that the right individuals reach the top. Rightness has not simply been Thatcherite sympathies, although it does not appear to be a disadvantage in the economic departments. But an essential and even more important qualification in her eyes is a matter of style: a belief that something can be done and an appetite to go and do it.

The distance which has opened between Thatcher and some of her fiercer advisers can be seen most clearly in the shifting debate over the creation of a Prime Minister's Department. The idea, which has a long history, was revived as the frustrations with Whitehall accumulated; they were accumulating faster in the Downing Street policy unit than elsewhere. Strauss wrote a paper not long after the election which argued that the preoccupation with industrial relations was out of date, since trade union power was already declining and set to do so further, and that the principal obstruction between the government and recovery was Whitehall itself. In June 1982, Alfred Sherman wrote a paper urging the establishment of a Prime Minister's Department to conduct strategic thinking and to ensure that policies were properly pursued. It would incorporate the functions of the Central Policy Review staff.

But Thatcher herself appears to be lukewarm about the idea. There was also some division among those urging the department on her over what it would be chiefly designed to do: is it to discipline ministers or to help cut the senior civil servants down to size? The former could be achieved by some rearrangement and expansion of the Prime Minister's administrative resources; the latter would be bound to involve a larger number of special outside advisers than at present. The appointments of personal defence and foreign affairs advisers in early 1983 were taken as a sign that the foundations of a new department were being laid. But as the election approached, it looked increasingly as if Thatcher did not favour a radical reorganisation. It appeared that she had not accepted the premise of Hoskyns' IFS lecture that unless the civil service could be driven the Government's way, little else would succeed.

A classic example of the kind of activity which Thatcher refused to delegate in the early days of government (and which a Prime Minister's Department might have found itself doing), was the anti-quango policy. The manifesto, taking its cue from a pamphlet by Conservative MP Philip Holland, promised to cut quangos substantially, alleged to be wasting large sums of government money. Characteristically, she had fired off sets of letters to government ministers in an attempt to get more of the symbols of waste and indulgence killed more quickly. It had not worked.

Sir Leo Pliatzky, an unconventional ex-Treasury official just retiring as Permanent Secretary at the Department of Trade was asked if he would conduct an inquiry. At a taut session in Downing Street attended by Sir Derek Rayner and others, Pliatzky established, with some difficulty, that he would be enabled to investigate the position before reporting. 'But we know what we want done,' retorted Thatcher, adding that Holland's pamphlet and Central Office could supply all the information he might need and that what the government wanted to do was to cut quangos down quickly. Pliatzky eventually turned in a low-key report, recommending some cuts but the preservation of most (the bulk of quangos are tribunals whose work would have to be transferred to the court system if they were abolished). He had killed the issue.

On a number of important issues, civil servants were caught in the crossfire between Number Ten and their minister, and accused of obstruction when they had been following the instructions of a minister who did not want to hurry. In a newspaper article published shortly after he left Downing Street, John Hoskyns alleged that Department of

Employment civil servants had been slowing down industrial relations legislation. They had, in fact, been doing no more than following Prior's intended rate of change. Hoskyns' colleague Norman Strauss took a slightly more charitable line about civil servants in general in September 1981: 'They have been proving increasingly irrelevant in an ability to generate imaginative policy options. So in a very real sense now, the ministerial desire is ... hampered by the fact that the Civil Service cannot provide the options even if the minister has come up with the correct objectives. I think they believe that because they understand all the issues and all the policy fields so well, they are genuinely laying before ministers all possible options ... in most cases they will abide by ministers' decisions.' From Downing Street, where Strauss had been working until shortly before that interview, the 'ministerial desire' would have looked clear cut. To the civil servants it seemed considerably less so; they sometimes found themselves acting as umpires of the Cabinet battle.

On three areas of policy there were pronounced differences between Thatcher and the relevant minister which served to undermine him and the policy he was attempting to run. It was made clear that although Lord Soames had been put in charge of the Civil Service Department, he did not direct the thrust of the government's policy towards Whitehall. Thatcher did not speak to him individually about her dislike of bureaucracy, nor did she brief him on how she wanted the civil service to be more tightly controlled and reduced. She considered his handling of the civil service strike inept, although Soames had advised the Cabinet to accept the final pay settlement figure six weeks before the strike ended. Their differences were well-aired in public. In the same way, Downing Street gave Prior's Ulster assembly legislation the minimum of public support during its rough passage through the Commons. Similarly, when new Home Office immigration rules began to encounter right-wing Conservative opposition in the Commons, Whitelaw approached Thatcher to obtain an assurance that he would not find himself in the same position as Prior – undermined by his backbenchers with encouragement from on high. His proposals were initially defeated by a backbench rebellion, but Thatcher's personal attitude remained ambiguous. He cleverly defeated her attempts to dissociate herself from his policy by making her decide the strength of the new legislation.

Thatcher genuinely dislikes anything which she feels to be impersonal. Dealing with civil servants and their departments, she has always made a distinction in practice between the institution and the individual. She is quite capable of singing the praises of an official while sounding vituperative about the department he or she belongs to. Much of the thrust behind the 'scrutinies' of Whitehall cost-efficiency led by Derek Rayner, the Marks and Spencer executive who had also given similar advice to Edward Heath, was against the institutions. When Rayner was first appointed – Keith Joseph had discussed the possibility with him just before the election – there was pressure inside the Thatcher camp for him to run a powerful central task force which would raid ministries in pursuit of savings. Thatcher herself had been reading, and was influenced by, the campaigning book written by ex-civil servant Leslie Chapman. Rayner argued that for there to be real savings and for these to stick, the groundwork would have to be done from within departments. He set up a small unit in the Cabinet Office and recruited bright middle-rank officials inside each department to examine costs in carefully-defined areas. Thatcher took a close personal interest. New relays of scrutineers would be invited to Number Ten for drinks served by the Prime Minister. She gave a Christmas party for the scrutineers in 1979 and held another so that they could bring their wives. There remained, however, a question mark over how much Rayner was actually saving the government. Although he had hoped to work towards cuts of up to 20% in departmental budgets, by the time he handed his small team over to civil servants and returned to Marks and Spencer as Chief Executive, Rayner's scrutinies had made little impact on the round numbers of civil service costs. He had, however, added powerfully to the impetus towards promoting bright civil servants faster than they were normally able to reach the top.

A Prime Minister handles two kinds of issues: those chosen for action and those which make action compulsory. She picked the complex and inconclusive issue of the civil service but did not choose to settle the future of British involvement in Rhodesia. But by the summer of 1979, decisions were inevitable.

In the last days of the 1979 election campaign, the Central Office tacticians had started to worry about a new anxiety to add to their daily list of things which could go wrong. The party had sent a team of observers to the Rhodesian elections then being held under a constitution agreed between Mr Ian Smith and Bishop Abel Muzorewa; led by the ex-colonial secretary, Lord Boyd, they were due to report on whether the poll was 'free and fair'. Party headquarters did not so much fear the observers' report – it seemed clear that they would say, as they duly did, that within their limits the elections had been reasonably conducted – as the inevitable consequence of their delivering any report at all: the issue would be on the campaign agenda. Any discussion would be unlikely to gain votes and would only serve to illuminate the divisions on the issue at the top of the party. Bishop Muzorewa became Rhodesia's first black prime minister during the campaign; the bush war continued unchecked and the constitution under which he governed included formidable entrenching clauses for the benefit of the white minority.

There had been divisions inside the Shadow Cabinet over Rhodesia, but they had been neither deep nor along the alignments which characterised discussions of the economy or industrial relations. Reginald Maudling had been irritated to be peremptorily hauled back to London by his leader while touring the capitals of southern Africa in 1975 in order to take part in a lost parliamentary vote and said that this fiasco had created the gap into which the ever-shuttling Dr Kissinger had stepped, excluding the possibility of any major British initiative for some time. Thatcher had considered having Carrington as her Foreign Secretary after the leadership election, but had taken the view that while a Foreign Secretary could sit in the Lords in government, a shadow spokesman must be in the Commons.

Carrington argued against the manifesto commitment, but it had been supported by the foreign affairs shadow of the time, Pym, and by Thatcher, who took a strong pro-Smith line. When the party rebels had defied the whips during one of the regular measurements of Westminster opinion on the issue – the Commons debate on the renewal of sanctions – Carrington had let it be known among his colleagues that he would have resigned from the Shadow Cabinet had the party leadership supported the ending of sanctions. Not only did Thatcher fail to support her rebels, but she very promptly sacked two of them. In the early months of government, Thatcher attended a series of seminars at the Foreign Office, designed to underline the realities of the situation. It was clear that her head and heart were pulling in different directions but it was also clear that she was open to persuasion. In Canberra in June Thatcher ignored warnings from Malcolm Fraser to be discreet on the subject and gave answers at a press conference which suggested that the manifesto commitment would be fully honoured: Parliament was unlikely to renew sanctions, recognition of the bishop was a possibility and Britain might not be alone in responding in this way to his fledgling regime. She had presented a straightforward argument: if the criteria for the established of decent government had been met, recognition should follow. Although it was questionable whether the Commons would, in fact, have voted to end sanctions – there was a well-organised group of liberal backbenchers which was determined to cancel out the effect of the pro-Rhodesia lobby – Carrington knew Thatcher's instincts to endorse the Muzorewa government were shared by a substantial majority in the party as a whole. As he set out to put party policy into reverse, he faced Thatcher's well-advertised distrust of the Foreign Office, balanced by her respect for his guidance in an area which she did not see as her highest priority for attention. She tended in private to describe Carrington as an old-fashioned Whig who was, in common with a number of his liberal colleagues, constantly pointing out obstacles and difficulties when he should be solving problems but who was at the same time an indispensable source of good tactical advice. The source of this advice was not optimistic about the prospects for the government in general under Thatcher. As soon as she returned from Australia, Carrington set about briefing her on a number of obstacles and difficulties which the following of her instincts would entail. He listed the probable consequences of recognition: little future trade with black Africa, increased Russian, East German and Cuban intervention, the disintegration of the Commonwealth, a diplomatic split with Washington (which was about to renew sanctions), and the possibility of United Nations sanctions deployed against Britain. The bush war would continue and would ultimately be won, after much more blood had been slowly shed, by the Patriotic Front; at the climax of the war, Britain would face appeals for help from the beleaguered white population. The arguments between the two were short and sharp and Carrington won. At the time when it was being rumoured that Thatcher might not even go to a Lusaka Commonwealth conference, which was to be attended by Muzorewa, Smith and herself, a message was filtered to Downing Street from Buckingham Palace. The queen disapproved: she considered herself head of the Commonwealth of which Britain was one member and she intended to attend, irrespective of what her Prime Minister did. On 25 July, five days before she left for the Commonwealth summit in Lusaka, Thatcher made a virtually unnoticed speech in the Commons which stopped short of accepting the Boyd report's implications and said that the government was preparing to go down the 'consultation route'.

Few Commonwealth governments had noticed the shift and the scene appeared to be set for a tough meeting. Sitting behind the Prime Minister on the flight to Lusaka, Carrington noticed that the contents of her handbag contained two large pairs of dark glasses. 'It's in case they get rough and start throwing anything like acid,' she remarked. She stepped straight off the plane into a milling crowd of journalists and some demonstrators and was swept into an utterly unorganised press conference, after which she looked profoundly shaken. Matters did not improve when she and Denis arrived at the VIP accommodation later on that hot night. It looked like a somewhat hastily erected building and Thatcher emerged from the bathroom to announce that there was no water. They commiserated on extra difficulties they could do without and Thatcher went back into the bathroom. No sooner had she done so than a portion of the ceiling collapsed onto her bed.

With the aid of some ingenious backroom coordination by the Commonwealth Secretary-General, Sonny Ramphal, Thatcher's enthusiasm for a settlement involving the Patriotic Front helped convince the key leaders at the conference – the heads of the 'front line' states bordering on Rhodesia – that the moment had come to put pressure on the guerillas to talk. Having been persuaded by Carrington's arguments, she advocated them with a convert's fervour. Zambia's president, Kenneth Kaunda, who had been hostile to her presumed approach at the outset was rapidly converted to singing her praises. Thatcher was, however, tiring herself, and a very long way from trusted advice and subjects with which she felt comfortably familiar. There was a caucus of Prime Ministers one evening and the gathering was debating the composition of the military force which should supervise the elections and keep order. It had been agreed that it should not be a United Nations force; Thatcher was arguing that it should be exclusively British. Kaunda pressed for the inclusion of Commonwealth units.

According to one source at the meeting, Thatcher was 'tired and close to the edge'. Denis, who had been sitting quietly in the outer circle of armchairs, got up and briskly announcing that it was time for bed, he put out his hand and led her out of the room. Whether he, or simply a good night's sleep, influenced the change of mind, the next morning his wife was ready to accept a formula which allowed for the principal duties to be done by British troops and for there to be Commonwealth observers alongside.

The Lusaka conference laid the foundations for the long and uncertain bargaining which preceeded the establishment of black majority government under Robert Mugabe. Carrington, periodically consulting and reassuring his

Prime Minister – and convinced until very near the end that everybody but Mugabe would agree – paid minimum heed to the rest of the Cabinet and steered the policy through the protracted talks at Lancaster House, the cease-fire and elections and the independence ceremony at which Britain's temporary governor, Lord Soames, finally set down the painful burden. The Conservative right wing tried occasionally afterwards to point to Thatcher's change of mind as evidence that she had been seduced, blackmailed, or both, by treasonous smooth-talking diplomats, but there was little evidence of regret from a Prime Minister who was quite capable when she wanted to of disowning Cabinet decisions by speaking of them as regrettable aberrations which had nothing to do with her. The episode was a potent example of what could be achieved when she was confronted with well-judged arguments. Carrington was shrewd enough to realise that it was not something which could be made to work in other areas of policy. He largely confined himself to foreign affairs until his resignation over the Falklands invasion – a departure received with great delight by the right-wingers who still resented his success and its international recognition.

There are few discussions in Whitehall in which Number Ten does not make an appearance, if only to be ruled out as a factor for consideration. Civil servants have only borrowed one other of the Cabinet nicknames – Mother. (The rest of the new generation of names spawned by government – the Bossette (Lord Carrington), Attila the Hen or the Leaderene (Norman St John Stevas) – have remained in the hands of the politicians.) But the frequency with which Number Ten has to be considered is a hallmark of Thatcher government. Even on issues in which she takes the minimum of Prime Ministerial interest there will be instincts to be catered and planned for. The best example is, perhaps, Northern Ireland.

An MP once commented that one could judge the level of Thatcher's interest in Northern Ireland by looking at the men she had appointed to look after it: she had won the leadership as a result of the efforts of Airey Neave, a man who would not otherwise have reached Shadow Cabinet rank but who deserved a place; she won the election largely thanks to the efforts of her Chief Whip Humphrey Atkins, who similarly had to be included to pay that debt. She then gave the job to her most outspoken Cabinet enemy, James Prior. But although this might have described her attitude to the troubled province at the beginning and end of the parliament, there was a brief moment when she believed that it was one of the most important issues she confronted. It has been the classic example of the tension between intellect and emotion.

She had made one Opposition speech which suggested that in government she might break away from the bipartisanship of party policy toward Northern Ireland and lean towards the Protestant and Unionist majority by returning some of the power which had been denied them by the suspension of the semi-autonomous Parliament at Stormont in 1972. A commitment to restore more powers to local government – understood as a small move in favour of the Unionists – was included in the manifesto. At the end of August 1979, Lord Mountbatten and members of his family boating party were killed in an explosion off the Irish west coast. On the same day, eighteen soldiers were killed by a pair of explosions at Warrenpoint in County Down. Both sets of killings were claimed by the Provisional IRA.

The immediate result was the appointment, arranged between the Cabinet Secretary John Hunt and the Permanent Secretary of the Ministry of Defence, Frank Cooper (who had previously been Permanent Secretary of the Northern Ireland Office), of Sir Maurice Oldfield as 'coordinator of security' in the province. There was clearly some doubt over Humphrey Atkins' ability to referee the differences over the conduct of the counter-terrorist campaign between the Royal Ulster Constabulary and the Army. Oldfield was given the right of direct access to the Prime Minister. Against the advice of his civil servants, but at the urging of a Prime Minister still ticking off action on manifesto commitments, Atkins embarked on an ill-considered series of round-table talks with local politicians which only ran into the sand.

In May 1980, the Irish Prime Minister, Charles Haughey,

came to London for a brief summit with Thatcher. He presented her with a Georgian silver teapot and a teaspoon inscribed with the quotation from St Francis which she had used on election day the year before. More seriously, the meeting laid the ground for the planning of an initiative which, although unsuccessful, was a reminder of the abrupt departures which could be achieved by those who persuaded the intellect to master the instincts.

Another summit was held in Dublin the following December. A communiqué, on which officials on both sides of the Irish Sea had worked for several months beforehand, was issued and its ambiguous and much-debated language disguised a U-turn in government policy towards Northern Ireland. In less than a year the government had travelled from saying firmly that the Dublin government had no business in discussions over the North to agreeing that Dublin and London should discuss the 'totality' of Anglo-Irish relationships. The phrase was instantly taken in the Republic as a sign that London was prepared to negotiate over whether Northern Ireland should remain inside, or leave, the United Kingdom. In Whitehall the phrase was interpreted as nothing more than a readiness to accept that if the Republic wished to organise ways of trying to persuade the reluctant majority in Northern Ireland to join the South, they were free to do so.

Thatcher's instincts – which, so far as she had any, were pro-Unionist – had been turned on their head. Persuaded after the failure of the early Atkins talks that a new approach was worth a try, she had taken Irish history books on her summer holiday and returned to Downing Street with a new and sober view of Northern Ireland's importance. She had accepted the case for an experiment which was being pressed by Cabinet Office officials. In return for the new stance, Mr Haughey assured British ministers that security cooperation at the Irish border would be maintained and that Dublin would do as little as possible to exacerbate the tensions caused by the first hunger strike which had started in the Maze prison outside Belfast several weeks before the summit.

Northern Ireland did not stay at the front of Thatcher's

thoughts for long. It quickly became clear that Mr Haughey had no serious intention of wooing Northerners into the South and another hunger strike began several weeks after the collapse of the first. As the tension mounted, Thatcher delivered a speech which described the strike as the IRA's 'last card'. The strike ended in victory for the government, although only after nine deaths and several months. But if the gambling metaphor was at all appropriate, it was the first card of a new hand. Thatcher told Jimmy Young that she had run out of ideas on what to do with the intractable Irish.

The appointment of Prior as Secretary of State for Northern Ireland suited her well. Prior needed to be kept as distant from economic policy as possible, but inside the Cabinet. He was tough and capable enough to withstand the emotional and physical strains of the job. His plan for a new consultative assembly in Belfast went through the Commons as legislative proposals in the summer of 1982 and ran into trouble from the Conservative right-wing and Official Unionists. They mounted a guerilla campaign against it which kept the House sitting for several long summer nights. Ian Gow, an ex-officer of the backbench Northern Ireland committee, was seen in frequent contact with the rebels while formally dissociating himself from Thatcher. He had many conversations with Enoch Powell. Those harassing Prior were left in no doubt that, although the decision to go ahead with his plan was a Cabinet decision, Thatcher was not wholly in favour of it. She had, it was explained, been outnumbered by the heavyweights. She did not speak a public word in Prior's defence. By early 1983, with the assembly created by that legislation bogged down, the debate within the Party had moved significantly rightwards. The manifesto would be most likely to contain a simple commitment to continuing efforts to make the assembly work. The only question at issue was whether the Westminster 'integrationists' (the grouping of High Tories and Official Unionists which advocated making Northern Ireland a part of the United Kingdom on the same basis as Scotland or Wales) would succeed in influencing the phrasing of the manifesto. All those involved were agreed on one thing: it was not a major issue in Thatcher's mind.

There is an important sense in which Thatcher would not wish to be judged by the achievement or otherwise of managerial objectives such as targets, policies, priorities and statistics. She would claim that more important than any of these are ideas, 'The battle of ideas,' she fervently told a lunch guest in early 1983. 'We must win the battle of ideas.' In the closing passage of a major speech to the annual gathering of the Institute of Directors shortly afterwards, she listed as her most important achievement so far: 'The comfortable illusions that accompanied our gradual decline have been shattered. The nation has woken up to the reality of the need to earn its place in the world.' On that priority, Thatcher's friends and enemies would agree, her intellect and her emotion send her in the same direction. 'When that happens,' said one adviser, 'she's a pretty well irresistible force.' An unexpected issue in 1982 brought that about.

CHAPTER TWELVE

Falklands

'Never forget,' James Callaghan once admonished one of his Foreign Office ministers, 'that it's never the big foreign affairs problems which cause real trouble. It's the pimples at the other side of the world which start wars.' At the beginning of 1982, nobody in Britain thought much about the bleak archipelago 6,700 miles from London, whose 1800 inhabitants were little known or regarded, save for their passionate and demonstrative loyalty to Britain and for their Foreign Office governor's official car, a maroon London taxi. When the islands were invaded, one opinion poll found that 60% of its sample thought that the islands were off the west coast of Scotland.

Even Thatcher's ministers were devoting relatively small quantities of time to the long-running headache which responsibility for islands so coveted by Argentina had given all British governments, Labour and Conservative alike. It was not a subject which attracted Lord Carrington, although no Foreign Secretary could hope to avoid it for ever. Before the islands came to dominate what Thatcher was later to call the most remarkable year of her life, she had only intervened on Falklands policy on one occasion of any significance.

Thatcher's career and the life of her government were about to be transformed by a sudden, unforeseen sequence of disaster and triumph. The Falklands campaign found Thatcher in her element: what often appeared to be obstinacy and a refusal to accept complexity and compromise came to be seen as a temperament suited to making and carrying out military decisions. By the end of the war she was the longest-serving leader among the European heads of government: victory in the South Atlantic made her a world figure and she had acquired a new appetite and instinct for foreign policy. Although her unpopularity had already begun to diminish before the Falklands, the war transformed her reputation at home as well.

After a visit to Latin America early in the life of the government, one of Carrington's junior ministers, Nicholas Ridley, had presented him with a firm proposal in favour of one of many solutions canvassed over previous years, but never seen through to success. He proposed conceding nominal sovereignty to Argentina (which was all their negotiators apparently required), after which the islands would be leased back to Britain for administration which would protect the inhabitants' traditional way of life.

Ridley's proposal was accepted by Carrington, who felt it necessary to raise it with the Prime Minister himself. She apparently declared immediate opposition and one Whitehall source reportedly described her reaction to the plan as 'thermonuclear'. She challenged Carrington to explain why it would be necessary to offend the feelings of backbenchers who championed the interests of the islanders in the House of Commons. On 20 September 1979, he sent a minute to her and to the other members of the Cabinet's Oversea and Defence Committee (DOPC) explaining the unattractive choices which the government faced: they could, at vast cost, garrison the islands against Argentine attack (this option had already become known in Whitehall as 'Fortress Falklands'); they could procrastinate for as long as possible in negotiations without giving any ground; or they could attempt to make the best deal possible for the islanders while giving Argentina some concession on sovereignty. He recommended the third option in the form of leaseback and asked for an early decision.

At this point, Thatcher appears to have hesitated, pulled up by a characteristic mixture of instinct and caution. She discussed the matter with both Carrington and Ridley – one version holds that she suspected the motives of Foreign Office officials and having failed to shake Carrington decided to try Ridley direct – and concluded, in the words of the Franks report, 'that a decision of principle on the Government's approach to the problem could not be rushed.' It would be discussed by the defence committee. Carrington kept up the pressure; once again, Thatcher delayed a decision on the grounds that the discussion should be delayed until the Rhodesian problem was out of the way.

By January 1980, the Ridley plan was finally in front of the committee. There was an anxious discussion which analysed the likely reactions of Tory backbenchers who would be on their feet at the slightest suggestion of concessions over sovereignty, a fear fully justified by later events. The leaseback plan was then drawn up in detail in the Foreign Office, again approved by ministers, put to the islanders during another visit by Ridley, and finally destroyed by the 'Falklands lobby' in the House of Commons during the notorious session of 2 December 1980. The Cabinet wrung its hands about the affair the following morning, but the energy had been drained out of the last constructive option which the Foreign Office had been able to devise. Lord Carrington received a proposal from Ridley and the officials for a campaign to educate islander and British opinion, but turned it back on the grounds 'that it would not have been agreed to by his colleagues and would have been counter-productive'.

After that, the gradual passing of British policy from active diplomacy to ingenious stalling can hardly have touched Downing Street or the Prime Minister. But there was an undercurrent of worry expressed by some of the Foreign Office officials most closely involved. They expected matters to come to a head some time before the 150th anniversary of the British retaking of the islands which fell in February 1983. Thatcher was fleetingly embroiled in an argument which developed after the publication of the 1981 defence review (or 'Command 8288' as it was known in Whitehall jargon) over the fate of HMS *Endurance*, the ice patrol ship operating in the waters around the Falklands. At a saving of £$\frac{1}{4}$m the defence review had announced the withdrawal of *Endurance* and Carrington immediately objected on the grounds that, for a paltry sum, a signal had been sent to Argentina that Britain was ceasing to care about the Falklands. Nott won the support of Thatcher and the decision was upheld.

Cutting and controlling the Ministry of Defence's massive costs had come to be a major theme of the Thatcher public expenditure reviews; she had repeatedly clashed with Nott's predecessor, Francis Pym, who was thought to be 'soft' on his department's budget and he was reported to have threatened resignation over particularly fierce cuts disputed earlier in the life of the government. So when *Endurance*'s withdrawal triggered off protests from backbenchers and Falkland islanders, Thatcher herself became briefly involved in defending a point of principle. One MP recalls being invited by Ian Gow to ask a question which would allow Thatcher to explain her reasons.

These brief communications and conversations took place amidst the normal crush of government business; it was an intractable problem with a gloomy future, but the idea that Britain would be at war over the islands within weeks would have been regarded (at the time) as laughable. None of the danger signs or the limited range of responses available to a government in London were ever discussed by the defence committee, still less by the full Cabinet.

Thatcher was, for example, seeing the important telegrams from the British ambassador in Buenos Aires. His report of 3 March contained enough that was ominous for her to write on it, 'We must make contingency plans.' Her office relayed the instruction that updated versions of the available emergency procedures were to be brought to the defence committee; she also spoke to John Nott to ask advice on how long it would take the nearest British ships to reach the islands.

The landing of the Argentine scrap merchants on South Georgia on 19 March raised the stakes. Five days later, Lord Carrington reported to his colleagues that there was a risk of confrontation with Argentina; the following morning he briefed the full Cabinet on the attempts which were under way to cool the dispute. Thatcher agreed later the same day to his request for naval contingency planning. Most of the decisions about the handling of the South Georgia incident were actually taken in bilateral conversations or meetings between Thatcher and Lord Carrington and John Nott; had it become too much of a habit to avoid full Cabinets or full

committees whenever possible? The Franks Committee
certainly thought that fuller and earlier discussion would
have helped.

Intelligence reports relayed increasing signs of military
preparations in Argentina, but also held that there had been
no decision by the junta to force the issue by invading. On
Friday 26 March, when few people in Britain were aware of
the increasingly frantic scurrying in Whitehall, Thatcher
received an amended version of the standard advice offered
by the Chief of Staff about what could be done if the
Falklands were invaded. It gloomily concluded that there
was no certainty that they could be retaken.

Thatcher and Lord Carrington were due to fly to Brussels
for an EEC ministerial summit on Monday 29 March; the
night before, after reading the latest telegrams, Thatcher
rang Carrington to express – as the stiff language of the
Franks Report expressed it – 'her concern that the government should respond effectively to the critical situation on
South Georgia and worsening relations with the Argentine
government'. But the choices of 'effective' response were
very few. On the flight to Brussels, they decided to send a
nuclear-powered submarine to the islands; destroyers,
frigates and fleet auxiliary vessels then on exercise off
Gibraltar were already being gathered for possible despatch
to the South Atlantic. They returned to London; on the
Tuesday, Carrington held some meetings on the crisis, made
a statement in the House of Lords and then flew to Tel Aviv
for talks on the Middle East situation with the Israeli
Government. The contingency preparations against a
disaster on the other side of the world accelerated.

In the early evening of Wednesday 31 March, John Nott
was shown the signals interception intelligence ('sigint')
which confirmed an Argentine plan to invade. He found
Thatcher in her room at the House of Commons. Foreign
Office junior minister Richard Luce and one of his officials
arrived soon afterwards. Sir Henry Leach, the First Sea
Lord, arrived back at the Ministry of Defence from a naval
ceremony outside London and followed his minister to the
Commons, still dressed in full regalia. It failed to impress
the Commons policeman, who parked Sir Henry on a bench

where he was spotted by a horrified junior whip who had to put him in his own office until he could be delivered to the Prime Minister's council of war. Other senior officials and ministers trickled in as the evening wore on.

Thatcher, although she appears to have given indications to the meeting that her instinct was towards a tough response, also accepted the reservations which were presented by those round the table. The Foreign Office side held to the view that since an invasion could not be prevented, nothing should be done which would give Argentina an excuse to make it more likely. From the MoD side came doubts about the feasibility of an operation so far from home. The one man who appears not to have shared these doubts, and who may have sensed the Prime Minister's own instincts in the matter, was Sir Henry Leach. He said that a full-scale task force could be ready by the weekend and that if Argentina did invade, Britain could reply in kind. When asked by Thatcher how he would react to that possibility if he were an Argentine admiral, he is said to have replied, 'I would return to harbour immediately.' Bombastic as it might have sounded to some participants at the meeting, it turned out to be an accurate prediction. Urgent messages were sent from the meeting asking President Reagan to intervene with the junta.

The following morning the Cabinet met to hear a progress report from Humphrey Atkins who warned that retaking and defending the Falklands would not be easy; in summing up the discussion, Thatcher said that the best remaining hope of avoiding confrontation lay in the influence of the American government over the Argentine. The defence committee met later to consider the options which were so severely limited by geography and diplomacy. The Americans had been assured that Britain would do nothing to escalate matters any further; the committee agreed not to try to fly troops to Port Stanley since they could not arrive in time. Thatcher told the committee that the Argentine task force could reach the islands in about 24 hours.

On Thursday evening, the group which had met the previous day at the House of Commons reconvened in

Thatcher's study at Downing Street; Thatcher herself returned from Windsor where she had been scheduled to stay with the queen that night. Whitelaw attended and Carrington arrived back from the Middle East before it ended. The fleet and the troops which make up the country's front-line assault forces were alerted. There was by now little debate about the rights and wrongs of deploying a task force; whether as bargaining counter or reinvasion force, it was clearly needed. Although the composition of the force had been largely decided by contingency plans which were already written, how it was to go about the job was not.

The strategic decisions which were made at the early informal meetings of what was to become the War Cabinet — Thatcher, Whitelaw, Pym, Nott and Parkinson — unleashed a hectic weekend of troop movement, planning, begging, stealing and borrowing of supplies for the task force to be able to meet Leach's promise that it could sail at the weekend. The intelligence officer of the commando brigade which was to lead the way, spent several hours in Plymouth City Library trying to learn what he could about Argentine military dispositions. Brigadier Julian Thompson, in charge of the Royal Marine preparations, already felt the influence of Thatcher's personality, although many of his colleagues doubted whether they would ever reach the islands, let alone fight for them. 'I was quite sure,' he said afterwards, 'that with our Prime Minister, if the Argentinians didn't fold, we would fight them.'

A crisis of this kind brings crushing pressures on prime ministers. Civil servants wondered about its effect on her. Their predecessors had noticed its devastating effect on Sir Anthony Eden, whose health was anyway uncertain at the time, during the Suez crisis. The day is lengthened by the five-hour time difference with the American east coast, meaning that discussions with Washington may not end until the early hours of the morning. That night, President Reagan had succeeded in speaking to President Galtieri with the aid of a State Department interpreter; 'I guess I spelt it out,' he said after hanging up, 'but it didn't sound as if the message got through.' At 2.45 a.m. London time, a message from the White House reached Downing Street relaying the gloomy outcome of the conversation.

At a Cabinet meeting which began at 9.45 a.m. on Friday 2 April, Thatcher announced that an invasion appeared imminent (it had in fact already taken place, although London did not know because of faulty communications) and at a later one beginning that night at half past seven, its members agreed that the task force should sail. The House of Commons was told that there would be a special sitting of the House on the following day, the first time that the House had sat over a weekend since the Suez crisis. The second Cabinet meeting of the day heard a presentation from service chiefs about the logistical problems of keeping a task force supplied at sea during the onset of the South Atlantic winter. It was agreed that Argentine assets in London would be frozen, export credits and imports suspended. Thatcher asked each minister in turn. Only John Biffen dissented. It was clear to most that a government which failed to take military action would fall, a feeling which was put into words by Mr. Whitelaw; if they had both watched an invasion of the islands and baulked at the risks involved in sending a task force, he said, they would have to resign.

The Commons on the morning of 3 April bore out Whitelaw's judgment: it was in a vindictive mood. Thatcher delivered her opening set piece without assurance or fluency. She was reading a speech dictated by the Foreign Office and dominated by the importance of avoiding the real confession: that her Government had risked a policy which did not add up. They could not detach the islands from Britain, neither could they defend them. They had inherited the dilemma, but as the options had steadily been running out, their gamble had been slightly greater. She could not discuss the nuances and minutiae of espionage and signals interception with the House. Her only defence was the task force: 'It is the government's objective to see that the islands are freed from occupation and are returned to British administration at the earliest possible moment.'

It was not enough to shield the front bench from an explosion of pent-up bellicosity and contempt which Tory die-hards had been wanting to detonate for some time. They had been frustrated over Rhodesia, immigration, Northern Ireland and a host of smaller issues. The Labour Party found itself in the enjoyable and unusual position of being able to hurl accusations of feebleness and lack of patriotism at a Conservative government, their position considerably reinforced by the calm solidity of James Callaghan, able to point to his despatch of a flotilla to the islands in 1977 at a time of tension.

Michael Foot, the Labour Party leader, was no less vehement than the Tory backwoodsmen: 'Even though the position and circumstances of the people who live in the Falkland Islands are uppermost in our minds ... there is the longer term interest to ensure that foul and brutal aggression does not succeed in the world. If it does, there will be a danger not merely to the Falkland Islands, but to people all over this dangerous planet.' Mr Foot said Tory MP Patrick Cormack a little later 'spoke for Britain'. The Foreign Office was regularly denounced as a nest of appeasers and the one Conservative who was himself an ex-diplomat and who tried to point out the longer-term dangers of going to war without knowing what you would do with victory when you had achieved it, was told that his old department had not been working for Britain and his speech was continually drowned by howling interruptions.

The newspapers of the following morning were no more gentle, reflecting the right-wing pressures on Carrington to resign. Carrington himself by this time felt he had to go and many ministerial hours were devoted on the Sunday to trying to make him change his mind. Besides Thatcher, Whitelaw, Chief Whip Michael Jopling, Lord Home and Harold Macmillan were all asked to add their persuasions. Whitelaw, who had lunch with Carrington at the latter's house in Ovington Square, could only extract an assurance that he would see what things looked like in the morning. Among other things, the morning brought a *Times* leader which made it brutally clear that he should go. Luce and Humphrey Atkins resigned with him. Among other factors in her mind, Thatcher must have given some thought as she urged him to stay, to the question of his possible successor. She had very little choice but to promote Francis Pym, perhaps the most formidable single challenger among her Cabinet opponents if she failed, and a man with whom she was to find herself frequently at odds during the politico-military diplomacy of the war.

Thatcher was now on the edge of an experience which falls to few modern prime ministers. Official machinery will respond sensitively and immediately to any command in a military emergency. But she would not be able to survive a failure. Occasional phrases in her speeches shortly after the end of the campaign to retake the islands suggested a little wistfulness for the simplicity of making and implementing decisions in wartime. By a curious irony, she had reminded herself of two British wartime leaders not long before the campaign began. Several months before, she had paid a visit to Churchill's underground war rooms which remain preserved much as they were when he used them. She had noticed a motto from Queen Victoria which Churchill kept on his desk: 'We are not interested in the possibilities of defeat: they do not exist.' She used the phrase in a television interview on the eve of the task force's departure: 'Do you remember what Queen Victoria said? Failure? The possibilities do not exist.' Just two weeks before the invasion, the National Maritime Museum in Greenwich had met a request from Downing Street for a portrait of Lord Nelson to hang in Thatcher's study.

Full Whitehall wartime machinery was not used: three ministers — William Whitelaw, Francis Pym, John Nott — and party chairman Cecil Parkinson were picked as a sub-committee of the Cabinet OD committee. With the initials for the words South Atlantic it became 'ODSA' and known in Whitehall as 'Odza'; it was instantly known outside as the War Cabinet. Parkinson fulfilled three roles: he represented the rest of the Cabinet, and to some extent, the party at large; he balanced the two heavyweights from the soggier end of the Cabinet and, as the only member of the committee without a department to run, he became the government's senior ambassador to the media after the Prime Minister herself.

The committee met virtually every day, starting at 9.30 a.m. to hear the overnight reports from the task force and late diplomatic news from Washington and New York. It was attended by a shifting cast of senior officials, the most regular attenders being Chief of the Defence Staff (CDS) Sir Terence (now Lord) Lewin and Sir Robert Armstrong. Lewin and Thatcher very quickly worked well and closely; they shared the same unprivileged background and stern, purposeful temperaments. 'He has beautiful manners and that sort of thing,' said one friend, 'but he's not exactly *funny*.' Sir Terence and John Nott had between them effected one of those important yet almost completely hidden moves by which the massive geological plates of Whitehall custom are shifted: they had finally established the CDS as an independent voice of military advice to the Cabinet and not as the conduit for the heads of the individual services. Independent junior ministers for each of the services had also been abolished. The Prime Minister undoubtedly shared the urge to cut down the power of what successive and frustrated defence ministers have come to regard as barely controllable service fiefdoms.

Sir Michael Palliser, the Foreign Office Permanent Secretary who had been in the process of retiring as the islands were invaded, was asked to return and set up a small group of officials in the Cabinet office which briefed other departments on developments and which prepared material for the War Cabinet on less immediate issues. He and his staff of two took over the Cabinet Office suite previously occupied by Sir Derek Rayner and his small team.

'When we started out,' Thatcher was to say after the campaign was over, 'there were the waverers and the fainthearts, the people who thought that Britain could no longer seize the initiative for herself.' It is probably just as true to say that many people's ambivalence was the same doubt which had afflicted many of those at the centre of events at the start of the affair. If a task force is mobilised does it work effectively as a bargaining counter in a search for a peaceful solution? Or does it acquire a momentum of its own and once despatched cannot easily be turned back? But as the campaign went on, public opinion – led and not followed by Thatcher – came round to her point of view. A series of Market Opinion and Research International polls with the same panel of interviewees found that satisfaction with the government's handling of the crisis had risen from 60% in mid-April to 84% after the Argentine forces had surrendered. Similar rises were recorded in support for: landing troops; sinking ships in Falklands waters; bombing Argentine bases (which even the War Cabinet baulked at); and the proposition that sovereignty was worth the loss of servicemen's lives.

On 9 April, 3 Commando Brigade sailed aboard the requisitioned passenger liner *Canberra*. President Reagan had given his Secretary of State Alexander Haig permission, on 7 April, to try some Kissinger-style shuttling in an attempt to stop two American allies going to war. Britain's diplomatic stance had been enormously strengthened at the start by two coups brought off by the much-vilified diplomats: partly by mobilising Thatcher to call King Hussein personally to swing his country's wavering vote, United Nations ambassador Sir Anthony Parsons had achieved a Security Council resolution ordering Argentina to back off. On Tuesday 6 April, Thatcher had sent a personal letter to the head of every government in the EEC asking for their support for a community-wide ban on Argentine imports; after some busy legwork from British officials in Brussels, the ban was settled over the following Easter weekend.

'We're friends of both sides,' President Reagan had announced at the start of the crisis. Haig was rightly thought to be strongly inclined towards Britain. But as he set off on his travels, there was some suspicion abroad that American peace-making would not necessarily assist its historic transatlantic ally. Haig's team arrived in Britain on 8 April and went to Downing Street after a brief stop at the Foreign Office. The opening session of talks was formal and stiff. Thatcher was lined up with Pym, the Foreign Office's new Permanent Secretary Sir Anthony Acland, Nott and Lewin. The group then moved to the study. Thatcher pointed out the portraits of Nelson and Wellington on the walls. Haig teased her by saying that General Galtieri was supposed to be a Thatcher fan. The Prime Minister pulled a face and everybody relaxed a little. At the end of dinner,

Haig outlined his approach again and it was clear that he was broadly sympathetic to Britain. Pym, Nott and Acland discussed theoretical concessions, but Thatcher was sceptical: she did not see how the Americans could find a window of opportunity to reconcile the two positions. She chided Haig with a phrase which was to become something of a slogan on the rest of the shuttle. 'They're just too woolly, Al,' she said when Haig spelt out his further ideas. 'It's your old friend, Woolly Al,' Haig was to say later, whenever the team concocted some idea that looked as if it was not going to get past Thatcher.

Haig went to Buenos Aires, tried to make it clear to an inchoate junta that Thatcher meant business, then returned to London. The British position, anchored upon the principle of self-determination for the islanders, had not softened, although Pym appeared keen to make every effort to help the American mission. He suggested at one point that the shock of invasion might have dissolved some of the intransigence of islander opinion; Thatcher commented that it was hardly likely to be altered in a pro-Argentine direction.

Haig's team was not finding it easy in either capital, but at least they knew where they stood when talking to Thatcher or the War Cabinet. One member of Haig's team commented later, 'I was struck by the strength of Thatcher's convictions. She felt more strongly I think than anyone in the Cabinet. She was the driving force, the leading edge. She was not at all tactical. What she wanted to talk about, initially at least, were the principles involved. And in a way it was refreshing; she looked at it in historical terms, in terms of the peaceful settlement of disputes and so on. I found that quite striking and it certainly affected the way we proceeded, because knowing the strength of her convictions, we had no doubt at all in our minds about the inevitability of the conflict and of the British success if diplomacy did not work out. It made us strive even harder to pull off a success.'

By the last week of April, the advance group of destroyers and Admiral Woodward's 'task group' were meeting in mid-Atlantic and Haig's criss-cross journeys were slowing down. A secret attempt to recapture South

Georgia, seven hundred miles south-east of the Falklands, was under way. During the operation, which came close to disaster several times in appalling weather, Thatcher had visited a nervous fleet headquarters at Northwood in Middlesex. To servicemen brought up with little respect for the inconstancy of politicians, her approach made much the same impression on the naval officers there as it had on Haig's men. On the night of 25 April, Thatcher emerged from the front door of No. 10 towing Nott in her wake, who was then instructed to read out the message from the task force reporting the recapture of South Georgia. Nott looked like an unhappy head prefect reading an announcement to school prayers. Questions immediately rained on them. 'Just rejoice at that news and congratulate our forces and the marines ... rejoice, rejoice,' said Thatcher before disappearing inside the door again, taking Nott with her. That instruction was not the last time during the campaign that the media were to hear the Prime Minister using that peremptory tone of voice.

Haig's mission ground to a halt and the American administration formally declared its support for Britain. At the beginning of May, covert patrols of the Special Air Service and the Special Boat Squadron were landed on the islands to begin reconnaissance for the landing on the Falkland Islands, which could not be attempted until the task force had established sea and air superiority in the area. To date, it had very largely been a 'phoney war', with negligible casualties.

On Sunday 2 May, Lewin arrived at the War Cabinet being held at Chequers to relay a request from Woodward for the submarine HMS *Conqueror* to sink the 14,000-ton Argentine cruiser *General Belgrano* forty miles outside the 'total exclusion zone', although such action would be justifiable under the rules of engagement. The order was issued after a unanimous War Cabinet decision and the *Belgrano* was sunk later that day. 368 members of her crew died.

Two days later, Thatcher was chairing a meeting of the Cabinet's 'E' committee, when at around six o'clock she was brought the first news that HMS *Sheffield*, a well-armed Type-42 destroyer, had been hit by an air-launched Exocet missile, caught fire and been abandoned. The casualty figures were unknown. Those who saw her that night — and she immediately convened a meeting at her room in the Commons — testified to the devastating effect of the news. Despite the strain, she had shown only slight signs of tiredness. Her traditionally enormous supply of adrenalin appeared to be pushing her through. Now she looked drawn and sad. From the date of the *Sheffield*'s sinking, colleagues began to worry that for a 'war leader' she was taking the deaths too personally and too much to heart. One or two approached Janet Young and tried to enlist her help in making Thatcher accept that war brings death in its wake. Throughout the campaign, Thatcher used to repair to the Downing Street flat late at night to write personal letters to the relatives of the victims.

The traditional debates over the reporting of wars had reverberated from the opening of the campaign; normal difficulties were exacerbated for journalists by the inescapable fact that the only way to get to the war was to sail with the task force. Thatcher took a strong personal interest in another traditional pastime in emergencies: attacking the BBC.

'The higher you get,' Lewin said after the war, 'the more aware you are of the great importance of public support and the part that the media play in providing you with public support and parliamentary support.' It was clearly Thatcher's view from the early days that the BBC was not playing its part. Early in May she had replied to a question in the Commons and criticised the broadcasters by saying that she understood that 'there are times when it seems that we and the Argentines are being treated almost as equals and almost on a neutral basis.' She closed her answer on a relatively detached and restrained note: 'I can only say that if this is so it gives offence and causes great emotion among many people.'

The parliamentary complaints, particularly about the 'even-handedness' of the BBC, rumbled on until the morning of 10 May, when the War Cabinet discussed the question of media management which was being dealt with in a day-to-day basis by two daily Whitehall meetings: the Information Coordination group, chaired at No. 10 by Bernard Ingham, and the section of the Chiefs of Staff committee meeting attended by the MoD's wry and measured spokesman, Ian McDonald. The War Cabinet meeting criticised the lack of television pictures from the South Atlantic. Ministers thought that carefully censored pictures would not endanger morale at home. That night the BBC's flagship current affairs programme *Panorama* devoted part of its time to a filmed report of doubts and dissenters among a few MPs and retired service chiefs. The Prime Minister was watching in the Downing Street flat.

'OUTRAGE OVER THE BEEB!' yelled *The Sun*'s headline the next morning, adding for good measure: 'Storm at *Panorama*'s "despicable" Argie bias.' One of Thatcher's former ministers, Mrs Sally Oppenheim, rose in the Commons the following afternoon to denounce the programme – which had also featured interviews with an Argentine representative at the UN and with Cecil Parkinson – as 'an odious, subversive travesty'. 'I share the deep concern that has been expressed on many sides,' Thatcher said, 'particularly about the content of yesterday evening's *Panorama* programme. I know how strongly many people feel that the case for our country is not being put with sufficient vigour on certain – I do not say all – BBC programmes. The chairman of the BBC has assured us, and has said in vigorous terms, that the BBC is not neutral on this point, and I hope his words will be heeded by the many who have responsibilities for standing up for our task force, our boys, our people and the cause of democracy.' Would it be 'useful', asked Mr David Winnick MP, if Thatcher and her friends stopped their 'constant intimidation' of the BBC? 'It is our great pride that the British media are free,' she replied, adding in case the BBC had missed the point, 'But we expect the case for freedom to be put by those who are responsible for doing so.'

There appears to have been a fault on Thatcher's line to the people. No survey of opinion could find widespread mistrust or even anger generated by the BBC's reporting and analysis. A survey commissioned by the BBC itself found that 81% of people questioned thought that it had behaved 'in a responsible manner'. A Gallup poll in the *Daily Telegraph* found that 62% thought it was reporting fairly. Separated by party affiliation the poll still showed that 57% of Conservatives disagreed with criticism of the BBC and that only 32% agreed.

Loss of life and the sudden notoriety of the sea-skimming Exocet briefly shook the nerve of the politicians conducting the war. The loss of the *Sheffield* was followed the next day, 5 May, by a full Cabinet and a complete presentation of the military position to date. Thatcher asked for views around the table, ticking off positions taken on the attitude to the fresh peace proposals being put forward by President Belaunde of Peru, over which she and Francis Pym had disagreed violently in the War Cabinet. Only two ministers, Lord Hailsham and Michael Heseltine, are thought to have dissented from the view that they should take the Peruvian proposals seriously and strain to meet their conditions. And in the Commons the following day, Thatcher took an unusually helpful line, although she was markedly less sympathetic to some new outline suggestions which had been formulated by the new UN Secretary-General, Perez de Cuellar. The junta promptly dismissed the Peruvian plan, leaving the UN proposal struggling against the odds. Thatcher contended that she would not fall into the Argentine trap of protracted talks while the winter grew worse. She was, however, changeable, one moment endorsing Pym's quest for common ground, one moment expressing doubt that there was any point in continuing to talk. Whatever was to happen would have to happen quickly; the War Cabinet was agreed that any landing would be hampered by a parallel drama of fine balanced negotiations. By the end of the second week of May, the service chiefs were ready to brief the War Cabinet on their landing plans, codenamed Operation Sutton.

Tory backbenchers were clearly not in the mood for compromise of any kind. Pym was given a hostile grilling by the 1922 Committee on 13 May, just after an acrimonious debate in the Chamber during which Thatcher had glared angrily while Heath had paid pointed compliments to Pym's work. Parsons and the Washington ambassador Sir Nicholas Henderson travelled to London for a War Cabinet. It was at this meeting that Parsons' consolidated his relationship with the Prime Minister to such a degree that, in spite of his being a Labour supporter, she later asked him to join her Downing Street staff as foreign affairs adviser. He was careful to avoid standard Foreign Office phrases which tended to suggest to Thatcher that the other side was being appeased and he did not hesitate to cut across her. 'Prime Minister,' he interrupted once. 'if I may finish what I was saying ... ' The document which emerged from that seven-hour meeting, although it was ultimately rejected by a junta trapped by its own adventurism, is remarkably conciliatory compared to the rigid 'Fortress Falklands' policy which has emerged since the end of the war. It accepted a mutual withdrawal of forces. It did not mention 'self-determination' but only an article of the UN charter covering some of the same ground. There would be no British governor but a UN administrator. Negotiations would proceed. Many of Argentine diplomats and their American supporters thought that Buenos Aires ought to have accepted it. Just before the news of the Argentine rejection was received, the Chiefs of Staff made their full-dress presentation of Operation Sutton to the War Cabinet. Immediately after the news from New York, Northwood ordered Woodward to proceed with the landing at his discretion.

The War Cabinet never settled into the regular division of opinion which its membership might have suggested. There were constant differences over peace negotiations between Thatcher and Pym, but Pym was not automatically supported by Whitelaw, and Nott and Parkinson did not regularly line up with the Prime Minister. Thatcher, Whitelaw and Pym formed the key triumvirate; Whitelaw, heading the least closely involved department, was the most frequent absentee and Parkinson's lack of departmental duties removed him slightly from the centre of detailed decision-making. Whitelaw and Pym, who both had wartime experience and who both hold Military Crosses, were two of the steadiest counsellors when men began to be killed. Nott, always a taut and wayward man, prone to sudden outbreaks of self-doubt, was to announce his retirement from politics not long after the end of the war.

The War Cabinet suffered a particularly nervy week after the landings at San Carlos Bay. Hobbled by the loss of all but one of the giant Chinook helicopters which had been sunk with the *Atlantic Conveyor* four days after the landings on 25 May, the task force moved east and south from its bridgehead only very slowly. Ministers struggled with the inclination to drive from the back seat.

With the task force gradually pushing towards Port Stanley, Thatcher once again came under pressure to negotiate. The Pope was visiting Britain, President Reagan was due to arrive soon and the longer-term future of the islands had to be considered. One of the recurrent divisions between Thatcher and her new Foreign Secretary was Pym's championing of the idea that the ending of the war could not be divorced from the starting of the peace. Was Britain to commit itself to garrisoning the islands indefinitely? At the very least it was beginning to look as if Thatcher did not wish to look any further than that. Lord Shackleton, whose report on the possibilities of economic development of the islands published in 1977 had effectively been shelved, was asked to update his conclusions. 'There are immense possibilities for development,' said Thatcher. 'I think she may be disappointed,' said a member of Shackleton's team as he got down to work.

On 1 June, the War Cabinet was presented with several options for 'internationalising' the problem once the military campaign was over — an approach which was being developed by the Foreign Office in consultation with the State Department in Washington. President Reagan formally presented Thatcher with an American 'five-point plan' when they met at a Western leaders' summit at Versailles in the first week of June. Reagan also suffered the painful embarrassment of sitting down to lunch one day next to a stony-faced Thatcher, apparently unaware that the previous night had seen an extraordinary about-turn in the United Nations Security Council. After voting to support a British veto against an unwelcome negotiating proposal, the

American ambassador to the UN, Jeanne Kirkpatrick, had been instructed to announce that her government would have abstained, had it made up its mind in time — a remarkable feat of diplomacy which succeeded in upsetting both friends and enemies alike.

'Magnanimous. It is not a word I use in connection with a battle on the Falklands,' said Thatcher during the final phase of the land campaign. On Saturday 12 June, news came through that the battle for Mount Tumbledown and Wireless Ridge was about to begin. Thatcher and Nott drove to Northwood to listen in the operations room. At 10.15 p.m. on the following Monday evening, she was able to say that the Argentines 'are reported to be flying white flags over Port Stanley'. Foot, who may have cast his opening speech in the six-hour debate of 3 April in the mould of a Prime Minister-in-waiting in case Thatcher should be sunk in the South Atlantic, nevertheless issued generous praise. 'I can well understand the anxieties and pressures that must have been upon her during these weeks, and I can understand that at this moment those pressures and anxieties may be relieved. And I congratulate her.' The crowd outside No. 10 sang 'Rule Britannia' as she returned home.

The war was over, but there was much else to follow. There were continuous post-mortems and analyses of the fighting and the diplomacy. A stream of ships and planes brought servicemen back to their families. The five members of the Franks Committee spent much of the summer in cubicles in a room in the Foreign Office building reading the secret papers. In October there was a victory parade through the City of London. According to one witness who saw her on the Commons terrace, Thatcher had been 'spitting blood' just after the thanksgiving service held at St. Paul's on 26 July. The Archbishop of Canterbury's sermon was apparently insufficiently patriotic and Thatcher was not the only one to think so; Edward Heath turned to Michael Foot just after it had ended to ask him with rich sarcasm if he had ghost-written it.

'She's very lucky, you know, to have been given a second wind at all,' said a junior minister assessing the government's transformed prospects. 'Most prime ministers don't get a second chance.' A MORI poll taken within a week of the Argentine surrender showed Conservative support at 48%, three points higher than the party achieved in the 1979 election and the first time in the life of the government that they had improved on that figure. What was remarkable about the trend of the figures, however, was that they made clear – contrary to the claims of Thatcher's opponents inside and outside her own party – that the rise in popularity had begun before the Falklands had been invaded. In MORI polls, the Conservative rating had been a steady 27% from September to December the previous year; it had risen to 29% in January, 30% in February and 34% in March. The same applied to her personal rating: satisfaction with Thatcher had fallen to 25%, the lowest point in a long decline since the general election, in December 1982. It had climbed back to 36% by March; after the Falklands campaign it was standing at 59%. The little-noticed recovery in popularity before April may help explain why the 'Falklands Factor' did not wear off as fast as pundits predicted that it might; wartime leadership, they said, does not necessarily appeal to peacetime voters and compared the aftermath to the slump in Churchill's popularity at the end of the Second World War.

'If you ask a person here what he would associate with Britain,' Thatcher said in an interview with the *Washington Post* at the beginning of June, 'it's not this talk about the welfare state or any sort of benefits or jargon. He would say, "We are a free country." I think what we are seeing now is something quite fundamental in the drawing together of the British people once liberty and justice are challenged once again.' On 3 July Thatcher delivered a speech to a Conservative rally at Cheltenham racecourse which poured out her instincts on the fusion of the spirit of war and peace. It is worth quoting at some length.

She began by saying that in spite of secret doubts about whether Britain was the nation it had once been, when 'called to arms' – 'then we British are as we always have been – competent, courageous and resolute.

'... yet why does it need a war to bring out our qualities

and reassert our pride? Why do we have to be invaded
before we throw aside our selfish aims and begin to work
together as only we can work together, as only we can
work, and achieve as only we can achieve? All over Britain,
men and women are asking – why can't we achieve in peace
what we can do so well in war? During this past week, I
have read again a little-known speech of Winston Churchill,
made just after the last war. This is what he said: "We must
find the means and the method of working together not only
in times of war, and mortal anguish, but in time of peace,
with all its bewilderments and clamour and clatter of
tongues."

'We saw the signs when, this week, the NUR came to
understand that its strike on the railways and on the
Underground just didn't fit – didn't match the spirit of these
times. And yet on Tuesday, eight men, the leaders of
ASLEF, misunderstanding the new mood of the nation, set
out to bring the railways to a halt. Ignoring the example of
the NUR, the travelling public whom they are supposed to
serve, and the jobs and future of their own members, this
tiny group decided to use its undoubted power. For what?
To delay Britain's recovery, which all our people long to
see.'

It might have come as a surprise to the executive of the
train drivers' union that they were holding up the entire
recovery of the British economy, particularly since they
appeared to enjoy substantial backing among their own
members for industrial action which was widely interpreted
as a defensive move against their NUR rivals who wished to
be the sole organising union on the railways. And peace in
general, with all its clamour and clatter of tongues, turned
out to be very much like the peace which had preceded the
Falklands campaign. If the unions appeared less aggressive,
their resolve seemed much more likely to have been
weakened by the fear of unemployment than the magic
force of the Falklands Factor. The remaining EEC
countries rapidly abandoned sanctions against Argentina,
the MoD returned unabashed to the business of cutting the
navy down to an economic size and the public showed no
special interest in the future of the Falklands themselves.

As the months after the campaign passed and the garrison, which vastly outnumbered the population, settled into making the best of a bad posting, Thatcher's closer colleagues became worried that she was unable to turn her thoughts away from the symbolic importance of the war to the nagging and intractable problem of what to do about the islands. Lord Shackleton reported again on their economy, proposing large amounts of aid as the only way of reversing the slow decline in the numbers of economically active islanders, without whom the community would eventually collapse anyway. Shackleton devoted some time to personally developing his ideas with the Prime Minister, but could not overcome two obstacles: implementation of Shackleton's key suggestion would mean government intervention in the land market in favour of new, smaller farms run by owner-occupiers. Thatcher apparently felt that the proposal hardly fitted Conservative economic doctrine and her officials were anxious about the risks of land profiteering. The second problem was simply the inescapable geographical fact of Argentina at close hand. There was no sign that Argentina, although bitter about the deposed General Galtieri's conduct of the war, was softening its claim to sovereignty. A substantial programme of development in the islands would amount to an announcement that 'Fortress Falklands' was to be the policy for ever. The government contented itself with a timid and gradual plan for the assistance of land reform, leaving the Shackleton team less than optimistic that it would make much difference. 'We are not running the country with them,' the Foreign Office junior minister said, defending this course of action to the Commons. 'We are standing guard to enable them to live their lives in their own way.'

It was to prove one of the most expensive guard-mounting operations which the British Army has ever conducted. Forward public expenditure figures released early in 1983 revealed that the cost over the next three years would amount to £1m for each of the 1800 islanders. The bill for replacing ships and hardware destroyed or used in the war stretches into the late 1980s; the government appears to estimate the annual cost of the garrison apart from those bills will be about £232m a year. A Gallup poll in the *Daily Telegraph* the previous week showed that 53% of people questioned agreed that it was not worth spending more than £400m a year (it will be well above that until at least 1986) to keep the islands British. Two adults in three, it found, thought that it would make sense to try and agree with Argentina on the future of the Falklands; no poll tested what kind of agreement the public might find acceptable and whether time had softened attitudes to the point where some concessions might be possible. There was some evidence from the polls taken during the campaign that while Thatcher was well-supported in her opposition to the invasion, she was not so well supported in her opposition, then and now, to going some way to meeting Argentina over a settlement.

Thatcher made no secret during and after the war that she felt that her long-time mistrust of the Foreign Office had been finally vindicated. 'There's no doubt,' Pym said, 'that Mrs Thatcher did feel let down at the time of the Falklands ... I don't think she felt let down by her Foreign Secretary. She did feel let down, I think, by the Foreign Office.' Carrington, watching at first bitterly from the sidelines and latterly in a somewhat more mellow frame of mind, disliked what he told associates were the wrong lessons being drawn from the war. Britain, he thought, should use its renewed self-confidence to achieve its foreign policy objectives, not draw into its own self-sufficient shell. The *Daily Mail*'s columnist, Andrew Alexander, had argued, as the campaign was reaching its climax, that 'we do not need others as much as we thought ... The idea that world opinion is something to which we must pay deferential regard has, I suggest, received a body blow in recent weeks.'

Thatcher and Pym disagreed frequently; their personal relationship never approached the Thatcher-Carrington rapport. Morale in the once-proud Foreign Office did not recover once the war was over. Sir Anthony Parsons' position halfway between his old colleagues and a Prime Minister on the warpath was delicate and its problems were reflected in an exchange with her when she was visiting Downing Street to discuss his terms of employment (three

days a week, five weeks' notice by either party). He said
that he would like to discuss his contract with his old
colleagues; 'Why?' she asked. 'It's got nothing to do with
them. You're becoming my foreign policy adviser.' But
Parsons won his way.

Lord Franks and his colleagues delivered their report to
Downing Street in the first week of January. One Saturday
Thatcher made the gruelling 23-hour journey to the islands.
The journey was a well-kept secret until she was airborne.
The television pictures beamed home, after a row between
Ingham and the BBC, provided some of the most potent pre-
election help which the Prime Minister was likely to receive
from the small screen. She was mobbed by the islanders and
edged herself neatly into regal territory by presenting some
campaign medals to servicemen who were still serving on
ships and who had been unable to return home to collect
them. Shops on the islands were doing a brisk trade in
photographs of Thatcher. She visited the grave of Colonel
'H' Jones, the hero of the Parachute Regiment, who had
died at Goose Green. She was filmed firing a large artillery
piece. By now she was the living embodiment of a principle
which she had enunciated to the *Washington Post*: 'Look at
a day when you are supremely satisfied at the end of the
day. It's not a day when you lounge around doing nothing.
It's when you've had everything to do, a real challenge, and
you've done it. Life really isn't just an existence. It's using
all the talents with which you were born. You can only do
that if you've got a government that believes that that is the
purpose of life as well.'

CHAPTER THIRTEEN

Future

In the autumn of 1982, around fifty Conservative MPs, MEPs, sympathisers, lobbyists and thinkers received a 'strictly confidential' letter from Sir Geoffrey Howe asking them to serve on a series of secret committees designed to 'identify programmes and measures for the second term of office of the present administration'. The Government was entering the last eighteen months of its parliamentary life, and perhaps more to the point, the predictions that Thatcher's Falklands popularity would prove short-lived had been wrong. The party's poll ratings stayed healthily above forty per cent through that autumn and into the new year. The planning and jockeying for position in a second Thatcher administration began in earnest.

The sources of advice competing for the ear of the Prime Minister were more numerous than those in opposition. As she has become more experienced and self-assured, Thatcher has continued to create interlocking networks of advisers from which she can pick and choose ideas. Some are inside Central Office machinery, some outside and some halfway. Some are inside government departments, some not. Some pick the brains of civil servants, some draw on the gurus of the CPS, the IEA or the Adam Smith Institute. The process was compared by one observer with the discarded American scheme for the siting of the MX missiles: 'Some empty silos are sited so as to encourage your friends, some so as to confuse your enemies, and only a very few to do a real job of launching a live attack when the war comes.'

Whatever the mixture of personalities, an important or sensitive issue is marked by the presence of a man or woman labelled – to the continuing embarrassment of even some of her loyalists – 'one of us'. Nine groups considering topics in the political economy were established to report to

Sir Geoffrey. Their subjects ranged from the quality of education (chaired by Lord Beloff) to the interplay of tax and social security (chaired by Terence Higgins MP). Manifesto submissions on other subjects were sent to Ferdinand Mount, the head of the policy unit at Downing Street.

There was some disagreement on the degree of radicalism which should be evident from the manifesto and over the quantity of detail it should include. Should it be open about its most extreme objectives, on the assumption that the electorate responds to bold ideas, and precise in its prescriptions in order to lessen the risk of obstruction by Whitehall? Or should it dampen the radicalism, in order to lessen the risk of Conservative voters defecting to the Alliance, and to cut down the hostages to fortune?

Some of these doubts reflected policy debates always present in the party, even the one led by Thatcher after the Falklands campaign. Thatcher's personal confidence was obvious enough after the war. She discovered a new appetite for foreign affairs and began to enjoy summits. The left wing of the Conservative party lapsed into sullen silence in the face of her unquestioned popularity and self-assurance. There was uncertainty about the exact reasons for the Government's continued popularity. Some of it was to be explained by the difficulties of both Labour and the Alliance. Labour's internal strife and Michael Foot's lacklustre leadership left the party weakened, despite a few by-election victories. The Alliance poll ratings and by-election performances were volatile and there seemed to be no pattern to the way in which they gained votes from either of their major rivals. But Conservative votes in by-elections were regularly around six per cent lower than the party's opinion poll scores, suggesting to some psephologists that there was a section of moderate Conservative voters very ready to move into the Alliance camp.

Opinion polls constantly reiterated that the issue of greatest concern to voters was unemployment, but the Thatcher government seemed largely to escape the blame. One of her ministers had remarked in opposition that one of their main tasks in government would be to place the responsibility for unemployment on the trade unions. They succeeded in shifting attitudes, although government economists were acknowledging in private that up to half a million of the unemployed had lost their jobs unnecessarily because of the early over-restriction of the money supply. The workless themselves blamed the international recession and if they were disposed to vote against Thatcher, they tended to be concentrated in seats which already boasted Labour majorities. By the beginning of 1983, those in work were enjoying increased earnings: the increase in average earnings was outpacing inflation by 8.25% to 4.9%.

There were some signs that many people were attracted by the image of a hard-headed leader who had convinced people that life would no longer be easy. In a by-election in the constituency of Northfield, on the outskirts of Birmingham, where 10,000 people had been sacked from British Leyland's Longbridge plant during the life of the Government, Labour won the seat on a recount with a majority of only 289 and a swing away from the government of only 0.48%. Vox pop interviewers came across unemployed people who said that they would nevertheless vote for Thatcher. The same was true during a later by-election campaign in Darlington. A MORI poll at the end of January 1983 combined a series of predictably high scores for Thatcher on leadership qualities ('good in a crisis', 'capable' and so on) with the highest score against the description 'out of touch'.

But there were also signs that groups which in 1979 had been powerfully attracted by the Thatcher line on unions and tax cuts were disenchanted. MORI polls found that the 18-24 group was not the only one swinging away from the Conservatives. While support had risen in the south, it had fallen slightly in the north and sharply in the Midlands. In 1979 the Midlands had swung further to the Conservatives than any other region but it was also where unemployment had risen faster than anywhere else under Thatcher government. Women, whose support for Thatcher has always been higher than men, seemed to remain loyal.

The imminence of the general election began to moderate a number of key decisions. To try to prevent the further deterioration of the Conservative vote in Scotland, the

Cabinet defied the economic arguments for closing the giant Ravenscraig steel plant and kept it open. Paradoxically, the self-confidence which Thatcher admirers felt about their heroine's electoral prospects gave free rein to their wilder dreams about what she could do in a second, and even a third term. The Falklands had brought forth a string of historical comparisons: Queen Victoria, Winston Churchill, Queen Elizabeth the First. Her own heroine was said to be Elizabeth. She was compared to de Gaulle, doing for Britain what he had done for France in consolidating the confidence of the nation around the idea of the national interest and making predecessors and competitors appear petty and inadequate. The comparison was inappropriate in more ways than one. Thatcher had not stepped in when a government was collapsing, and her concept of the 'nation' was hardly all-embracing, excluding as it did various important categories of citizen (immigrants, offenders and many public servants to name but a few). But the comparison was an accurate reflection of the scale of the hopes which some of her followers had for the future.

Thatcher came to power advocating a prescription for the country which was seen as an economic solution. Even in her own terms, she had had mixed success. The management of the economy had come to dominate government business, as the results of monetarism proved to be less certain and swift than had been assumed. In a second term, she would want to shift the emphasis towards other areas: the EEC, defence, health and welfare and 'the family'. The late success in temporarily depressing the inflation rate has masked the fact that many initial economic aims have been discreetly abandoned or modified and that, in a second term, the economy is likely to prove once again more troublesome than anticipated. The commitment to reduce taxation has collided with the desire to limit the extent of public borrowing. So at the time when the PSBR was finally beginning to fall as a proportion of Gross Domestic Product, the Treasury was admitting, in April 1983, that the real increase in the average family's tax payments since 1979 was equivalent to 7p on the standard rate of income tax. Thatcher began to talk of first seeing growth in the economy and then making the cuts; at the beginning of the government the emphasis had been on the reverse – tax cuts were supposed to precede and stimulate activity which would lead to growth. By early 1983, predictions of a recovery – albeit from a very low base – were being aired with increasing frequency, but they had been made, and proved wrong, before.

Thatcher considered a second term necessary to implement policies of what Keith Joseph would call the 'social market': greater privatisation – some of it in areas which have not been hinted at as targets before – and the continued dismantling of public services. 'Let us pledge ourselves,' she told an adoring audience at the annual convention of the Institute of Directors, 'to build a nation strong in its defence, its commerce and its standards.' A second term would be heavily preoccupied with the nuclear arms debate, due to be brought to a climax with the deployment of Cruise and Pershing missiles in Britain and other European countries at the end of 1983. The appointment of Michael Heseltine as Minister of Defence signalled a new propaganda offensive against the renaissance of the Campaign for Nuclear Disarmament. Thatcher has complained on many occasions about what she regards as low standards in schools, although she has seldom been able to articulate what exactly she thinks should be done. A new government is likely to renew efforts to raise standards and continue the tentative changes – in the training of teachers, for example – proposed so far by Keith Joseph. Joseph's reign at Education has been characterised by some detailed attention to the politics of educational small print which may give some indication of the direction which a future Thatcher administration might like to take. The DES intervened to ask a public examination board to change its terms of reference for a physics course so as to discourage teachers from discussing nuclear war during science lessons.

But the main thrust is to be privatisation. 'The second term will be the Privatisation Period' said one close adviser. It is the group of policies which has been pushed forward by classic Thatcher tactics. The psychological and ideological ground is prepared as one stage and the policy is implemented in a second stage. Her government since 1979 has sold majority shareholdings in British Aerospace, Cable and Wireless, the National Freight Corporation and Amersham International in addition to a slice of shares in BP. The National Enterprise Board has been required to sell its shares — a list of firms including ICL, Ferranti and Fairley. Perhaps the most significant privatisation success of the first term was the dissolution of the Post Office monopoly. It was split in two, between postal duties and telecommunications, and private firms were encouraged to compete in the profitable fields of equipment sale and hire and special parcel and messenger delivery. There was little public discussion about the changes and Thatcher was able to take advantage of the traditionally moderate postal workers' union and a long-standing disenchantment with the Post Office standard of service. With the ground prepared, the next stage is ready to go ahead: a bill setting up the sale of British Telecom is ready to go through Parliament.

A new company, Britoil, was created to sell the government stake in North Sea Oil. British Airways is planned for sale. Its workforce and operations are being reshaped by one of Thatcher's favourite businessmen, Sir John King. There are plans to sell the nineteen ports of the British Transport Docks Board, British Gas's oil interests, British Shipbuilders, open-cast mines and part of the National Bus Company. These plans have already been well-rehearsed in public and prepared for execution.

There is at least one nationalised industry waiting uncertainly for a clue to what a second Thatcher term might bring. British Rail so far only faces plans for the privatisation of some of its subsidiaries, but its executives are in little doubt that these will not satisfy Thatcher's dislike of the rail monopoly. The Serpell report, which proposed drastic reductions of the subsidised, public service elements of the network, was put in cold storage when it appeared in early 1983 as too controversial and too late in the government. A second term would be likely to see it re-examined.

So worried did British Rail's senior executives become at one stage about Thatcher's hatred of railways that a member of the board was detailed to see if there was a way to soften her attitude through Denis. The board member was the organiser of an annual outing to a Scottish rugby international on which he took friends and business contacts. The party travelled to and from the match in a luxury private coach, well-stocked with drink. Denis was duly invited and came. He enjoyed himself hugely, drank a good deal and by the end of the day was a thoroughgoing convert to the railways. His conversion received short shrift back at Number Ten. When he began to mention his new-found enthusiasim, his wife promptly told him that he must have been nobbled.

If Thatcher continued to dismantle or denationalise British Rail, it is probable that real action might be deferred until a possible third term. For the psychological preparation of the public for major change has barely begun. Michael Edwardes persuaded the government not to break up British Leyland when the idea was raised, but under a new government and a new BL chairman, it might be debated again.

The pace of change which Thatcher wishes to bring about has sometimes been altered by the installation or discovery of the right individual to drive the policy forward. Sir Ian MacGregor, the Scottish-born industrialist who was lured back from the autumn of his American career to be chairman of British Steel, had been earmarked as a likely candidate for that type of job by the previous Labour government. But he immediately struck up a rapport with Thatcher, signalled by his unusually rapid access to Downing Street when he wants it. His transfer to the chairmanship of the National Coal Board is likely to see an attempt to speed up the programme of shrinking the industry, its jobs and its losses — a move likely to coincide with the start of the next government. It will be a tougher job than the job losses and closures he saw through at British Steel: the miners will not accept such things as easily as the steelmen.

Much more controversial and less advanced are the

outline ideas produced in the summer of 1982 by the Think Tank for privatising parts of the NHS. This exercise arose less from fulfilment of previous commitments to denationalise and privatise, and more from calculations about the future taxation and welfare budgeting. The Think Tank analysis was leaked and Thatcher, who had herself asked for it, was forced to announce that it had been shelved. But at the Cabinet meeting which debated the shelving, Howe warned his colleagues that they could no longer assume that the economy would support public services along the lines which most people now took for granted. Other economic commentators pointed out at the time that the predicted future shortage of money to support national health and social security networks appeared to be due not to unavoidable future population changes, but to large increases in the defence budget. At the beginning of 1983, the government asked hospitals to test the cost-effectiveness of their domestic, catering and laundry services with a view to putting them out to private tender.

The arrival of Ferdinand Mount in Downing Street revived Thatcher's interest in the family. Mount's book on the importance of family life, bemoaning its disintegration, had been an important reason behind his appointment, and he set about coordinating a group of ministers to consider future government policy affecting families, particularly in the context of a diminishing welfare state. When the tentative proposals were leaked, a furious controversy developed. The plans included suggestions that mothers should be encouraged by tax relief to abandon work in favour of looking after their children; that parents should be helped to set up their own schools; and education vouchers should replace 'free' state education. Such leaks have the short-term effect of shutting down public discussion of the issue after the initial controversy has died down. But the idea has been seeded in the public mind and a determined government can return to such an issue after an interval if the public reaction has not been so hostile as to rule it out for good. Although the Family Policy Group leak probably came from a civil servant disturbed by the implications of its deliberations, it may have helped prepare the ground for a government with a renewed mandate and the confidence to press ahead.

Thatcher continued to move with enthusiasm in the world of more abstract ideas. 'The Prime Minister plays with ideas as though they were ping pong balls. She just likes to knock them about a bit. It makes her feel relaxed,' said one participant at a meeting of the Conservative Philosophy Group, the private group of dons, politicians and journalists which meets periodically to discuss Conservative theory and practice. Thatcher is a surprisingly frequent attender and takes part with relish. She attended one meeting in Cambridge which heard a paper from Dr Edward Norman, Dean of Peterhouse, on religion and politics. At around eleven o'clock, the chairman thanked the meeting and said that they would understand that the Prime Minister had to get back to London. 'Not at all,' retorted Thatcher. 'We've only just started,' and proceeded to wade into the debate for another hour. She spars with Enoch Powell, admonishing him, 'Enoch, please be serious', or 'Be constructive, Enoch, be *constructive*'. When Friedrich Hayek addressed the group, she sat reverently at his feet.

The group had its informal origins at a dinner conversation between Hugh Fraser MP, a defeated candidate for the leadership in 1975, Jonathan Aitken MP, at whose house in Lord North Street – once owned by Brendan Bracken – the group meets, and two young dons, Roger Scruton and John Casey. Airey Neave was initially suspicious of the group and asked if the new leader could attend. Its debates are normally inside the Thatcherite wing of the party – between, for example, free marketeers and more authoritarian strains of Conservative thinking. It is a source of worry to the party's liberal heavyweights who, as a Thatcher second term becomes more likely, fear that the group may successfully whisper unpalatable ideas in her ear. It has listened to advocacy of voluntary repatriation of immigrants, integration of Northern Ireland into the United Kingdom and the ending of overseas aid. But it has also been addressed by the former Labour minister, Lord Lever, the left-wing economist, Professor Wynne Godley, and

Lord Sieff, the Marks and Spencer's chief who lectured Thatcher in private in Number Ten on the need to alleviate youth unemployment.

After the Falklands campaign, Thatcher began to mention the importance of Victorian values with increasing frequency. It was not immediately clear whether their emphasis was a prelude to specific preparations or simply the general direction Thatcher wanted for the country. It became something of a set piece recital, to be dropped into interviews.

'Look at the enormous increase in industry and commerce in this country during Victorian times, which brought with it a consciousness of duty to others. They built the hospitals. They built the schools. They built the prisons. They built the industries. They built the town halls.' (July 1982)

'... As people prospered themselves, so they gave voluntary things to the state. So many of the schools we replace now were voluntary schools, so many of the hospitals we replace were hospitals given by this great benefaction feeling we have in Britain, even some of the prisons, some of the town halls. (January 1983)

Not all Thatcher's ministers shared her admiration for Victorian philanthropy. 'I am glad to see,' said Norman Tebbit while presenting awards to the disabled, 'that it is not the bleeding hearts, or the Victorian philanthropists, who are winning these awards.' He observed that only one health authority had qualified for an award against five for companies owned by the electronics conglomerate GEC. Nor did Victorian virtues consort easily with the drive to establish cable television with few of the kind of quality controls imposed on past broadcasting by the BBC and the IBA. The decision was made in principle during the first government and will go ahead during any second term. Any other party would be likely to impose greater restrictions on cable operators.

The abandonment of the Reithian ideals of public

broadcasting is not confined to cable. In an appointment only likely to become significant during a second term, Thatcher appointed Stuart Young, brother of the Manpower Services Commission chairman and Thatcher adviser David Young, as the next chairman of the BBC. Young, a solicitor, described himself as non-political but promptly admitted that he was a member of the traditional Conservative gentleman's club, the Carlton. In a second Thatcher term, the idea of financing BBC expenditure by broadcasting advertisements will be explored and BBC subsidiaries will be scrutinised to see if they are suitable for privatisation.

Any new government will face mounting pressure to take action on the diplomatic and military stalemate in the Falklands. Thatcher seems set, however, to ignore it as long as possible. She accepts advice she is receiving from Anthony Parsons that an interval of several years has to pass before anything constructive can happen. No Argentine government can take part in serious negotiations and hope to survive. In a second Thatcher government, Falklands policy will remain static. The Foreign Office and the Ministry of Defence will confine themselves to administering the status quo and the garrison.

One veteran observer of post-war foreign policy-making in Whitehall and Downing Street remarked that Thatcher was the first Prime Minister of his experience not to hold grandiose ideas of the country's influence among the superpowers above its actual position in the world.

The war with Whitehall will continue. Michael Heseltine's appointment at Defence has been largely interpreted as inaugurating more aggressive government policy promotion on defence, but is significant also as the transfer of Heseltine, the initiator of the MINIS and Joubert management systems, to the departure with a budget which every government has found hard to control. The Rayner unit drafted a suggestion in 1982 that there should be a charter spelling out the duties of Permanent Secretaries and making them formally responsible for efficient and cost-effective management. Unsurprisingly, there were objections and the document moved only slowly through the machinery, but it will be driven with more force by a government with a renewed mandate. A new Thatcher administration would continue to debate with itself the pros and cons of a more powerful Prime Minister's Department. The size of the Downing Street staff (68 and five special advisers at January 1983) is still almost exactly the same size as it was in May 1979. The attractions of enlarging Downing Street's staffing and power are likely to vary depending on the degree of control she has over her own Cabinet. One adviser is recommending that she should make use of referendums to appeal to the country over the objections of her colleagues and Whitehall.

At the start of her government she sought out and constructed bypasses round ministerial obstruction. An overall majority would give her the chance to dispense with at least some of the obstructions. The principal figures in this calculation are Pym, Prior and Walker. Pym occupies an unusual position. Thatcher has been unable to prevent him moving nearer to the centre of power during the life of the Government; should she suddenly cease to be leader or Prime Minister, he is the most likely successor. He does not, however, cultivate a band of followers in the Commons and if he failed to survive into a second Thatcher Cabinet, he would be an unlikely focus for revolt. Thatcher will attempt to keep Prior at the Northern Ireland Office for as long as she can. A Thatcher victory would face Prior with a dilemma. If he resigned Northern Ireland and left the Cabinet, any eventual revolt from the left of the party might well look to a younger leader. If he stays in the Government, he has little power to influence its key policies and he may find himself fighting a rearguard action against Conservative and Unionist hardliners who are pressing for a more decisively anti-nationalist strategy in Northern Ireland. Walker has been lucky to steward a traditionally 'wet' and interventionist department like Agriculture. His Cabinet future remains an open question.

Thatcher faces a problem in finding experienced replacements for ministers whose commitment she does not trust, although with the promotion of men like Leon Brittan and Norman Tebbit the problem is not as acute as it was in her earlier years as leader. Some of this problem could be

solved by an idea being canvassed among her supporters:
Whitehall amalgamations. There is a strong possibility that
the departments of Trade and Industry will be reunited as
they were in the early seventies. There has been a suggestion
that such a new department might also include the presently
independent Department of Energy.

The politics of a new Thatcher Cabinet will turn, as they
have in the old, on William Whitelaw. His wife Cecilia has
been urging him to retire from politics, but MPs on the
centre-left of the party have been urging him to stand at the
next election so that he would be in place to steer the party
into coalition negotiations if no party commanded an
overall majority. He ignored hints from Thatcherite
quarters that he should announce his intention not to stand
and move gracefully aside in order to make a pre-election
reshuffle easier.

After four years, she is careful to say, the country had so
far merely 'woken up' to the 'reality of the need to earn its
place in the world'. The second term might be expected to
be a period of fast change, building upon the foundations of
the hard lessons learnt in the first term. The economy, and
above all, the size of her majority, would temper her
behaviour. And the extent of the changes are hard to
predict. There is no master plan and she is not appealing to
the public on a specific, coordinated programme of
concerted reform. The very lack of detailed planning of a
grand strategy has dispirited many of her close advisers,
such as Hoskyns, who would prefer a more ordered way
forward.

What makes Thatcher different as a British Prime
Minister are not her convictions or intentions. It is
combining them with a purely political skill of assembling
and managing an electoral coalition of votes and interests
which puts those convictions and intentions in power. The
coalition of the middle-class and those with conservative
and nationalistic instincts is neither as narrow as a British
Poujadism, nor as broad as 'one nation'. She is the first
Prime Minister to have rejected the post-war consensus, and
to have explicitly attacked what she identifies as its
weakness: 'that sense of ... self-criticism, which affects

those ... who cling to a relatively comfortable life while feeling a troublesome pang of conscience because there are others less well off.' John Biffen identified one troublesome pang of conscience which had been felt by the politicians who remembered the thirties, and particularly the MP for Stockton, Harold Macmillan. 'There are no Stockton-on-Tees skeletons in the Grantham cupboard,' Biffen said of Thatcher. She is the only post-war Prime Minister not to have been involved in the bi-partisan cooperation during wartime which led to the founding of the Welfare State.

One loyalist defined 'the centre of what she feels' as an objection to the vast majority of people being told what to do and what to want by a small minority who think that they know what's best. But she is only anti-elitist in the sense that she wishes to put a new elite in position to 'roll back the state' and turn back what she sees as the ratchet of post-war centre-left policies. She may be unlike the majority of Conservative grandees in that she feels a distaste for the inhabitants of some traditional Conservative constituencies like the City, but she has done nothing to discourage their financial support for the party machinery which keeps her coalition together. In the election, Central Office expects to spend around £15 million – three times the amount spent on the 1979 campaign, five times the money available to the Labour Party and ten times that budgeted by the partners of the Alliance.

After four years in government she made increasingly frequent references to her father's ideas and guidance. 'Pa said this, Pa wouldn't say that,' one close friend described her as saying. One interviewer asked her if her approach to another government would be 'tough'? 'No, it's the sincere approach ... Born of the conviction which I learned in a small town by a father who had a conviction approach.' But ultimately what changed during those four years was the style of government at the top. What respect she has won, has been won for her determination and less for specific achievements. 'The reason I am in politics,' she said, 'is because I believe in certain things and try to put them into practice.'

Appendix

The full text of Margaret Thatcher's remarkable lecture delivered on behalf of the Conservative Political centre at the conference in Blackpool of 10 October 1968.

Criticism of politics is no new thing. Literature abounds with it.

In Shakespeare we find the comment of King Lear:

'Get thee glass eyes;
'And, like a scurvy politican, seem
'To see the things thou dost not.'

Richard Sheridan, reputed to have made one of the greatest speeches the House of Commons has ever heard (it lasted 5 hours and 40 minutes), commented that 'conscience has no more to do with gallantry than it has with politics'. Anatole France was perhaps the most scathing: 'I am not so devoid of all talents as to occupy myself with politics.'

Nor have political leaders escaped criticism:

'Disraeli unites the maximum of Parliamentary cleverness with the minimum of statesmanlike capacity. No one ever dreams to have him lead. He belongs not to the bees but to the wasps and the butterflies of public life. He can sting and sparkle but he cannot work. His place in the arena is marked and ticketed for ever.'

This from the Controller of the Stationery Office, in 1853, quoted in *The Statesman* by Henry Taylor.

There is no need to remind you how utterly wrong that judgment was.

There are even some things that have improved over the years. Bribery and corruption, which have now gone, used to be rampant. The votes of electors were purchased at a high price. The famous Lord Shaftesbury when he was Lord Ashley, spent £15,600 on successfully winning Dorset in 1831. It is interesting to note that £12,000 of this went to public houses and inns for the refreshment of the people. And this when gin was a penny a glass! Some forty years before, Lord Penrhyn spent £50,000 on his campaign – and then lost!

But we can't dismiss the present criticisms as easily as that. The dissatisfaction with politics runs too deep both here and abroad. People have come to doubt the future of the democratic system and its institutions. They distrust the politicians and have little faith in the future. Let us try to assess how and why we have reached this pass. What is the explanation? Broadly speaking I think we have not yet assimilated many of the changes that have come about in the past thirty to forty years.

First, I don't think we realise sufficiently how new our present democratic system is. We still have comparatively little experience of the effect of the universal franchise which didn't come until 1928. And the first election in this country which was fought on the principle of one person one vote was 1950. So we are still in the early stages of dealing with the problems and opportunities presented by everyone having a vote.

Secondly, this and other factors have led to a different party political structure. There is now little room for independent members and the controversies which formerly took place outside the parties on a large number of measures now have to take place inside. There is, and has to be room for a variety of opinions on certain topics within the broad general principles on which each party is based.

Thirdly, from the party political structure has risen the detailed programme which is placed before the electorate. Return to power on such a programme has led to a new doctrine that the party in power has a mandate to carry out everything in its manifesto. I myself doubt whether the voters really are endorsing each and every particular when they return a government to power.

This modern practice of an election programme has, I

believe, influenced the attitudes of some electors; all too often one is now asked 'what are you going to do for me?', implying that the programme is a series of promises in return for votes. All this has led to a curious relationship between elector and elected. If the elector suspects the politicians of making promises simply to get his vote, he despises him, but if the promises are not forthcoming he may reject him. *I believe that parties and elections are about more than rival lists of miscellaneous promises — indeed, if they were not, democracy would scarcely be worth preserving.*

Fourthly, the extensive and all-pervading development of the welfare state is also comparatively new. You will recollect that one of the four great freedoms in President Roosevelt's wartime declaration was 'freedom from want.' Since then in the Western world there has been a series of measures designed to give greater security. I think it would be true to say that there is no longer a struggle to achieve a basic security. Further, we have a complete new generation whose whole life has been lived against the background of the welfare state. These developments must have had a great effect on the outlook and approach of our people even if we cannot yet assess it properly.

Fifthly, one of the effects of the rapid spread of higher education has been to equip people to criticise and question almost everything. Some of them seem to have stopped there instead of going on to the next stage which is to arrive at new beliefs, or to reaffirm the old ones. You will perhaps remember seeing in the press the report that the student leader Daniel Cohn-Bendit has been awarded a degree on the result of his past work. His examiners said that he had posed a series of most intelligent questions. Significant? I would have been happier had he also found a series of intelligent answers.

Sixthly, we have far more information about events than ever before and since the advent of television, news is presented much more vividly. It is much more difficult to ignore situations which you have seen on film with your own eyes than if you had merely read about them, perhaps skimming the page rather hurriedly. Television is not merely one extra means of communication, it is a medium which because of the way it presents things is radically influencing the judgments we have to make about events and about people, including politicians.

Seventhly, our innate international idealism has received many nasty shocks. Many of our people long to believe that if representatives of all nations get together dispassionately to discuss burning international problems, providence and goodwill will guide them to wise and just conclusions, and peace and international law and order will thereby be secured. But in practice a number of nations vote not according to right or wrong even when it is a clear case to us, but according to their national expediencies. And some of the speeches and propaganda to explain blatant actions would make the angels weep as well as the electorate.

All of these things are a partial explanation of the disillusion and disbelief we encounter today. The changes have been tremendous and I am not surprised that the whole system is under cross-examination. I welcome healthy scepticism and questioning. *It is our job continually to retest old assumptions and to seek new ideas. But we must not try to find one unalterable answer that will solve all our problems for none can exist.*

You may know the story of the soldier of fortune who once asked the Sphinx to reveal the divine wisdom of the ages in one sentence, and the Sphinx said 'Don't expect too much.'

In that spirit and against the background I have sketched, let us try to analyse what has gone wrong.

I believe that the great mistake of the last few years has been for the government to provide or to legislate for almost everything. Part of this policy has its roots in the plans for reconstruction in the postwar period when governments assumed all kinds of new obligations. The policies may have been warranted at the time but they have gone far further than was intended or is advisable. During our own early and middle period of government we were concerned to set the framework in which people could achieve their own standards for themselves, subject always to a basic standard. But it has often seemed to me that from the early 1960s the emphasis in politics shifted. At about that time 'growth' became the key political word. If resources grew by X per cent per annum this would provide the extra money needed for the government to make further provision. The doctrine found favour at the time and we had a bit of a contest between the parties about the highest possible growth rate. Four per cent or more. *But the result was that for the time being the emphasis in political debate ceased to be about people and became about economics.* Plans were made to achieve a 4 per cent growth rate. Then came the present government with a bigger plan and socialist ideas about its implementation, that is to say if people didn't conform to the plan, they had to be compelled to. Hence compulsion on Prices and Incomes policy and with it the totally unacceptable notion that the government shall have the power to fix which wages and salaries should increase.

We started off with a wish on the part of the people for more government intervention in certain spheres. This was met. But there came a time when the amount of intervention got so great that it could no longer be exercised in practice by government but only by more and more officials or bureaucrats. Now it is difficult if not impossible for people to get at the official making the decision and so paradoxically although the degree of intervention is greater, the government has become more and more *remote* from the people. The present result of the democratic process has therefore been an increasing authoritarianism.

During July the *Daily Telegraph* published a rather interesting poll which showed how people were reacting against this rule of impersonal authority. The question was 'In your opinion or not do people like yourselves have enough say or not in the way the government runs the country (68 per cent not enough), the services provided by the nationalised industries (67 per cent not enough), the way local authorities handle things (64 per cent not enough — note this rather high figure; people don't like remote local authorities any more than they like remote governments).'

Recently more and more feature articles have been

written and speeches made about involving people more closely with decisions of the government and enabling them to participate in some of those decisions.

But the way to get personal involvement and participation is not for people to take part in more and more government decisions but to make the government reduce the area of decision over which it presides and consequently leave the private citizen to 'participate', if that be the fashionable word, by making more of his own decisions. What we need now is a far greater degree of personal responsibility and decision, far more independence from the government, and a comparative reduction in the role of government.

These beliefs have important implications for policy.

First Prices and Incomes policy. The most effective prices policy has not come by controlling prices by the government, through the Prices and Incomes Board, but through the Conservative way of seeing that competition flourishes. There have been far more price cuts in the supermarkets than in the nationalised industries. This shows the difference between the government doing the job itself and the government creating the conditions under which prices will be kept down through effective competition.

On the Incomes side, there seemed to be some confusion in the minds of the electorate about where the parties stood. This was not surprising in the early days because a number of speeches and documents from both sides of the House showed a certain similarity. For example, here are four separate quotations – two from the Labour Government and two from our period of office. They are almost indistinguishable.

1. 'Increases in the general level of wage rates must be related to increased productivity due to increased efficiency and effort.' (White Paper on Employment Policy, 1944)

2. 'It is essential therefore that there should be no further general increase in the level of personal incomes without at least a corresponding increase in the volume of production.' (Sir Stafford Cripps, 1948)

3. 'The Government's policy is to promote a faster rate of economic growth ... But the policy will be put in jeopardy if money incomes rise faster than the volume of national production.' (Para. I of Incomes Policy, *The Next Step*, Cmnd 1626, Feburary 1962)

4. '... the major objectives of national policy must be ... to raise productivity and efficiency so that real national output can increase and so keep increases in wages, salaries and other forms of income in line with this increase.' (Schedule 2, Prices and Incomes Act, 1966)

All of these quotes express general economic propositions, but the policies which flowed from those propositions were very different. We rejected from the outset the use of compulsion. This was absolutely right. The role of the government is not to control each and every salary that is paid. It has no means of measuring the correct amount. Moreover, having to secure the state's approval before one increases the pay of an employee is repugnant to most of us.

There is another aspect of the way in which Incomes policy is now operated to which I must draw attention. We now put so much emphasis on the control of incomes that we have too little regard for the essential role of government which is the control of money supply and management of demand. Greater attention to this role and less to the outward detailed control would have achieved more for the economy. It would mean, of course, that the government had to exercise itself some of the disciplines on expenditure it is so anxious to impose on others. It would mean that expenditure in the vast public sector would not have to be greater than the amount which could be financed out of taxation plus genuine saving. For a number of years some expenditure has been financed by what amounts to printing the money. There is nothing *laissez-faire* or old-fashioned about the views I have expressed. It is a modern view of the role the government should play now, arising from the mistakes of the past, the results of which we are experiencing today.

The second policy implication concerns taxation and the

social servies. It is no accident that the Conservative Party has been the one which has reduced the rates of taxation. The decisions have not been a haphazard set of expediencies, or merely economic decisions to meet the needs of the moment. They have stemmed from the real belief that government intervention and control tends to reduce the role of the individual, his importance and the desirability that he should be primarily responsible for his own future. When it comes to the development of the social services, the policy must mean that people should be encouraged if necessary by taxation incentives to make increasing provision for themselves out of their own resources. The basic standards through the state would remain as a foundation for extra private provision. Such a policy would have the advantage that the government could concentrate of providing things which the citizen can't. Hospitals are one specific example.

The other day I came across a quotation which you will find difficult to place.

'Such a plan as this was bound to be drastic and to express nothing less than a new pattern ... (for the hospitals of this country) ... Now that we have it, we must see that it lives. As I have said before it is a plan which has hands and feet. It walks and it works. It is not a static conception stated once and for all but something which is intended to live and to be dynamic ... My Ministry will constantly be carrying this review forward so that there will always be ten years work definitely projected ahead.' (*Hansard, 4th June 1962, Col. 153.*)

No, it doesn't come from Harold Wilson. It is not about our enormous overall plan, but a very limited plan in a small area in which the government could make a distinctive contribution. It was Enoch Powell introducing his ten-year hospital plan in the House of Commons on 4th June 1962.

To return to the personal theme, if we accept the need for increasing responsibility for self and family it means that we must stop approaching things in an atmosphere of restriction. There is nothing wrong in people wanting larger incomes. It would seem a worthy objective for men and women to wish to raise the standard of living for their families and to give them greater opportunities than they themselves had. I wish more people would do it. We should then have fewer saying 'the state must do it.' What *is wrong* is that people should want more without giving anything in return. The condition precedent to high wages and high salaries is hard work. This is a quite different and much more stimulating approach than one of keeping down incomes.

Doubtless there will be accusers that we are only interested in more money. This just is not so. Money is not an end in itself. It enables one to live the kind of life of one's own choosing. Some will prefer to put a large amount to raising material standards, others will pursue music, the arts, the cultures, others will use their money to help those here and overseas about whose need they feel strongly and do not let us underestimate the amount of hard earned cash that this nation gives voluntarily to worth causes. The point is that even the Good Samaritan had to have the money to help, otherwise he too would have had to pass on the other side.

In choice of way of life J.S. Mill's views are as relevant as ever.

'The only freedom which deserves the name is that of pursuing our own good in our own way so long as we do not deprive others of theirs, or impede their efforts to obtain it ... Mankind are greater gainers by suffering each other to live as seems good to themselves than by compelling each to live as seems good to the rest.'

These policies have one further important implication. Together they succeed at the same time in giving people a measure of *independence from the state* – and who wants a people dependent on the state and turning to the state for their every need – also they succeed in drawing power away from governments and diffusing it more widely among people and non-governmental institutions.

The second mistake politics have made at present is in some ways related to the first one. We have become bewitched with the idea of size.

As a result people no longer feel important in the scheme of things. They have the impression that everything has become so big, so organised, so standardised and governmentalised that there is no room for the individual, his talents, his requirements or his wishes. He no longer counts.

It is not difficult to see how this feeling has come about. In industry the merits of size have been extolled for some years now and too little attention given to its demerits. Size brings great problems. One of the most important is the problem of making and communicating decisions. The task of decision tends to be concentrated at the top, and fewer people get used to weighing up a problem, taking a decision, sticking to it and carrying the consequences. The buck is passed. But even *after* a decision has been made, there is the problem of communicating it to those who have to carry it out in such a way that it is understood, and they are made to feel a part of the team. In a large-scale organisation, whether government, local government or industry, failure to do this can lead to large-scale mistakes, large-scale confusion and large-scale resentment. These problems, can, and must be, overcome, but all too often they are not.

The third mistake is that people feel they don't count when they try to get something done through government agencies.

Consider our relations with government departments. We start as a birth certificate; attract a maternity grant; give rise to a tax allowance and possibly a family allowance; receive a national health number when registered with a doctor; go to one or more schools where educational records are kept; apply for an educational grant; get a job; start paying national insurance and tax; take out a television and driving licence; buy a house with a mortgage; pay rates; buy a few premium bonds; take out life assurance; purchase some shares; get married; start the whole thing over again; receive a pension and become a death certificate and death grant, and the subject of a file in the Estate Duty Office! Every one of these incidents will require a form or national government office. *The amount of information collected in the various departments must be fabulous. Small wonder that life really does seem like 'one damned form after another.'*

A good deal of this form-filling will have to continue but I think it time to reassert a right to privacy. Ministers will have to look at this aspect in deciding how to administer their policies. There is a tendency on the part of some politicians to suggest that with the advent of computers all this information should be centralised and stored on magnetic tape. They argue that this would be time-saving and more efficient. Possibly it would; but other and more important things would be at stake. There would be produced for the first time a personal dossier about each person, on which everything would be recorded. In my view this would place far too much power in the hands of the state over the individual. In the USA there is a Congressional enquiry sitting on this very point because politicians there have recognised the far-reaching dangers of such a record.

Fourthly, I believe that there is too great a reliance on statistical forecasts; too little on judgment.

We all know the old one about lies, damned lies and statistics, and I do not wish to condemn statistics out of hand. Those who prepare them are well aware of their limitations. Those who use them are not so scrupulous.

Recently the economic forecasts have been far more optimistic than the events which happened. The balance of payments predictions have been wrong again and again.

For example, in February this year the National Institute of Economic and Social Research forecast predicted a *surplus* of £100m. in the second half of this year. In August they predicted a *deficit* of £600m. for the whole of this year, but a surplus of £250m. *next* year.

They commented, 'The balance of payments forecasts taken year by year look a lot worse than previously estimated, but the difference is largely one of timing – with the movement into surplus coming later, and with a still larger rate of improvement.'

The truth is that statistical results do not displace the need for judgment, they increase it. The figures can be no better than the assumptions on which they are based and these could vary greatly. In addition, the unknown factor which, by its very nature is incapable of evaluation, may well be the determining one.

Fifthly, we have not yet appreciated or used fully the virtues of our party political system. The essential characteristic of the British Constitutional system is not that there is an alternative personality but that there is an alternative policy and a whole alternative government ready to take office. As a result we have always had an Opposition to act as a focus of criticism against the government. We have therefore not suffered the fate of countries which have had a 'consensus' or central government, without an official opposition. This was one of the causes of trouble in Germany. Nor do we have the American system, which as far as Presidential campaigns go, appears to have become almost completely one of personalities.

There are dangers in consensus; it could be an attempt to satisfy people holding no particular views about anything. It seems more important to have a philosophy and policy which because they are good appeal to sufficient people to secure a majority.

A short time ago when speaking to a university audience and stressing the theme of second responsibility and independence a young undergraduate came to me and said 'I had no idea there was such a clear alternative.' He found the idea challenging and infinitely more effective than one in which everyone virtually expects their MP or the government to solve their problems. The Conservative creed has never offered a life of ease without effort. Democracy is not for such people. Self-government is for those men and women who have learned to govern themselves.

No great party can survive except on the basis of firm beliefs about what it wants to do. It is not enough to have reluctant support. We want people's enthusiasm as well.

CHAPTER FOURTEEN

9 June, 1983:
The General Election

Margaret Thatcher has always said that she would need at least two terms to carry out the fundamental reforms she felt were needed in Britain. As 1983 progressed, she came under increasing pressure from her supporters to call a general election while the going was good. The Conservative Party was substantially ahead in the opinion polls and had been for many months. Her personal rating was high, as it had been since the Falklands war. The Labour Party was in obvious disarray and the support for the SDP-Liberal Alliance had ebbed away. One by one, her senior Cabinet ministers came to the conclusion that it would be a grave error not to cash in their chips. Of them all, only John Biffen was vehemently opposed. William Whitelaw was at first against an early election, then became an agnostic.

In her public statements she said that she had not given any serious consideration to the date of the election and that she had until May 1984 to make up her mind. In private she was exploring the prospects for the final year. Most of the immediate party programme had been enacted and there was little legislation in the pipeline. However – a major consideration – all estimates showed that the key indicators of the nation's health were at their best for the foreseeable future. By the autumn, inflation would begin to rise, unemployment would further increase and interest rates would remain high. The improvement in the US economy was taking a long time to filter through to Britain. Although a relaxation of the Chancellor's tough economic measures had put more money in people's pockets, monetary controls had been relaxed far beyond what was considered prudent. The sooner the election, the sooner tough action could be taken to bring the money supply back in line.

An election summit was set for the weekend of 7–8 May at Chequers. Speculation had been allowed to continue about the prospect of a June election throughout the spring and although Thatcher appeared to dampen any suggestion of going to the country a year early, she allowed her aides to keep the subject alive. She even joked about it to the CBI, quoting the popular song 'Maggie May'. She was particularly vulnerable to the accusation that she was about to 'cut and run' before the economic situation got worse. An early election also ran counter to her preferred image of a steadfast, resolute leader, unswayed by electoral considerations and determined to continue to govern for a full term. To call a June election would not only refute the highly popular 'resolute approach' to leadership which she had established, but would doubly undermine that image by allowing it to be thought that she was being forced into calling an early election against her better judgment by the weight of public speculation.

The very fact that an election summit was to be held brought public speculation about an early election to screaming pitch. She drove down to Chequers on Friday 6 May, still undecided about what she ought to do. She had let it be known to the press that she would announce nothing during Saturday and Sunday, but there was extraordinary pressure upon her to announce something, if only that there would not be an election, in the early part of the week. Her lack of decision was being spoken about as indecision. On Sunday morning, when, at ten in the morning, Gordon Clough and 'The World This Weekend' radio news programme came to interview her for broadcast that lunchtime, she told them, unconvincingly, that she would not be 'hustled' into a decision. That Sunday morning, the top Tories arrived. They were led by Whitelaw, her loyal deputy, Parkinson, the head of the Party machine, and Howe, in charge of drafting the manifesto. With them were Biffen, Tebbit, David Wolfson, head of her political office in Number Ten, Ferdinand Mount, head of her policy unit, Christopher Lawson, head of Conservative marketing, Anthony Shrimsley, the recently appointed head of Tory press and publicity, and Ian Gow, the ever-present PPS. After lunch, they sat down to discuss the election in detail.

Every clue pointed to the fact that if there were a general election in June, the Conservatives would win it handsomely. All opinion polls pointed the same way. Just as important, the polls at last began to show that Conservatives would not be so disgruntled with what many of them considered an unnecessary election that they would not vote. Also, the previous Thursday, the biggest electoral test had taken place in the shape of the local government elections in England and Wales. On Friday the results had been fed into a new £750,000 computer which had recently been donated anonymously to Conservative Central Office. It was important to translate the local election results into the revised boundaries which would operate at the general election – a revision which had made traditional comparisons and therefore judgments difficult.

The discussion soon moved from whether June was a suitable date to when in June the election should be held. The two most favoured dates were 9 June, the first available Thursday, and 23 June, by which time the last remaining parliamentary business could be cleared out of the way. The arguments in favour of 9 June were formidable. The need for an early announcement to curb the accusations of indecision coincided with the need to make a statement before the Speaker called a by-election for the seat of Cardiff North West the following Tuesday. To have allowed the Speaker to announce the date for Cardiff, then overrule it with a general election announcement, would have left the Government open to charges of holding parliamentary procedure in contempt.

But the pressures to hold the election on 9 June were also due to the need to minimize the length of the campaign. If an announcement were made on Monday or Tuesday 9 or 10 May that the election would be on 23

June, there would be a full six and a half weeks of campaigning. During that time, it was argued, the electorate would have become bored, there might have been unforeseen accidents and mistakes which would be blown up into major electoral issues. There was the example of the June 1970 general election in which an unappealing Opposition leader, Edward Heath, had plodded through a summer campaign in which the then Wilson government held a large lead in the opinion polls: unexpectedly he became Prime Minister.

By the time the senior Tories left for London that Sunday night, most felt that Thatcher had become convinced that 9 June was the most favourable date. It was suggested by those returning from Chequers that night that the Prime Minister was still undecided. However, Anthony Shrimsley was confident enough to telephone the editorial staff of the BBC current affairs programme, Panorama, who were due to broadcast an hour-long assessment of the readiness of the Labour Party for an early election. Shrimsley asked whether they had any alternative plans made, because the announcement of an election would cause the intended programme to be counted as part of the Labour share of coverage under the strict equal-time regulations which govern the BBC during elections.

The following morning, Parkinson visited Thatcher at Number Ten and arrived beaming. A Cabinet meeting was quickly summoned and the lobby correspondents were informed that the election would be held on 9 June and that Thatcher would shortly be asking the queen for a dissolution of Parliament. At 2.15 p.m. an official statement was given from Downing Street that the election would be held on 9 June and that Thatcher had confirmed in her own mind that morning a provisional decision to go to the country made the previous evening. Later that Monday evening, she gave her reasons for the election, stressing that election fever was bad for business confidence. Michael Foot, the Labour leader, swiftly accused her of 'cutting and running'.

The long build-up to the general election meant that

the principal issues of the campaign proper had been prepared for months. During the latter part of 1982 and increasingly during 1983 the debate on defence, nuclear arms, the siting of Cruise missiles and the future of the American military bases in Britain had been waged by the Labour Party through the surrogate offices of the Campaign for Nuclear Disarmament. Similarly, the trade union movement was gradually building up an assault upon those government policies which had increased unemployment. A People's March for Jobs had set off with Labour Party blessing from Glasgow and was due to arrive in London on 4 or 5 June. The estimated economic indicators for the autumn and the following year were gathered and held in readiness by the Labour Opposition for highlighting with the full fanfare of publicity during the expected campaign.

While Labour and the Alliance were hoping for a broad-based campaign about issues not personalities, basing what little optimism they could muster upon the opinion-poll findings which said that voters were most concerned about unemployment, the EEC and nuclear weapons, and that they did not, in general, support the government line on those issues, the Conservatives were preparing to hang the main thrust of the campaign upon the personality of Margaret Thatcher. She was to be treated with dignity and reverence, in an attempt to exploit her Prime Ministerial aura, painting her as a world statesman while the others squabbled about domestic politics.

As the election campaign began, there seemed little chance that Labour and the Alliance would be able to cut back on the Conservative lead during the four and a half weeks before 9 June. But opinion-poll experts warned of the electorate's unpredictable volatility. What had seemed impossible only two years before, with Thatcher the most unpopular Prime Minister since opinion polls began and Britain severely disrupted by rioting in cities as the summer wore on, had been transformed. On either side most politicians put this down to her success as a national leader during the Falklands war. Certainly the confident woman who led the Conservatives into electoral battle in 1983 was a more skilful and accomplished politician than the woman who beat Callaghan in May 1979. In no campaign since Churchill's in 1945 had one person so dominated the political landscape. Most Conservatives hoped the comparison would stop there.